DYSPHORIC MODERNISM

MODERNIST LATITUDES

MODERNIST LATITUDES

JESSICA BERMAN AND PAUL SAINT-AMOUR, EDITORS

Modernist Latitudes aims to capture the energy and ferment of modernist studies by continuing to open up the range of forms, locations, temporalities, and theoretical approaches encompassed by the field. The series celebrates the growing latitude ("scope for freedom of action or thought") that this broadening affords scholars of modernism, whether they are investigating little-known works or revisiting canonical ones. Modernist Latitudes will pay particular attention to the texts and contexts of those latitudes (Africa, Latin America, Australia, Asia, Southern Europe, and even the rural United States) that have long been misrecognized as ancillary to the canonical modernisms of the global North.

Nergis Ertürk, *Writing in Red: Literature and Revolution Across Turkey and the Soviet Union*

Cate I. Reilly, *Psychic Empire: Literary Modernism and the Clinical State*

Adam McKible, *Creating Jim Crow America: George Horace Lorimer, the Saturday Evening Post, and the War Against Black Modernity*

Hannah Freed-Thall, *Modernism at the Beach: Queer Ecologies and the Coastal Commons*

Daniel Ryan Morse, *Radio Empire: The BBC's Eastern Service and the Emergence of the Global Anglophone Novel*

Jill Richards, *The Fury Archives: Female Citizenship, Human Rights, and the International Avant-Gardes*

Claire Seiler, *Midcentury Suspension: Literature and Feeling in the Wake of World War II*

Elizabeth Outka, *Viral Modernism: The Influenza Pandemic and Interwar Literature*

Ben Conisbee Baer, *Indigenous Vanguards: Education, National Liberation, and the Limits of Modernism*

Aarthi Vadde, *Chimeras of Form: Modernist Internationalism Beyond Europe, 1914–2014*

For a complete list of books in this series, see the CUP website.

DYSPHORIC MODERNISM

UNDOING GENDER IN FRENCH LITERATURE

MAT FOURNIER

Columbia University Press   *New York*

Columbia University Press
Publishers Since 1893
New York   Chichester, West Sussex

Copyright © 2025 Columbia University Press
All rights reserved

Library of Congress Cataloging-in-Publication Data
Names: Fournier, Mat, author.
Title: Dysphoric modernism : undoing gender in French literature /
Mat Fournier.
Description: New York : Columbia University Press, 2025. | Series: Modernist
latitudes | Includes bibliographical references and index.
Identifiers: LCCN 2024021665 (print) | LCCN 2024021666 (ebook) |
ISBN 9780231209526 (hardback) | ISBN 9780231209533 (trade paperback) |
ISBN 9780231557986 (ebook)
Subjects: LCSH: French literature—20th century—History and criticism. |
Gender identity in literature. | Sex role in literature. |
LCGFT: Literary criticism.
Classification: LCC PQ307.G35 F68 2025 (print) | LCC PQ307.G35 (ebook) |
DDC 840.9/353809042—dc23/eng/20240624

Cover design: Chang Jae Lee

CONTENTS

Acknowledgments vii

Introduction 1

1 A Case Study: Schizophrenic Splits in
La femme qui était en lui 31

2 Gide's Failed Marriages 71

3 Cross-Pollination: A Trans Reading of Marcel Proust 107

4 On Queer Crooks, Abjection, and Moving Sideways:
Maurice Sachs's Dysphoric Smuggling 139

5 Intermittent Miracles: Queer Time
and Temporal Dysphoria 181

Notes 219
Bibliography 257
Index 265

ACKNOWLEDGMENTS

This book has been written with few financial and institutional resources but with the help and support of a group of brilliant people and a generous land.

The 2017 Deleuze Studies Conference and Camp was instrumental in shaping the concepts that gave life to this book. I want to thank its organizers, Markus Bohlmann and Jane Newland. I am also extremely grateful to Anne Sauvagnargues for her seminar, her talk, and our conversations. An earlier version of the introduction was published in 2022 *Deleuze, Guattari, and the Schizoanalysis of Trans Studies*. Many thanks to Ciara Cremin for editing this wonderful volume and for her support and encouragements. My project had become quite a lonely endeavor at this point, and her sharp mind and energy were just what I needed. Diane Brown took the time to help me shape a book proposal; her thoughtful lessons in academic publishing have been useful in many occasions. Jen Spitzer proofread and edited an entire chapter in its early stage and provided me with feedback, advice, support . . . she has been an amazing reader, colleague, and friend throughout the years. Chris Coffman, Benjamin Kahan, and Sandrine Sanos read parts of the book and helped me with their generous insights. I'm all the more grateful for their support that their various works have been inspiring me and guiding me along the way. I'm also grateful to Chris Coffman for introducing me to the Modernist Studies Association Conference and for our common work and conversations at the conference over the years. Many thanks also to Aaron Stone for co-organizing a seminar on trans modernism with me. Isis Sadek, the best editor one can hope for, gave to this book a life of its own and taught me to find joy amid the frustration of writing in a second language. Federico Fridman, Meridith Kruse, and Abraham Weil have been my partners in philosophy, continental or not. Talking to them makes me feel like someone speaks my language. Todd Reeser has been supportive of my research over the past twelve years and has provided me with many opportunities to expand it in new directions. Thank you also to Teagan Bradway for her insights and for our conversations.

At Columbia University Press, I want to thank Philip Leventhal, Michael Haskell, and their teams for their availability and their swift and thoughtful work. Paul Saint-Amour and Jessica Berman have been amazingly generous series editors and readers, supporting me at every step of the way. I'm also grateful to a number of anonymous reviewers at different presses, among whom a very angry one, who, in calling me a structuralist (I've been called worse), gave me a better understanding of what I was trying to accomplish.

At Ithaca College, I want to thank the Center for Faculty Excellence and the Dean's Office at the School of Humanities and Sciences for their financial support. Thank you to Claire Gleitman and Raul Palma for making this happen and for their kindness along the way. I also owe a lot to generous colleagues and friends. Marella Feltrin-Morris helped me with translations and taught me how to become a better translator. Carla

Golden welcomed me to the Women's and Gender Studies Program and made it possible for me to build bridges between research and teaching. Patricia Zimmerman made me better equipped to stand up for myself, as she did for anyone who had the privilege to know her. Last but not least, Jonathan Ablard, Sumru Atuk, and Camilo Malagon, have been great friends, interlocutors, patient listeners to many a rant, and providers of resources and support of all kind.

This book has been written on the homelands of the Gayogǫhó:nǫʔ Nation, sometimes known as the Cayuga Nation. I want to acknowledge their role past and present, and I also want to express my immense gratitude to the land itself: to the waters that carried me, to the soil that fed me, to the woods that sheltered me, and to the birds that kept me in good company.

I couldn't do anything at all without my very queer posthuman family. Sica, a cat made all too smart by seven lives lived to the fullest, has relentlessly supervised my writing until he had to abandon my desk (our ship) in his last days. Meanwhile, other companions from other species, among whom Belka, Sangha, Selma, Nyama, Kevin, Josepha, Eliane, Gaspard, and Ita make life thick with joy, creativity, and resourcefulness. And Cécile: I would like to say love is all, but you always give me even more than that.

INTRODUCTION

Writing has a double function: to translate everything into assemblages and to dismantle the assemblages.
   —Deleuze and Guattari, *Kafka: Towards a Minor Literature*

I now understood . . . how . . . I had managed to arrive at the conclusion that M. de Charlus looked like a woman: he was one!
   —Proust, *In Search of Lost Time*

TRANSWANDERINGS: ON QUEERNESS, DYSPHORIA, AND GENDER NORMATIVITY

It's been a while now, but I still have no idea what men are. Almost ten years ago, I started hormone replacement therapy, giving myself a weekly injection of testosterone ever since. At the time, I didn't engage in any of the rituals that mark one's "coming out as trans." I never gave the "I identify as a man" speech, if only because I was too shy and too afraid to be exposed as a fraud. If anything, the "I identify as a man" narrative had, for years, prevented me from beginning to take hormones or from even beginning to think about it. As a French radical born in the 1970s, I didn't envision identity as something to achieve but as a process to undo.

The first thing I knew about gender, and about identity, was: "I am not a woman," however "woman" was defined. As for men—where to begin? I would have liked to have been one, particularly when I was a child, but I didn't consider myself capable of this. Nor did I have much of a sense of what a man really was. I envied men and boys, all of them, and I firmly believed that had I been born one, my life would have been not only easier but better. I suffered from dysphoria: a particular type of intimate hatred, hovering at the border between body and mind, between physical pain and mental distress, between the material and the spiritual.

After I decided, at the age of forty, to start taking hormones and to undergo "gender reassignment therapy," it took me a couple of years to consistently pass as male. In the meantime, "I am transgender" became a catchphrase to explain the discrepancies between my appearance and the gender specified on the documentation that I showed when I had to cross the checkpoints of state capitalism: airport check-ins, doctors' offices and bank counters, state borders . . . I sometimes even, for lack of time, resorted to the T word, particularly when traveling in France: "je suis transsexuel," "I am a transsexual" (from which most of my interlocutors understood that I was working very hard to become a woman, but this is another story).

I continue, however, to identify as queer. Or, more accurately, queer is something that I can relate to, for lack of identifying with it. Queer is what keeps me going when the dysphoria is too hard to bear. Queer is the voice of hope, not so much the hope of undoing gender but of riding the wave and having fun in the process. Queer means embracing weirdness and turning it into a game, a body, a costume, an attitude—queer means that you get to do as you please, and this is how I started hormone replacement therapy. I started it not so much to take care of the dysphoria, though it certainly helps, but just because I could. Queerness cannot get rid of dysphoria because they don't operate on the same plane. In a way, dysphoria is the opposite of queerness: the latter is a way out, while the former is what keeps you in—in the realm of social interactions and constraints. Dysphoria is your answer to gender norms, your go-to place when you don't understand them, at the most basic level, when you don't know what men are or what women are or how you are supposed to act around them. To put it another way, dysphoria and gender normativity respond to each other, engaging in an endless conversation. This process, as I will argue in this book, doesn't only affect a queer/trans minority but (virtually) everyone because dysphoria is the byproduct of gendered societies of control. For the same reason, queerness, in its manifold twisting virtuosity, also hovers within reach for us all, like a magical power only manifesting itself to those who truly need it. As a way out—as any way out when it comes to societies of control—queerness is a temporary, elusive, parenthesis in the inexhaustible conversation of gender norms and dysphoria. But as Proust's readers well know, sometimes a parenthesis makes all the difference.

PROUST KNOWS BETTER

Upon discovering his neighbor's homosexuality, the teenage narrator of Marcel Proust's *In Search of Lost Time* exclaims: "I now understood . . . how . . . I had managed to arrive at the conclusion that M. de Charlus looked like a woman: he was one!"[1] Thus begins Proust's depiction of gay men as "men-women" who reveal their feminine nature through their quest for male partners but also, more importantly, because they "look like women." Often read, incorrectly, as the first discussion of male homosexuality in French literature, Proust's work has been in turn praised for being ahead of its time or belittled for its inner homophobia.[2] The first time I read *Sodom and Gomorrah* with a class, my students felt that, when it came to describing homosexuality, the backward spirit of the time had gotten the better of Proust. He had been brave enough, but there was only so far he could go. His "men-women" theory was simply a confused and vaguely homophobic attempt to avoid depicting an authentic male-to-male romance. The truth had to wait a few more decades.

My students' frustration frustrated me until I remembered that it had been mine too. As a closeted lesbian looking for straightforward answers, I had found Proust didn't do much for me. In the intervening years, though, he would teach me how to live with dysphoria—that is, how to navigate the gender assemblage. Later on, I will elaborate on the concept of assemblage and on the reasons I rely on it to describe the gender binary. But the path that led me there started with Proust and, more precisely, with Charlus. How could he look like a woman, let alone be one, when he also looks like a man, sufficiently so that *he* is assumed to be one throughout most of the novel? As soon as I gave up on expecting Proust to tell me who or what I was (and for that matter, what or who his characters were), he began to show me what I longed for and how I longed for it: the whole spiel of desiring (someone) while desiring to be (someone else), and the volatility of it. In reading Proust, Deleuze and Guattari write, "we are struck by the fact that all the parts are produced as asymmetrical sections, paths that suddenly come to an end, hermetically sealed boxes, noncommunicating vessels . . . in which there are gaps even between things that are contiguous, gaps that are affirmations, pieces of a puzzle belonging not to any one puzzle but to many."[3] What Proust revealed to me was the mirror game of gender with its narcissistic trapdoors, its social choreographies and choruses, and its deep kinship with sex, intimacies, desire, and romance, and how we connect to other (gendered) beings. Gender doesn't work, and dysphoria thrives in these "gaps that are affirmations." The pieces of the puzzle do not fit, or they overlap. In describing Charlus as a woman *while* he obviously wasn't one, Proust's narrator was asserting a new reality. If Charlus could be a woman, not hidden but smiling, inside of a man's body, then the very definitions of masculinity and femininity were at stake. What is made apparent through the body and the posture of Baron Charlus is no less than the modern gender binary and the reason why it doesn't work.

This book takes a detour via French literary works in order to analyze the Foucauldian moment of the crystallization of modern sexuality *and* gender and of sexuality *as* gender. Along with Proust, I propose to revisit the French modernist canon with queer and trans readings of works of André Gide, Maurice Rostand, Maurice Sachs, Colette, Raymond Radiguet, Jean Genet, and René Crevel. What did they know that we don't know? As Proust and his contemporaries witnessed the slow shaping of the gender assemblage, they were able to see or feel its contours, its lines of fracture, its places of concatenation, and its blind spots through observation points that have become less accessible to us. Once the gender assemblage was built and the scaffolding had been removed, it became impossible to glimpse the construction from the same perspective. The French modernist writers discussed in this book have the ability to guide us through the maze of the assemblage that we have inherited, which they translate and dismantle as described in this introduction's first epigraph.

As authors such as Laura Doan, Benjamin Kahan, and Michael Lucey have recently demonstrated, this crystallization happened in an undefined space between gender and sexuality.[4] Following in their footsteps, my reading is indebted to queer theory and its epistemological inquiries into "the mutual boundaries between the political and the sexual."[5] But it is also a trans reading, insisting on situated embodiments and the violence performed by gender assignments. In pairing the pathologizing term "dysphoria" with the Deleuzo-Guattarian concept of assemblage, I aim to provide a critical perspective on the modern gender binary while acknowledging its violence: the gender-variant individuals discussed in this book do not constitute a limited group of ill-fated people. Like the members of Proust's "cursed race," their numbers expand and their ranks spread once you learn how to recognize them. What they reveal is how the gender assemblage's reach extends to such deep and vital places that no one can avoid being affected by it. They expose how the very notion of gender was constructed in relation to violent systems of exclusion, discrimination, and oppression, and they show how dysphoria was built into the gender assemblage as a side effect of these discrimination systems.

Dysphoria, then, cannot be understood without a discussion of gender's political entanglements in the capitalist and imperialist framework in which we still live. Historians have demonstrated how modern gender is a racialized construct that took shape alongside a colonialist project.[6] Yet the literary works discussed in this book expose the political and racial entanglements of gender in ways that have often been overlooked. They reveal, first of all, a two-sided racializing process. One of these sides, antisemitism, is highly visible, from Proust's engagement with the Dreyfus affair to the discrimination faced by Maurice Sachs.

But this visibility obscures another racial divide, which goes merely unquestioned: the cut separating colonizers from colonized and white bodies from Brown bodies. Here again, Proust's Charlus operates at a crossroads. He is, of course, a ferocious "anti-Dreyfusard" but also shares a silent involvement in French colonization: among the several personalities by whom his character was inspired was the very conservative Maréchal Lyautey, the orchestrator of the French colonization in Morocco.[7] Lyautey was, like Charlus, an authority figure, vocal about his support for French monarchy and the enforcement of (gendered) social hierarchies. Unlike Charlus, he was married, but he never hid his preference for men. What Charlus as Lyautey reveals about gender echoes Gide's sexual preference for Arab boys and his Orientalist musings in Northern Africa: the encounter between dominant white masculinity and its fugitive, feminized counterpoint is tied to the colonial borderlands and the exploitation of Brown bodies.[8]

Carolyn Dean has shown how France's relative political stability during the interwar years makes it "a forum for exploring the role of fantasy in the life of liberal democracy."[9] European and American historians, philosophers, feminists, and queer scholars of theory and literature have been thinking about gender, sexuality, and biopolitics through French literary productions either directly or indirectly, through a genealogy of influences. In reflecting on the history of the present, this book tells a century-long story of transatlantic queer intellectual exchanges. While two celebrity pairings share the spotlights, Sedgwick and Proust[10] and Bersani and Gide,[11] they are but hallmarks in a complex narrative also featuring writers and thinkers as different as Genet, Colette, Cocteau, Jouhandeau, Leduc, Deleuze and Guattari, Foucault, Jonathan Dollimore, and Judith Butler. Kadji Amin exposed in *Disturbing Attachments* how Genet's case reveals the "affective tendencies" at work in queer theory's history.¹² Like Genet, the writers discussed in this book, from Proust to Gide, Colette, and Radiguet to the lesser-known Maurice Sachs, Maurice Rostand, and René Crevel, belong to a modernist canon that influenced, directly or not, discussions on gender in critical theory, queer theory, and trans studies.

In *Feeling Backward*, Heather Love takes "impossible love as a model for queer historiography."¹³ Love's interest in "failed or interrupted connection," drawing from Foucault via Carolyn Dinshaw, anchors queer historiography in desire and discontinuity. Following their path, Leah Devun and Zeb Tortorici underscore the necessity to acknowledge "our own cravings for queer and trans histories."¹⁴ I want to acknowledge here a craving of my own: my endeavor in this book is attuned to the queer desire for history described by Love and Dinshaw, as is my insistence in revisiting the French canon that ruled, albeit counterintuitively and unsatisfyingly, my coming of age in queerness and in literature. In so doing, I have been, in Love's words, "reaching out to queer historical figures who may be turning their backs on [me]."¹⁵ We are now, two decades after the end of the twentieth century, only beginning to grasp how these cultural productions that we thought about as counterculture, namely, the French modernist canon and its legacy, queer theory, contributed to nurture the very system we thought they helped us escape.¹⁶ This book is my attempt to come to terms with past and present failed connections and to open new doors to the flows of unsatisfiable literary desires.

ASSEMBLAGE: BLURRING DISTINCTIONS

In order to map this genealogy of modern gender, I borrow the concept of assemblage from the coauthored works of Deleuze and Guattari.¹⁷ Describing gender as an assemblage allows for the cartographic combination of precision and fluidity required to do justice to the complexity of the phenomenon while avoiding the dead-end of essentialization. It also makes it possible to expose the entanglements of gender with race, class, and citizenship without singling out any of these aspects. Similarly to Foucault's apparatus of control, the concept of assemblage in Deleuze and Guattari's works describes the stable yet contingent networks in which lives (human, but not exclusively) are embedded. It is much more complex, however, than a network because it is more like a concatenation, encompassing the vastly heterogeneous elements that make possible the physical, material, social, intellectual, spiritual, etc. existence of any given group. An assemblage allows for consistency and permanence while also being able to evolve and to incorporate elements as diverse as bodies, language, science, laws, sexuality, social infrastructures, and so on. The concept of assemblage enables us to think about organic and inorganic elements without dissociating them; more importantly, it renders visible the articulations between these elements. This makes it particularly apt for describing what Gayle Rubin referred to as the "sex/gender system": a "set of arrangements" organizing the connections between socially validated forms of kinships and of intimacies, imposing itself as permanent, self-sufficient, and, more often than not, "natural."[18]

In this regard, the concept of assemblage also allows us to unfold the intersectional aspect of gender: its cartographic dimension makes it apt to describe gender in terms of race, class, citizenship status, geopolitics . . . while offering a contextualized understanding of the complex interactions at play. In *Terrorist Assemblages*, Puar demonstrates how the concept can be used to understand gender in all its heterogeneous entanglements. Analyzing how the turban worn by Sikh men triggers racist reactions tainted by misogyny and homophobia, Puar writes:

And here we are pressed to rethink race, sexuality, and gender as concatenations, unstable assemblages of revolving and devolving energies, rather than intersectional coordinates. The fusion of hair, oil, dirt, sweat, cloth, skin, the organic melting into the non-organic, renders a turban . . . as an otherwise foreign object acculturated into a body's intimacies between organic and inorganic matter, blurring the distinctions between them, blurring insides and outsides.[19]

Gender, like race, cannot be grasped without "blurring the distinctions," particularly since they operate on the belief that the distinctions sustaining them are firm. Organic and inorganic matters are held together by energies rather than being located on binary coordinates such as inside versus outside, individual versus world, subject versus object, and so on. To paraphrase Deleuze in *Foucault*: "Gender has no essence; it is simply operational."[20] Like power, to which the original sentence refers, the gender assemblage is "operational": it *works*, if not uniformly, then powerfully.[21] But gender is only operational insofar as it operates as an assemblage, enmeshed in heterogeneous elements and systems, such as race, that extend beyond it.

Yet—and this is how the concept differs from the Foucauldian apparatus of power—an assemblage is as prone to variation as it is to stability. Its organic cohesion is maintained by tumultuous forces that both reinforce and threaten it: "An assemblage, the perfect object for the novel, has two sides: it is a collective assemblage of enunciation; it is a machinic assemblage of desire."[22] Machinic, here, means not only that the assemblage "works" but that it works to produce constant streams of desire that contradict the appearing stability of its cohesive enunciation—hence its affinities with literature. To the "set of arrangements" of the sex/gender system, the assemblage adds the mess and mesh of dysphoric desires plugging themselves into these arrangements and dismantling them. The reason Proust's narrator was led to think that Charlus looked like a woman in the first place was, in fact, a smile: "Blinking his eyes in the sunlight, he seemed almost to be smiling, and I found in his face seen thus in repose and as it were in its natural state something so affectionate, so defenseless."[23] Smiling in the sun, Charlus interrupts the flow of enunciations associated with him (such as masculinity and authority), revealing a "gap that is an affirmation," and sets in motion streams of desires that will lead him to have sex with another man, that will lead the narrator to divest from his botanical quest, and that will lead the author to give a new turn to the Darwinian narrative of sexual difference.

Reading gender as an assemblage, then, allows for a trans reading of any representation of gender, beyond the question of whether a given character can be described as trans. Transgender studies, Susan Stryker notes, is "concerned with anything that disrupts, denaturalizes, rearticulates, and makes visible the normative linkages" between bodies, social roles, a "gendered sense of self," and "the cultural mechanisms that work to sustain or thwart specific configurations of gendered personhood."[24] Thinking about those "normative linkages" as an assemblage allows us to grasp both their consistency (necessary to preserve a norm) and their contingency while avoiding the dead end of questioning gender's very existence. The fact that an assemblage is contingent doesn't mean that we can choose to operate outside of it. Dysphoria stems from this impossibility: it is triggered by the normative linkages that function as hard limits that we find ourselves running into over and over. There is, literally, no way out: the gender assemblage has a grasp on heterogeneous elements (bodies, objects, traditions) that makes it able to sustain its existence by incorporating new elements according to circumstances. Consider the fact that the gender assemblage has a hold on or is constituted of the following: bodies, real and fictional; abstract notions, such as nature and humanity; sciences, human and natural, applied and pure (from psychology and anthropology to anatomy, endocrinology, ethology, embryology, sociology . . .); medicine and technologies of bodily modifications, from pharmacology to surgery; languages as well as intensive and extensive systems of coding, including "body language," clothing, fashion, accessories and their cohort of surplus values, symbolic and economic, cosmetics, purses, wristwatches, guns, cars, smartphones, cigarettes, alcohol; family, both as a way of life and an ideological token; religion and the law; schooling and education; buildings, public and private spaces and their division and accessibility (bathrooms, bedrooms, classrooms); and so on. Who wouldn't be dysphoric?

GENDER: A WORD

My use of the word "gender" in the context of the interwar years is a deliberately anachronistic choice, and particularly so in the French context. In the United States, the notion of gender as distinct from biological sex appeared only in the late 1950s, in the context of sexology and discussions of gender reassignment.[25] It is worth noting, in this regard, that the genealogy of "gender" is already a trans genealogy: dysphoria and gender are codependent from the start, in more ways than one. As for France, the use of the word "genre" as an equivalent to "gender" is even more recent and still disputed. In his 2012 introduction to one of the first French academic publications dedicated to the topic, Daniel Welzer Lang notes that there isn't yet any consensus on the definition of the word *genre* or on the academic framework of its uses.[26] Furthermore, the overlapping uses of *genre* and *sexe* in French academic conversations are to this day fraught with tensions exacerbated by the prevalence of psychoanalysis and by the French feminist tradition rooted in Beauvoir's *The Second Sex*. The latter was written before the word "gender" was coined in the United States and was so influential in French second-wave feminism that Beauvoir's terminology continued to prevail until the end of the twentieth century.[27] Meanwhile, Lacanian psychoanalysis insisted on imposing its own account of gender through the concept of sexual difference, which it crystallized into a very specific account of the relationships between language and bodies, one that I believe to be incompatible with a trans approach.[28]

I chose nonetheless to rely on the anachronistic use of the term "gender" because my aim is to investigate the genealogy of the gender assemblage: gender, as we know it here and now, was already taking shape then and there. Ultimately, my object is a discussion of gender as we understand it now, and I argue that it found its premises in the modernist era. The mutually exclusive definitions of masculinity and femininity that still inform our contemporary gender assemblage emerged during the first decades of the twentieth century, along with modern capitalist states and their definition of citizenship, which was intended to mark irreducible lines between sexes, races, colonizers, and colonized.[29] As Laure Murat demonstrates in her discussion of the history of the "third sex," the notion of sex, at the turn of the twentieth century, matches our understanding of *gender*, which is "a cultural, social, and political construction" and a "linguistic act coordinating a series of theories and enunciations."[30] In "The Law of *Gender*: A Cultural History of the Third Sex," Murat bridges the epistemological gap created by the shift from one term to the other.[31] Opting to examine the third sex *as* gender, she takes into account both the contemporary concept (gender) and the historical term (sex). This strategy emphasizes the contiguity and the overlap between the two terms in French cultural history. In tracing them to a feminist history, Murat also draws from Beauvoir's conceptualization of the second sex: Murat's history of (the third) sex is "a political history of gender and of the domination imposed on the 'feminine' by the 'manly.'"[32] This balance of power doesn't end when "sex" is replaced by "gender." Even in the United States, as Kathryn Bond Stockton has argued, the contemporary use of the term wasn't meant to break down binaries but to obstruct their contestation, to "shore them up."[33]

Lastly, I want to emphasize that I do not intend here to give a universal description of gender nor to give a complete account of its conceptual history but to depict the biopolitical consequences of its crystallization in a given time and place (modernist France), which I believe to be a turning point—but certainly not the only one. Neither do I intend to universalize transness or dysphoria. Rather, I use this particular turning point to emphasize, as Stockton does, how "gender is queer": "irredeemably strange, ungraspable, out of sync with 'male and female' . . . since live gender fails to conform to normative ideals."[34] Or in the words of Marquis Bey, how gender is a "cistem failure."[35]

DYSPHORIA: AN AFFECT

The word dysphoria was modeled upon its opposite, "euphoria," "bearing well," an etymology particularly relevant to address modernist discussions around gender deviance. While the prefix "dys" is often understood as indicating division or duality, it refers in fact to absence or abnormality. Dysphoria suggests both lack and excess (too much ill-being or not enough well-being), which were recurring notions in the descriptions of gender incongruences from the turn of the nineteenth century.[36] Both notions point toward a misdistribution in the balance of sexual difference that needs to be readjusted in the choice of a mating partner—that is, a man suffering an excess of femininity finds himself attracted to a man. Most importantly, both lack and excess articulate gender identity with sexual orientation, reading both of these as defections from gender norms we now describe as queer. Thus, dysphoria points back toward the arrangement of gender and sexuality as it appeared in the sexologists' works and was unmade in modernist literary works and toward the "mutability" asserted by Kahan.[37] In reclaiming the term from its pathologizing past, I also mean to inscribe it in a longer history encompassing other forms of assignments as well as creative tensions between vernacular and medical. Even though trans scholars have recently pointed out the complexity and the critical potential of dysphoria, I am calling here for a conceptual use of the term that both eschews pathologizing interpretations and allows for a critical understanding of the gender binary.[38] Practices of linguistic reclamation in queer communities have been widely discussed.[39] When used by their former victims, stigmatizing terms gain a new meaning, one that encompasses layers of negativity. Far from constituting a clean slate, reclaimed words also serve as reminders: they never entirely lose their capacity to harm; the victory of reclaiming them remains tainted by bitterness.

The fifth edition of the *Diagnostic and Statistical Mental Disorders* (DSM-5), the current standard classification of mental disorders used in the United States, defines gender dysphoria as "a conflict between a person's physical or assigned gender and the gender with which he/she/they identify."[40] This definition raises many problematic points, such as what a "physical gender" can be and what it means to "identify with" a gender. Also noteworthy is the change between DSM-4 and DSM-5. In the latter, the diagnosis of "gender dysphoria" has replaced the previous "Gender Identity Disorder" (GID) in order to "avoid stigma." The criteria for the 2013 revision of the DSM produced by the American Psychiatric Association (APA) specify that "gender nonconformity is not in itself a mental disorder." The term "dysphoria" shifts the diagnosis (and the need for treatment) from gender disruption in itself to the pain that it causes: "the critical element of gender dysphoria is the presence of clinically significant distress associated with the condition."[41] Dysphoria, in its institutional use, is defined as a specific form of mental suffering calling for psychiatric help, a gesture that tautologically reasserts the pathologizing effect it is supposed to negate, in the same way as the medical use of the term "gender" ultimately reasserts sexual difference.

The diagnosis of "gender dysphoria syndrome" was first used in the 1970s by Stanford University's Gender Dysphoria Program. As one of its members, the psychiatrist Norman F. Fisk, reports, this diagnosis became relevant when the previously defined category of "transsexualism" revealed its limits. The main issue it raised was that "all patients [who came to the Stanford Program] . . . presented as virtual textbook cases of classical transsexualism . . . [because] they had availed themselves of the germane literature and had successfully prepared themselves to pass initial screening." In other words, patients knew how to get the diagnosis they needed, which led the program to shift from differential diagnosis to the assessment of "phenomenologically oriented" criteria, that is, to acknowledge "the patient's status here and now."[42] Thus the medical concept of dysphoria emerged in an unstable context, blurring the line between institutional categories of assignment and self-defined gender fluidity.

At its mildest level, Fisk states, gender dysphoria "might well be demonstrated by an apparently normal, well-adapted male . . . who chooses to . . . cross-dress as a can-can girl" in his "civic club's annual skit."[43] Beyond the doctor's demonstration of good will lurk the indicators (or the syndrome) of a wider issue: the fine line distinguishing a pathologizing spectrum from a general dysfunction. What does dysphoria, as a syndrome, tell us about gender? Dysphoria's relationship to gender is as wide as gender itself. Would anyone be able to assess one's appearance, clothing, figure, face, body, or hygiene outside of gender? Examining the "durability of negative affects in trans lives," Hil Malatino rightly argues that trans affects are not entirely encompassed by dysphoria.[44] In the same way, dysphoria isn't encompassed by trans lives but constitutes a variable response to a global constraint; it is less an affliction than a defense mechanism. When used in the trans community, this familiar term can describe a feeling or a state of mind ranging in intensity from mild to overwhelming. "Feeling dysphoric," like feeling depressed, can be temporary and trivial, or continuing and devastating, or both. It can hover at the back of your mind, or it can create the kind of intense distress that would have the members of the American Psychiatric Association nod approvingly.[45] It can lead you to hurt yourself; it can prevent you from leaving your house—or your bed—for days. It can make you laugh at yourself while shopping for clothes (you know this won't fit, don't you?). It can cause you to leave a party where you were doing just fine until suddenly it became so isolating to be surrounded by so many cis people that it brought you back to your particular brand of self-hatred and discomfort. Or you can be fine, really, most days, as long as you don't stay too long in front of the mirror—as few cis people do. While it relates to bodily incongruence, feeling dysphoric, like feeling nostalgic, can happen to anyone.

My dysphoria doesn't belong to me: it is constituted of and traversed by collective injunctions shaping and repeatedly failing to shape how I relate to my body and to others. In this regard, dysphoria is an affect, in the sense Deleuze and Guattari drew from Spinoza. It "does not refer to emotion but to forces" and traverses the gender assemblage in its entirety before becoming the personal feeling, or array of feelings, just described.[46] Affects aren't personal, nor can they be felt or expressed in any discursive form. Feeling dysphoric, overwhelming as it might be, is only the tip of the iceberg, an identifiable consequence of dysphoria as the affect itself. I was affected by dysphoria long before I knew of the word, but the ways in which it traversed me then found different outlets and triggered different escape routes. Charlus certainly doesn't *feel* dysphoric. As an affect, as "the gap that is an affirmation," dysphoria is both constraint and defense mechanism, antidote and poison, and has more kinship with desire than with identity. There might be a Spinozan joy in dysphoria. Not, obviously, in dysphoria as a feeling but in dysphoria as an affect, dismantling, like Charlus's smile, the assemblage's stable enunciations. This book tracks dysphoria as a vessel of disruption, a fugitive manifestation of forces at work beneath the surface, whose emergence can be joyful or desperate, liberating or destructive, creative or reactionary, world-changing or deadly. Dysphoria is the devil in Radiguet's teenage narrator's flesh, with its thirst for destruction; it also hovers in the hotel room where Crevel plans his suicide and glimmers in Sachs's extravagant web of lies.

Dysphoria is an insistent and willful affect, one that is at the same time object and method of inquiry, tracing and being traced.[47] As an affect, dysphoria bypasses the division between subject and object (or passive and active, or any binary, for that matter): the capacity of being affected is also a capacity to affect.[48] Michael Snediker describes how chronic pain fosters a paradoxical form of intellectual and intuitive awareness, one attuned to the body and its fugitive inputs. Neither phenomenological nor discursive, chronic pain casts "a shadow" on reading and thinking, one that gives it an edge to track forces at work below the surface.[49] Like chronic pain, dysphoria is a figure of insistence, persistence, and attunement. "One of the strange things about the fatigue of chronic pain, Snediker writes, is that nerves are indefatigable.... In trying to understand the experience of feeling constantly (a limb, a joint, an angle, a humidity) what other bodies disregard, learning to be attuned to *like* ... has become a way for me to think about the non-inurable body's response to ongoing affliction."[50] Similarly, not to be inured to gender assignment means not to be inured to the ways in which collective gendering injunctions exert their pressure on bodies and practices. Gender assignment, modern subjectivity, and dysphoria come together in a single package. Dysphoria affects us all: what differs is how and when you and I might *feel* dysphoric, or not.

TRANS: A STRATEGY

If gender is queer, what do we mean when we say "trans," particularly when looking at periods when neither the practices nor the word existed? "Exploring trans before trans," or "gender before gender," as Rachel Mesch exposes, involves not so much looking for trans people than it does using a "new set of critical tools."[51] Unlike Mesch, I am not, strictly speaking, looking at "gender before gender," since I focus on a later period than she does. Yet my aim is somewhat similar: I am not trying to locate and assert trans subjectivities. Rather, I am interested here in the desubjectifying potential of transness, the "trans-ing" that "takes place within, as well as across or between, gendered space."[52] The Anglo-European term "trans" has come to designate at least three overlapping groups of people: the Western contemporary group of those of us who either explicitly identify as trans or whose practices of discourses and embodiments align with those who do; those who stray, with various degrees of intentionality and visibility, from cultural gender norms; and those who live in a gender that doesn't match the way in which cultural norms understand their (naked) bodies. This book operates at the junction between the first and the last two categories and considers how the emergence of the contemporary category of trans makes room to look at gender deviance of the past.[53] What can these strategies of nonalignment teach us about gender or about cisness and transness? And if we acknowledge the fundamentally oppressive structure of the gender binary, how consistently does dysphoria affect each of its sides?

Approaching gender as an assemblage enables one to eschew the question of the "realness of gender," which probably constitutes the most important site of dissension between transgender studies and queer theory.[54] In *The New Woman*, Emma Heaney argues that queer theory, by privileging the analysis of sexuality over gender, has consistently erased transfeminine lives and experiences. Tracing back the origin of queer theory to French philosophy and particularly to the works of Foucault, Heaney unveils a consistent history of transmisogyny in which transwomen's existence has been used as an allegory to deconstruct the gender binary. In response, she calls for a materialist transfeminist approach that will "produce accounts of women's embodiment that do not assume cis experience."[55] While I fully agree with this analysis of transmisogyny, I also believe that the gap between queer theory and trans studies can be productively bridged, precisely because queer theory is rooted in this materialist approach. The array of theoretical thinkers usually considered poststructuralists, from Foucault to Butler, have been occupied with the question that Karen Barad sums up as the "nature of nature." Far from denying its materiality, questioning the nature of nature amounts to acknowledging the gap between nature, speech, and meaning while exploring ways to do justice to their materiality. Challenging the idea that "beings exist as individuals with inherent attributes, anterior to their representation," doesn't amount to negating materiality. On the contrary, it is an attempt to bring materiality to the foreground: only in letting go of the idea of an adequacy between words and things or between an object and our ability to represent it can we engage with the world. As Barad demonstrates, the poststructuralist conception of subjectivity is a materialist one. "Rejecting both poles, that subjectivity is either internally generated or externally imposed, post-structuralists eschew not only the very terms of the debates over agency versus structure and free will versus determinism but also the geometrical conception of subjectivity, which would validate 'internally' and 'externally' as meaningful terms in the debate."[56]

Subjectivity and interiority are key points here: this book understands that gender is a subjectification process, a making of political subjects, *and* a making of bodies. Like disability, dysphoria is an embodied encounter with norms.[57] As such, it counters with a willful insistence the abstraction that sometimes accompanies the constructivist approach of gender. Although the femininity it evokes is a misogynist construction, Charlus's smile is not an allegory but a line of flight cracking the surface of a very real gender assignment. As Abraham Weil underscores, assemblages "are best understood by what they *do*, rather than by what they *are*."[58] In this case, the dysphoric assemblage is holding together the contradictory impulses of assignments and corporeality, of desires and of enunciations, making them work together in unpredictable ways.

"THEN" AND "THEM": ENGAGING WITH THE CANON

In order to learn from Proust, I first had to learn, unsurprisingly, about time. As many queer scholars have aptly exposed, time is not a straight line.[59] In order to understand literary works from the past and shed light upon our own time in the process, we need to do away with the teleologic idea of progress. Attempting to read Proust or any modernist "gay writer" as a *first* attempt to describe what *we* know *now* paves a path lined with frustrations and misinterpretations. Gender and sexuality aren't for Proust what they are for me, even though the place from where I look at them is not fundamentally different from his own (think of a country whose borders have moved, not so much that you couldn't find your way around, but enough that the distances and the relational gaps between landmarks would change your travel plans). Instead of the straightforward directional line of temporality, the mapping of persistent places enables us to read "them" in a way that can make sense in our own cartography.[60]

The beginning of the twentieth century has shaped our relationship to gender and sexuality and to literature and art to such an extent that we often forget that "we" started "then." But while the history of modern gender and sexuality has been well documented, a similar discussion has yet to occur regarding literary productions. Heaney's critique of the allegorical use of transfemininity leaves us with a question: how can we engage with modernist texts and their queer reception without perpetuating the same type of instrumentalization? How can we still read, teach, and learn from works of the modernist canon while acknowledging their racism and their misogyny? The answer is in the question: we need to confront the fact that structural racism and sexism are lingering presences in those modernist texts we value precisely for their contestation of gender and sexual norms.

All of the authors discussed here, except for Genet, were more or less privileged members of the Parisian intellectual bourgeoisie.[61] Of course, this statement needs to be nuanced: Colette suffered the social and financial burden of divorced women; Sachs came from a bankrupted family and made a living by embezzling his wealthier friends' money; Proust and Sachs belonged to the Jewish minority. But all of them were deeply influenced by the racial and gendered divides at work in French imperialism. These discriminative systems emerge as blind spots in their critique of gender, ambiguously enabling them to draw lines of flight and carve free spaces for themselves while contributing to the enforcement of a violent world order. While it may seem counterintuitive to give even more space to an already overrepresented group, my concern here isn't representation—nor do I believe that representation should be the main purpose of trans studies—but the analysis of entanglements that are still weighing on us.[62] In so doing, I also hope to contribute to transatlantic discussions of the ways in which French imperialism and its creation of race and gender echoes and interacts with but also differs from its North American counterpart.[63]

By situating the texts discussed in this book within the scope of trans studies, I do not intend to reclaim their characters or their authors as transgender. With the exception of Gide's early works, they were written at a time when what we now call "gender transition" was already a publicly discussed practice. Surgical gender reassignment technologies and legal sex change were mediatized in the interwar years through a number of cases, from Lili Elbe to Violette Norris.[64] I do not intend to discuss those cases here. Again, my concern here isn't representation. Rather, I read these works as roadmaps, guided by a practical, personal question: how does one navigate a dysphoric assemblage? This is also why, with the exception of Colette, all the writers I am discussing are cisgender males. Even though their main focuses are sometimes solely masculinity (Gide) or femininity (Rostand), most of them describe the gender assemblage from the dominant position of white cismasculinity. My choice of corpus can be perceived as limited, and my hope is that eventually many other French modernist works, either canonical or little known, could be analyzed with the same tools. Yet exploration of the French modernist gender assemblage initiated in this book opens with analyses of white cismasculinity because, as I will discuss in my first two chapters, it defines itself in relationship to citizenship and thereby offers that a guiding thread through the biopolitical structure of the assemblage. Similarly, the dysphoria affecting or, rather, traversing those individuals who find themselves assigned to dominant positions allows a glimpse into the power dynamics dividing and cementing the assemblage.

A common trait among the texts discussed here is the very fine line they draw between autobiography and fiction, a trait Michael Lucey identified and exposed in *Never Say I*. Some are self-proclaimed autobiographical, even apologetic, first-person writings, and most keep a safe/unsafe distance from the actual life of their authors, which have been subjected to endless discussions since the time of their publication. In his analysis of French gay or protogay modernism, Lucey examines the conditions of emergence of a collective identity. The "glass closet" situation created by a problematic and fluid use of first-person narratives opened the path toward the possibility of naming and owning queer feelings and practices. Since my main interrogation points toward gender, not sexuality, what is at stake for me is not the formation of a community but an array of individual attempts to navigate a collective gender assemblage. In this regard, to borrow a term from Lucey's later work, the individuals discussed in this book are also "misfits." They belong together solely because "they find themselves unfit or misfit, decategorized, but to an uncertain degree."[65] This position, or lack thereof, also leads them to play with genres as they do with genders. The undetermined relationship between the personal and the fictional, while underscoring the danger of sexual and gender deviance, also points toward the dysphoria at work in the assemblage. The impossibility of a resolution, of finding a livable space within the binary, leads to textual explorations, which find themselves, as well, in undetermined spaces between life and fiction, between imaginary and real, between experience and resolution.

WRITING GENDER IN THE FRENCH INTERWAR YEARS: A NEXUS AND A NETWORK

Each chapter of this book looks into a particular way in which French modernist literary works translated and dismantled the dysphoric assemblage of gender. I work with a close-knit corpus of authors, whose works and whose critics echo one another. Some of them, like Proust, Gide, Genet, and Colette, are still major figures in literary history; others, like Sachs, Rostand, Crevel, and Radiguet, never achieved this level of fame or have faded from attention. Yet the Parisian literary and artistic circles of the interwar years were a small world, and most of the authors discussed here personally knew and interacted with at least some of the others. There were famous and well-documented exchanges between them, such as Proust's conversation with Gide on first-person writing.[66] There were less-known collaborations, as when Rostand used his minor fame to help Proust on the path toward his major fame[67] and when Crevel introduced Gide to gay Berlin.[68] There were sex, gossips, and queer alliances: Sachs took Radiguet's place as Cocteau's protégé and falsely claimed Proust as a relative. And there were also missed encounters, such as between Sachs and Genet, queer brothers in crime who probably never met nor interacted: at the time of Sachs' death in 1945, Genet's first novel had only been published for two years. This open-ended group of writers forms a nexus in a wider network that could be expanded toward other names, other cultural productions, and other assemblages.

Chapter 1 uses Maurice Rostand's 1933 novel, *La femme qui était en lui* (The woman in him), as a case study to describe key aspects of the interwar years gender assemblage.[69] Rostand's novel is riddled with contradictions. While it portrays alternative masculinity as an escape route from the violent assignments of the gender assemblage and relies on pacifism and homosocial desires to draw the contours of a resistance to the violence of masculine subjectification, *La femme qui était en lui* does so by enforcing structural misogyny and racism. The plot centers on a gay man who, feeling hampered by his inner femininity and his unfortunate love affairs, seeks the help of a doctor, who literally severs him from "the woman in him." But this surgery comes at price: the woman, who now possesses a body of her own, exerts a deadly attraction over him. The fantasy dimension in Rostand's novel makes it a perfect paradigm to understand the contradictory feelings crystallized around the scientific apparatus of psychiatry and sexology during the interwar years. Here, dysphoria emerges as a reaction to the modern alliance between masculinity and warfare, but while the novel displays a series of caring fathers and lovers, its portrayal of femininity acts as a foil that makes it an untenable, and unrelatable, position. Similarly, its cast of racialized servants manifests the strong delimitation between the masters of the empire and their Orientalized subjects, enforcing the white masculinity it seeks to question. This series of contradictions makes Rostand's novel exemplary not only of the gender assemblage of its time and its racialized configuration but also of the body of texts discussed in the following chapters.

Chapter 2, "Gide's Failed Marriages," looks at the gender assemblage's most dysfunctional feature: heterosexual marriage. To do so, I trace the paradoxes at work in Gide's accounts of marriage, from his essay *Corydon* to *Madeleine*, the memoir he dedicated to his wife, and to the twin novels *The Immoralist* and *Strait Is the Gate*.[70] Queer theory has portrayed Gide as a "gay outlaw" and as a "sexual dissident," yet, as Lucey has highlighted, Gide also "finds in sexuality [the] confirmation of conservative ideologies."[71] Focusing on his description of marriage sheds a new light on this process. Marriage, by crystallizing mutually exclusive definitions of femininity and masculinity, keeps the two genders estranged and crushes its subjects. But, while women are either, in fiction, killed in the process (*The Immoralist*, *Strait Is the Gate*) or reduced to a subaltern position in reality (*Corydon*, *Madeleine*), men are granted the escape route of disruptive desires. Marriage fosters an erotics of misogyny in which sexual dissidence finds its political value as the rejection of a social order whose stability is attributed to women. To this social order corresponds the geographical space of the French colonial empire: it is no accident that North African territories are the place where

Gide's heterosexual relationships always end up and always end. Race, here, reveals itself once again as a central component of the assemblage: the erotization of Brown bodies answers the erotic of misogyny. The colonial borderlands provide dysphoria with a space where the gender assemblage embraces its own contractions, in an endless loop of failed escapes: Gide's marriage is in itself a dysphoric assemblage.

In chapter 3, "Cross-Pollination," I revisit the appearance of Charlus-as-a-woman in Proust's *Sodom and Gomorrah*. My analysis draws on a combined reading of Sedgwick and Deleuze, whose essays on Proust have never been examined side by side, and on Simon Porzak's analysis of Proust's passion for evolutionary biology.[72] Unlike Gide, Proust embraces the conflation of gender with sexuality, but in depicting homosexuality as inversion, he draws a complex landscape in which all his characters are engaged in a game of social metamorphosis, a game that, I argue, revolves around the Darwinian questions of change and fecundity. As Sedgwick has shown in her discussion of the scene in which Charlus and his future lover Jupien are compared to a bumblebee and an orchid, Proustian botanical metaphors are far from endorsing gender binarism.[73] Rather, Proust dwells upon the findings of evolutionary biology and uses them to complicate the naturalizing narratives of heteronormativity. Proust's men-women literally hack into the gender binary and become free agents, both orchids and bumblebees, initiating a process of cross-pollination that traverses social categories. Inversion, not heterosexual reproduction, is the real source of change and evolution in Proust's textual landscape, and dysphoria is the affect that triggers it.

Chapter 4 focuses on a lesser-known author, but a central figure in more ways than one: Maurice Sachs is connected in some way or another with most of the writers discussed in this book.

A master at networking, Sachs was a socialite, a con artist, a thief, an art dealer, and a talented writer who produced a series of autobiographical texts. As a writer and a criminal, Sachs blurs the boundaries between reality and fiction: while his memoirs are inspired by reality and by literature (Charlus and Jupien are recurring names in his works), they are also written with the aim to improve Sachs's image and financial situation. Sachs is a spider, in the sense that Deleuze attributed to Charlus, but while a fictional Charlus controls whole networks of meaning and *logos*, a very real Sachs trades in currencies, goods, people, and information.[74] As a highly visible queer and crooked Jew in the Paris of the interwar year, Sachs embodied for some of his contemporaries the fascist trope of abjection.[75] Utterly devoid of gay shame, he crystallized traits that made him a threat to white masculinity and the values associated with it in a much more threatening way than Rostand's tender pacifists. Dysphoria, in Sachs, manifests as an escape strategy, a game of fraud and cunning, emerging in gender-bending and physical metamorphosis but eventually shaping an entire mode of existence.

The fifth and final chapter, "Intermittent Miracles," explores how temporality is framed by the gender assemblage. Queer theory scholars have described queer temporality in ways that emphasize its intensity and its connection to the present, as opposed to futurity and continuity.[76] I introduce a new element to these discussions: a dysphoric temporality made of absence as much as presence, a disjunctive time born out of the impossibility of finding one's place in the assemblage. Temporal dysphoria, unlike queer time, is a temporality of disengagement rather than attunement, even though both modes of temporality share a disruptive, unstable kinship. This final chapter explores queer and dysphoric time through four texts. The first two, Raymond Radiguet's *The Devil in The Flesh* and Colette's *The Vagabond*,[77] follow a somewhat traditional chronological narrative but translate and dismantle the temporal constraints imposed by the gender assemblage. The last two, Jean Genet's *Our Lady of the Flowers* and René Crevel's *My Body and I*,[78] bend temporal normativity in their form as much as in their content. Set in a single space—a prison cell (Genet) and a hotel room (Crevel)—these two texts use space as the anchor for a spiraling temporality that escapes linearity and defies boundaries. Genet's transfeminist characters disrupt the gender binary, blurring identities and boundaries. Queer time and dysphoric time are given a textual presence that ultimately yields an account of common experiences triggered by the gender assemblage.

1

A CASE STUDY

Schizophrenic Splits in *La femme qui était en lui*

And what of the woman, Doctor, that mysterious woman, what will you do with her?
—Maurice Rostand, *La femme qui était en lui*

CIVILIZATION AND ITS DYSPHORIA

A tale of forbidden desires, of tender fathers, loving sons, and their caring Oriental servants, of cruel women and evil scientists: the entire gender assemblage of the French interwar years can be glimpsed through the plot of a fantasy novel. Maurice Rostand's *La femme qui était en lui* (The woman in him), published in 1933, hardly qualifies as a classic, let alone a masterpiece.[1] Yet in bringing together fantasy, confession, gay romance, and queer coming of age, Rostand brings to life the tangle of contradictions and irreconcilable divides of the gender assemblage. In *La femme qui était en lui*, tender men wander in search of modes of relation that would escape the violence of heteronormativity while they are cared for by racialized servants who validate and facilitate their dramas, imaginary women rule over an aesthetic universe of music and passion while actual women hinder true romance, and Swiss doctors are all too ready to insert their normalizing scalpels into throbbing flesh and hearts. This chapter uses Rostand's novel *La femme qui était en lui* as a case study and entry point into the salient tensions at work in the gender assemblage of its time, tensions that will keep surfacing throughout the rest of this book—the crisis in men and the foil of femmes fatales, the lure of Orientalism, the constant seesaw between the fixation of object choice and the quest for alternative subjectivities—along with their historical and ideological contours: European wars and colonial expansion, as well as evolutionary biology and modern psychiatry.

The book's preface cryptically states: "Those who understand me know that if I wrote *La femme qui était en lui* it is because I had to."[2] A prolific writer as well as a successful playwright, Rostand has a paradoxical literary profile: while his flowery style and romanticized aestheticism seemed outdated to his contemporaries, his choice of topics and thematic explorations are attuned to modernist investigations into gender.[3] The sentimentality of his prose shouldn't obscure the part he played in the gay community and his visibility. His use of the first person, notably, aligns with the premises of a representation of gay identity in the French modernist literary canon described by Michael Lucey.[4] Born in 1891, Maurice Rostand was the eldest son of Edmond Rostand, the playwright and author of *Cyrano de Bergerac*, and of the poet Rosemonde Gérard. Through his famous parents and their aristocratic connections, Maurice became a socialite before he had any say in the matter. A repertoire of anecdotes from his childhood years includes the fact that he spoke in verse before he was five, wrote his first play at eight, and spent his afternoons in Sarah Bernhardt's dressing room, whose hairstyle he strove to imitate.[5] A queer icon since his teenage years, Maurice cut a hypervisible figure in the literary Paris of the interwar years: wearing makeup and jewelry, cultivating his own mannerisms and style, he inspired the young Jean Cocteau, and even though his literary fame never matched Cocteau's, he remained one of the most emblematic queer personalities of his time, the "national flag" of the gay Paris.[6]

His visibility also made him a key influence on his contemporaries and inscribed him in a queer lineage extending to the present. Rostand is notably the author of *L'homme que j'ai tué*, (The man I killed), which was adapted to cinema by Ernst Lubitsch under the title *Broken Lullaby* and more recently by François Ozon as *Frantz*.[7] Yet contrary to Gide, whom I will discuss in the next chapter, Rostand has no interest in the politics of sexual dissidence. Both his politics and his writing style remain on the conservative side. He doesn't advocate for any kind of radical change, and his interventions in favor of pacifism and same-sex love, albeit courageous, are limited to the bourgeois circles within which he thrives. A well-meaning conservative, Rostand makes a perfect case study precisely because he grapples with contradictions but doesn't devise any strategy to resolve them. In revealing white masculinity as an inhospitable position while taking for granted that all others are subalterns, Rostand enforces the alienation of people of color. Similarly, his account of gender deviance reifies women, portraying them as a token of a sexual and social disruption only beneficial for men, a process that Emma Heaney has described as the "transfeminine allegory."[8] In other words, *La femme qui était en lui* offers an entry point into the ambivalent strategies adopted by modernist writers in attempting to translate and dismantle the gender assemblage of their time.

While Rostand's career as a playwright started under the aegis of his illustrious father, another family member exerted a less visible but probably more significant influence on him. Maurice was the elder brother of the biologist and popular science writer Jean Rostand, who published in 1933, the same year as *La femme qui était en lui*, *Les problèmes de l'hérédité et du sexe* (The problems of heredity and sex). During the first part of his scientific career, Jean Rostand conducted groundbreaking research on the genetics of amphibians and notably on the role of sexual hormones and parthenogenesis. Jean's study of the genetics of sexual difference cannot be ignored when looking at Maurice's flirtation with Shelleysian witch doctors. *Les problèmes de l'hérédité et du sexe* includes sections on "intersexuality" and "sex change."[9] Even if Maurice never commented publicly on his brother's research interests other than to praise him, Jean's specific experiments with sexual hormones gave him an actual insight into the scientific developments of his time.[10] Like Radclyffe Hall's *The Well of Loneliness*, *La femme qui était en lui* bears the influence of turn-of-the-century sexology, but Rostand's novel also manifests, albeit in an allusive form, a closeness to the issues at the core of contemporary scientific and psychiatric endeavors.[11] In this regard as well, *La femme qui était en lui* echoes and gives shape to the contradictory impulses, phobias, obsessions, and incongruences at work in the descriptions of gender variance and same-sex desire.

Published a year after the French translation of *The Well of Loneliness*, Rostand's novel is introduced as a confession in a manner somewhat similar to Hall's and opens like an autobiographical narrative focusing on gender variance and same-sex love, emphasizing the singularity of its main character from childhood on.[12] Rostand's narrator begins his confession by disclosing that there always was, in him, a "feminine presence," who prompted him to fall in love with men for as long as he can remember. Like Hall's, the narrator recalls a sheltered childhood in a rich mansion and a loving father who suffered an early death, then evokes a hectic coming of age marked by desperate romances.

On its premises, Rostand's novel is, like *The Well of Loneliness*, "feeling backward": it is imbued with the sense of loss and the nostalgic undertones described by Heather Love.[13] But its subsequent incursion into fantasy complicates things: reaching beyond nostalgia, it reveals the schizophrenic divides that fracture the gender assemblage of its time and extend into ours. In his adult years, Rostand's narrator embarks on a successful career as a composer and meets Emmanuel, the man he loves and to whom his confession is dedicated. After months of happiness, Emmanuel leaves him at the insistence of his wife. Desperate, the narrator resolves to seek a cure for his condition and meets with a Swiss "doctor and sorcerer" who offers to sever him from the woman in him: he will conjure her to life, force her to incarnate herself in her own body, and kill her. After submitting himself to this treatment, the narrator discovers that his talent for music has left him, along with any possibility of happiness. His wandering life leads to his childhood home, which he realizes is now occupied by a mysterious woman. He falls in love with her at first sight before discovering who she really is: the woman that was in him, who managed to escape her fate by killing the doctor. The novel ends with a letter informing Emmanuel that the author of the confession was found dead, lying near the body of a woman that he had shot.

CIRCULATING ACROSS: DYSPHORIA AS NAVIGATION

The turn toward fantasy in *La femme qui était en lui* builds upon the nineteenth-century tradition of narratives of possession. In the vein of Maupassant's *Le horla*,[14] Rostand gives a literal version of the *"anima mulieribus virili corpore inclusa,"* "a woman's soul in a man's body" argument used to describe gender deviance at the turn of the century.[15] Possession, here, with its suggestion of split personality, materializes the question of the gender binary: what does it mean to be haunted by a gender, or to be a gender, for that matter? But the split, it turns out, is not so much within the narrator as it is around him—not a split but rather a series of splits, consolidating and undermining the gender assemblage. The lines of fracture separating woman and man, colonizer and colonized, German and French, tender (gay) men and "normal men," form "the hydra-headed creature of the coloniality of being" described by Yv E. Nay and Eliza Steinbock, which "splits colonial difference into the heads of racial difference, sexuality difference, and sex/gender difference."[16] With all its contradictions, dead-ends, and juxtapositions, Rostand's novel exposes the interconnectedness between sexuality, gender, and race, while the "Jekyll and Hyde" aspect of his plot materializes the violent intrusions of psychiatry and science, which deepen the splits in their pretense to cure them.[17]

Dysphoria, as an affect, flows around these splits, not as another split but as their side effect: an attempt to reconnect, to reconcile, to circulate across and beyond splits. In Rostand, as in many of the works discussed in this book, dysphoria first emerges under the guise of male same-sex desire, a destructive yet assertive force cutting across and reconfiguring the gender assemblage and its lines of fracture. Rostand's dysphoric attempts at reclaiming femininity are fueled by streams of desire that point toward what can best be described as the gender/sexuality seesaw of inversion. As Benjamin Kahan has shown, the turn-of-the-century scientific apparatus of sexology vastly emphasized the "stabilization of gender as object choice."[18] But this very move ensured that inversion remained elusive, oscillating between the gendered and the sexual, an ambiguity on which modernist literature endlessly plays. As with *The Well of Loneliness*, the question of whether the narrator of *La femme qui était en lui* is to be read as a gay man, a fantasized case of sexual inversion, or a model of male femininity is irrelevant.[19] Rather, this chapter uses the case study of Rostand to explore the stabilization of object choice as a dysphoric attempt at unraveling the sealed boundaries dividing the social field.

Dysphoria also emerges in *La femme qui était en lui* under the motif of pacifism. Rostand's most famous novel, *L'homme que j'ai tué*, is a pacifist manifesto in which the narrator atones for the "murder" of a German soldier on the battlefield, a victim he comes to consider as his brother. The underlying homoerotic tone of the novel brings together pacifism and tender masculinity, which *La femme qui était en lui* takes to the next level. In picturing a world of interwoven male tenderness, the novel gnaws at dominant masculinity and patriotic warfare and reveals the weight of a political context shaped by wars. Historians have shown how actual wars and their consequences, as well as the ghosts of future conflicts, shaped the mutually exclusive definitions of masculinity and femininity in the modernist era.[20] As Carolyn Dean has shown, the French context distinguished itself in its unique combination of relative stability and widespread anxieties. "During the tumult of the interwar years, [France] remained a liberal democratic state whose elites sought to reconcile individualism, secularization, and the rule of law with perhaps unparalleled, irrational fears and fantasies about national decline."[21] In France, the enforcement of secularization implemented by the government and the bourgeois elites was accompanied by an active defense of the heterosexual family. National decline, gender deviance, and a fantasized decline in birth rates were understood as being in direct connection to one another.[22] Rostand's pacifism can be read as a dysphoric attempt at navigating these contradictions, exposing war as a heteronormative regulating trope and a cornerstone of the modern gender assemblage.

Yet the hypervisibility of European wars tends to obscure the presence of another war, felt but not shown, in Rostand's novel: the constant warfare of colonization. In this regard as well, Rostand's novel is exemplary. Although few French modernist texts directly engage with race, these works feature an impressive cast of racialized servants, sex workers, estranged family members, all bringing the colonial presence to the metropolitan terrain. In *La femme qui était en lui*, dysphoria also emerges in the discrete attachments formed with racialized subalterns and adjuvants, who act as intermediaries leading toward a fantasized space beyond gender, or as guides enabling a deterritorialization of sorts. *La femme qui était en lui*, as a case study, thus also brings to light the connections between evolutionary theory and the gendered birth of modern citizenship. Both of these tropes, citizenship and science, played a central part in the shaping of the modern gender assemblage we inherited. European imperialism "seeded the development of *scientia sexualis*, psychiatry, endocrinology, surgery, and other medical fields engaged in . . . the 'better breeding' programs of nation-states."[23] Antisemitism plays a queer part in this process, manifested in Rostand's novel through the portrayal of the Jewish "witch doctor," who embodies sexology in all its contradictions. Again, Rostand's narrative doesn't resolve anything: rather, it bears witness to the iterations of dysphoria triggered by the network of irresolvable contradictions traversing the gender assemblage.

In order to map these contradictions, this chapter first goes back to late-nineteenth-century theories of inversion. Rather than looking at the emergence of sexology from an Anglo-American perspective, I focus on its German origins, namely the works of Heinrich Ulrichs and Magnus Hirschfeld. Their influence on French modernist literature, manifest through the figures of Gide and Proust, is also intrinsically tied to evolutionary biology, a thread I introduce in this chapter but will pursue in more depths in the following chapters. My purpose is to focus on the gender/sexuality seesaw that fuels Rostand's narrative and makes it emblematic of modernist narratives of inversion. While the modernist ambivalence between gender and sexuality, crystallized in the trope of inversion, is often addressed as an overlap, I propose to look at it from a dynamic perspective: the movement of the seesaw is triggered by the fundamental unbalance between genders, that is, by the misogyny structuring theories of inversion.

The next two sections of this chapter, "The Archipelago of Tender Masculinity" and "Femininity's Tragic Enigma," illustrate how the mutually exclusive definitions of gender and the gender/sexuality seesaw fuel each other. As Rostand's novel amply illustrates, the representation of inversion itself, with its tender sons and lovers, crystallizes the discriminative definitions of masculinity and femininity by enforcing a perception of femininity as a sheer negative foil.

The following sections, "Dysphoric Pacifism" and "There Aren't Any Sins . . .," introduce Rostand's pacifism and his description of male homoeroticism, bringing out the articulation between modern masculinity and the nation-state. While Gide's writings offer a much more complex and subtle exploration of the same trope, Rostand's opposition of gay love to warfare allows me to introduce the historical context of the French interwar years and its particular combination of familialism and patriotism. Far from advocating for male homosexuality as sexual dissidence, Rostand's dysphoric pacifism mirrors the masculine anxieties and the structural misogyny at work in the gender assemblage.

In "Invisible Attachments," I address the ways in which racial divides structure the entire plot of *La femme qui était en lui*, even though the novel's protagonists are white men and its main settings are Paris and the Provençal countryside. The French colonial empire is represented by a racialized cast of subaltern characters whose care and allegiance are taken for granted, a situation that reflects the geopolitical truth of the unquestioned pilfering of resources sustaining metropolitan bourgeois cultural life. Yet the novel's racialized servants also serve a deeper motive: they are agents of gender trouble, facilitating the narrator's dysphoric quest. The antisemitic portrayal of the doctor serves a similar purpose. While the servants are portrayed as primitive, he is described as decadent: both of these dehumanizing and Orientalizing traits insist on the ungendered nature of the racialized Others leading the narrator to uncharted territories at the border of the assemblage.

Lastly, "The Cut" delves into Rostand's enactment of his fantasy of *scientia sexualis*. The figure of the Swiss doctor, and his Shelley-like attempt at gender reassignment surgery, offers a troubling synthesis of medical science, psychology, psychiatry, and the nascent biology of the sexes. The disastrous cure enacted by *scientia sexualis* makes a murderous woman and a suicidal man out of a talented gay man. This lethal intervention reflects not so much the inaccuracy of the diagnosis but the ways in which the diagnosis, with its conflation of gender dysphoria and schizophrenia, enacts the violence at work in the gender assemblage itself. The split is the problem, not the cure, and its victims are gendered bodies.

In lieu of a conclusion, "Impossible Embodiments" traces Rostand's quest for a satisfying form of embodiment through its musical structure: dysphoria acts as a refrain in the novel, always returning, never being resolved. While its plot is based on the fantasy account of a missed incarnation, *La femme qui était en lui* keeps eschewing the presence of actual bodies: male bodies are only portrayed through their (painful) affects and keep circling around an idealized, and inhuman, female body. Again, the most interesting aspect of *La femme qui était en lui*, except maybe for its ability to work with clichés while pretending to invent them, is its unresolved contradictions. Rostand's refrain manifests over and over the impossibility of truly satisfying forms of embodiment in the gender assemblage.

THEORIZING INVERSION: THE GENDER AND SEXUALITY SEESAW

At the end of the nineteenth century, the Prussian jurist Karl Heinrich Ulrichs became famous for advocating for those individuals practicing what he first called "manly love," then "Uranism" and "third sex."[24] Described as the initiator of "a conceptual revolution that transformed erotic, same-sex love from an idea of deviant acts into a full-blown sexual orientation," Ulrichs is mostly remembered as a gay rights pioneer.[25] Less discussed is the fact that his argument pertains to gender as much as to sexuality. Ulrichs's depiction of male homosexuality is based on an account of gender, that is, a series of traits and behaviors deemed as natural and stable even though they aren't necessarily associated to bodily functions or organs. As Emma Heaney states, Ulrichs's figure of the Urning "initiates the project of carving out a defining set of desires and characteristics that are 'of woman' but present in 'male bodies.'"[26] Ulrich's explanation of "manmanly" love relies on the fact that the individual prone to it is partially female: "the Urning is not a man, but rather a kind of feminine being when it concerns not only his entire organism, but also his sexual feelings of love, his entire natural temperament, and his talents."[27] This point forms the root of Ulrichs's theory of the third sex. Far from negating the gender binary, he uses it to naturalize male-to-male attraction: a man who desires another man is actually not male but female.[28]

Ulrichs's argument is rooted in evolutionary biology, as are most of the turn-of-the-century accounts of gender variance. He relies on, specifically, the emerging science of embryology: "A dual sexual germ is latent in each embryo approximately until the twelfth week of its existence, a male one and simultaneously a female one. The germ of the sexual organs of the embryo is then able to develop male sexual parts ... and *at the same time* to develop female sexual parts." The human Urning is the product of the abnormal growth of a single and normal "seed" (Ulrichs uses the German word *Keim*, "nucleus"). The hybrid nature of the Urning is the result of an accident, the wrong development of this kernel, which contains the potential for both male and female individuation. While Ulrichs's ultimate goal is to inscribe Urnings in the realm of the natural, he relies on the logic of sexual difference to rationalize what he describes as an evolutionary error. Urnings owe their unnatural inclinations for other males to the fact that their "seed of latent sexual desire develops into the female, not corresponding to the development of the sexual organs."[29] Urnings are abnormal, but this abnormality is the result of natural circumstances, much like the development of any disease. Ulrich's thesis contains the seed of the contradiction at work in the repressive hypothesis, which Rostand's novel carries to its point of rupture: deviance is both a *nature* and an *error* (that might be fixed). Through his emphasis on gender, Ulrichs carries over the cut he is aiming to transcend in conceptualizing a new category.

During the first decades of the twentieth century, while Ulrichs's theory was being elaborated on by Magnus Hirschfeld in Germany and popularized by Marcel Proust, among others, in France, a competing model to describe male homosexuality also emerged, one that emphasized the idea of male bonding rather than inversion.[30] In his essay *Corydon*, published in 1920 but written before World War I, André Gide states his disapproval of the third-sex theory and its proponents:

> The theory of woman-man, of the *Sexuelle Zwischenstufen* (intermediate degrees of sexuality) advanced by Dr. Hirschfeld . . . which Marcel Proust appears to accept—may well be true enough; but that theory explains and concerns only certain cases of homosexuality . . .—cases of inversion, of effeminacy, of sodomy. . . . Even granting that Hirschfeld's theory accounts for these cases, his "third sex" argument certainly cannot explain what we habitually call "Greek love": pederasty—in which effeminacy is neither here nor there.[31]

"Inversion," "sodomy," and "effeminacy": the first term refers to a medical category, the second one to a sexual practice, and the third one to gender appearance. Substituting one for the others shows that, even though Gide argues for a different perspective on homosexuality, he operates in the same assemblage as Ulrichs. His argument, like Ulrichs's, relies on the evolutionary perception of sexual difference. Gide later refers explicitly to Darwin's description of sexual selection. Since, Gide argues, evolution gave male birds brighter feathers and more sophisticated singing abilities, it is only natural that the male individuals of a species favor aesthetic perfection in their quest for mating partners.[32] How, while they are so brightly attired, could they satisfy themselves with their duller nesting counterparts?

Imposing a paradoxical twist on sexual difference, Gide's central argument is that shared attractions between men aren't the product of an excess of femininity but of masculinity:

> Yes, the sexual instinct exists . . . but it is compelling only at certain times. . . . In order to respond infallibly to the female's momentary proposition, the sexual instinct confronts her with the permanent desire of the male. . . . The only heterosexual relations (of animals) are for the purpose of fertilization.
>
> And the male is not always satisfied with these.[33]

The model that accounts for male bonding relies on the same evolutionary conception of gender as the proponents of inversion. Neither Ulrichs nor Gide question sexual difference and its mutually exclusive definitions of masculinity and femininity. The only point on which their arguments diverge is the question of femininity. The former incorporates it in his definition of male homosexuality; the latter bases his on utter rejection. The first one explains and legitimizes male homosexuality by an excess of masculinity; the other argues for an excess of femininity. Operating in a common framework, both models are, as Heaney has shown, highly misogynist and trans misogynist.[34] In pushing masculinity toward its point of rupture, whether through excess or lack, they expose it as an unachievable imperative weighing on every male-assigned individual and depriving of her agency every female-assigned individual—or, in Foucauldian terms, subjectifying the first while depriving the second of her status as subject. Both theories endorse and reinforce the cut imposed by the gender binary that they sought to escape.

Evolutionary biology plays a seminal part in both theories, in which it serves the same purpose: to make room for same-sex alliances, relationships, and desires. But it is no accident that these arguments are concerned first and foremost with the male homosocial continuum: a female homosocial continuum doesn't even register in the gender assemblage. Male homosexuality and gender deviance, understood either as lack or as excess of masculinity, are an argumentative seesaw whose perpetual movement is triggered by the imbalance built into the descriptions of sexual difference. Femininity is offered as an option allowing one to escape heteronormative masculinity, but only as a form of fetishized countervalue. Since femininity derives its disruptive power precisely because it is the undesirable side of the gender binary, it never constitutes a satisfying end. More often than not, as Heaney has demonstrated, femininity is used as a foil in narratives and conceptualizations of gender deviance and queerness, a recurring process she calls the "transfeminine allegory." Depersonalizing actual transwomen, the allegory allows for the reclaiming of deviant uses of femininity or the positing of femininity as deviance or dissidence in ways that only benefit the masculine side of the binary.[35]

The transfeminine allegory leads to the impasse manifested in *La femme qui était en lui*. Male-to-male attraction is blamed on sexual difference, that is, the intrusion of femininity. The novel's fatal conclusion remains ambiguous. When the narrator's dead body is found lying near that of the woman, the investigation establishes that he shot her in the heart and spontaneously died, "as if he had died from killing her." But is the narrator a victim of the Woman or of the mistake he made in trying to kill a part of himself? Is the Woman so lethal because she was orphaned from her better half or because she is a *woman*? Which is deadliest: inversion or its refusal? And would acceptance of same-sex love solve the matter? The novel closes with a letter by the narrator's lover, Emmanuel, in which he asks a priest to tend to the graves of "the man and the woman who played such a great part in [his] life."[36] Emmanuel's acknowledgment of his lover's dual nature rings as an acknowledgment of dysphoria itself, not as faulty embodiment but as the impossibility of any livable embodiment across the gender divide.

AN ARCHIPELAGO OF TENDER MASCULINITY

In the first decades of the twentieth century, Magnus Hirschfeld expanded Ulrichs's third-sex theory toward a more open-ended model. In his theory of sexual intermediaries, Hirschfeld distinguished six main types of sexual inclinations.[37] Ranging from the "total man" to the "total woman" and including various degrees of "psychological hermaphrodites" and "Uranians," those types were categorized according to their sexual objects of predilection—the total man being attracted to the total woman, for instance—but the types corresponded at the same time to what we now describe as genders. Hirschfeld's scale, not unlike the one Kinsey would advance a few decades later, is a continuum. As a chart, it would gather the coordinates of both gender and sex to map every possible position—the six original types being only dots on a line between which many more could be inserted. Hirschfeld's understanding of gender can be summarized through three underlying principles: every position on the chart is "natural," that is, morally acceptable; there isn't any clear-cut distinction between sexual orientation and gender identity; and there are as many positions as there are individuals. Eventually, the gender/sexuality seesaw, like the gender binary, is broken into an archipelago of idiosyncratic "minor perverts," according to the expression coined by Benjamin Kahan.

The word "archipelago," here, refers to Deleuze's concept of archipelagic systems, which describe, rather than a group of distinct and stable entities, a contingent process bringing together elements floating, so to speak, in relation to one another.[38] Comparing Hirschfeld's theory of sexual intermediaries to contemporary queer and trans vernacular classification systems, Kadji Amin has argued that although they both provide empowering tools to queer individuals, their taxonomical aspect implies an identitarian and universalizing aspiration ultimately irreconcilable with a queer ethos.[39] In Hirschfeld's case, however, taxonomy is more an archipelagic move than an identitarian one: first, because the multiplicity of types included in his system is always already susceptible to expansion and subdivision to the point of implosion, thus defeating the categorizing endeavor of the sexology of his time. Second, because, as with any archipelagic system, each individual type represents the entirety of the system but also wouldn't exist without it. Hirschfeld's taxonomy-like description of gender deviance seeks to describe gender and sexuality as a contingent formation and not as the reification of universalizable types. Here, the taxonomy provides a map of the assemblage rather than pinpointing its individual subjects.

Like Hirschfeld, whose work he was undoubtedly familiar with, Rostand's narrator understands gender as a continuum. Using the word "man" only when referring to mankind, rather than to a gendered individual, he prefers the word "being" (*être*) to designate male characters and argues that "all that happens ... is human.... Each being is its own special case: special cases are all there is."[40] Yet in practice this variation only applies to masculinity, and the archipelagic system remains on the male side of the binary. In spite of its title, *La femme qui était en lui* features an almost exclusively male cast of characters. Beyond the narrator's inner Woman, a fantastical creature, the sole feminine presences are the singers who give their voices to the narrator's operas, the fictional characters whose parts they are playing, and Fernande, Emmanuel's jealous wife. All of the friends, relatives, or servants mentioned in the course of the narrative are male, as is the witch doctor, who isn't even granted a female assistant. In this regard as well, *La femme qui était en lui* is exemplary: gender disruption and nonheteronormative sexualities, far from being markers of liberal "progress," only offer an enforcement of the masculine position, by granting it access to domains from which it was excluded. If tender men form an archipelago, it is only because of the structural unbalance of the gender/sexuality seesaw.

Even though the narrator emphasizes the singularity of his condition, none of the other male characters would qualify as Hirschfeld's "total men." Instead, they are characterized by their "tenderness," a recurring word in their portrayals.[41] Sweet-tempered, soft-spoken, caring, articulate, prone to romance, they also seem to possess a tendency to self-sacrifice that leads many of them to an early death. Most of them are defined by their affective relationship to the narrator: the novel follows a serial pattern, in which the male characters' function is to repetitively assert the validity of various forms of attachment and care between men. Since the narrator's mother died during his infancy, his father is the first person he remembers, along with his "tenderness," and the fact that he dreads being separated from him. Well aware of his son's gender deviance, thanks to his "vibrant sense of intuition," he considers it with "humane mercy" and never mentions it.[42] This loving father is the first of many masculine figures who comfort and assist the narrator, validating his feelings. After his father's early death, he is entrusted to a benevolent guardian, then cared for by teachers, lovers, and servants. This cast of masculine characters can be divided into three series: fathers, lovers, and servants. The first series, the fathers, precipitate the original loss that casts the male narrator as a figure of vulnerability. The second series, the lovers, asserts the erotic and social ties within the male community—Sedgwick's homosocial continuum—portraying same-sex love as the natural outcome of the gender divide. The third series, the servants, reveals how tender masculinity both questions and asserts racial boundaries.

DOMESTIC AND PREDATORY: FEMININITY'S "TRAGIC ENIGMA"

In spite of his affinities with Hirschfeld's theory of intermediaries, Rostand also endorses the male-bonding model through a homage to its most infamous proponent, the Austrian philosopher Otto Weininger, who gives his surname to the witch doctor who attempts to cure the narrator.[43] Weininger's essay *Sex and Character* argues, like Ulrichs, that each individual initially possesses male and female characteristics. But the male type, he claims, is undoubtedly superior. Women, according to Weininger, are "completely occupied and content with sexual matters, whilst the male is interested in much else, in war and sport, in social affairs and feasting, in philosophy and science, in business and politics, in religion and science." Weininger's reasoning reaches the same conclusion as Gide's: male superiority. Since women are "possessed" by their sexual organs, Weininger also argues that they are incapable of intellectual thinking, artistic creation, independent action, or courage.[44] Similarly, Rostand's portrayal of women reveals the tension between the dysphoric desire for gender deviance and the dissymmetry undermining the binary. In *La femme qui était en lui*, transfemininity is less an allegory than an impossibility. The only two female characters are Emmanuel's wife, Fernande, and the narrator's inner Woman, who becomes autonomous after being severed from him; they both are deprived of any positive personality traits. Care, empathy, skills for intellectual and physical intimacy: these are exclusively men's. In opposite but complementary ways, both Fernande and the Woman are "possessed by their sexual organs": Fernande in her bourgeois possessiveness and the Woman in her vampiric craving for men's love. They exemplify the two sides of the "sexual matters" feared by Weininger: one as domestic and the other as predatory.

Fernande, Emmanuel's jealous wife, acts as a foil highlighting the perfect accord between her husband and the narrator. The two men become aware of their mutual feelings in the theater box where they attend, with Fernande, Debussy's opera *Pelléas et Melisande*.[45] As Debussy's music draws them closer, it erases Fernande's presence: "we were alone together, Emmanuel, as if art had created for us a superior country where one can love freely." Earlier, the narrator had praised Fernande for being "a clever piano player," adding that she "even possessed some musical sense." The triviality of Fernande's actual skills underscores the depth of Emmanuel's and the narrator's affinities. But soon, she begins to trouble the idyll. Thanks to "her feminine instinct," she "understands the importance" of what is happening between the narrator and her husband; she is also upset by the rumors "bearing judgment on [their] tenderness." Tenderness is precisely the opposite of Fernande's modus operandi, and she threatens Emmanuel through "continuous tantrums."[46] Years after his separation with the narrator, Emmanuel eventually leaves Fernande, and she reveals her true colors by marrying a drunkard gambler. Thus Fernande assumes all the misogynistic traits of the petty wife, possessive, intellectually and morally inferior, abusive, and vulgar.

At first glance, the narrator's inner woman appears as Fernande's complete opposite. She is associated with music to the point that she sometimes appears to personify it, as the source of the narrator's inspiration. "Every time I played . . . she was the one playing . . . I could feel her in my fingertips, in my skittish, restless play. . . . It was Her, Emmanuel, who was giving me this loving soul, this burning soul, this artistic soul." She prompts him to start his musical career, and after she is severed from him, he loses the source of his talent. He completes the last act of the opera that he had started writing during his idyll with

Emmanuel, but "the public wasn't fooled: whereas the first two acts were a triumph, the last one was a disappointment. . . . As I listened to it myself, I could feel an absence; it sounded like the work of a deceased composer which had been completed by somebody else." The narrator's musical talent appears as quintessentially feminine, a manifestation of "women's hearts": upon hearing him play, "women wept as if they recognized [in his music] their heart and the cursed way in which they suffer."[47] Yet the feminization of artistic skills doesn't contradict Weininger's theory: to the Woman, music is only a means to an end, or it would be if she possessed any kind of intentionality, if instinctive seduction weren't her sole purpose.

The Woman makes her first appearance when the narrator is eleven years old. She is lured by the presence of Silvestre, a handsome neighbor who will be the narrator's first love. Aware of his son's change, the narrator's father stares at him "as if he had glimpsed on [his] face a troubling presence" and mentions his own sister Diana, who was "extraordinarily beautiful and whose death always remained a tragic enigma . . . either suicide or murder."[48] Crystallizing the Baudelairean association of beauty and death, Diana evokes the "monstrous femininity" of decadent femmes fatales.[49] The Woman will remain unnamed throughout the novel, but she carries the attributes associated with the name "Diana," the hunting goddess whose arrows pierce the hearts of men. Combining beauty and blind cruelty, the Woman charms innocent men into a feverish state that kills the narrator's young lover Robert, sparks off a "crazed passion" in his philosophy teacher, drives Silvestre to suicide, and causes the death of the narrator and of the doctor who had tasked himself with getting rid of her. After Emmanuel leaves the narrator, the Woman gives in to her sexual cravings. The "horror of the debauchery she inspired in [him]" then drives the narrator to seek a radical cure, more so than his wish to recover from the loss of Emmanuel.[50] A Beauvoirian alienated Other, the Woman is unable to love but is addicted to the love of men.

A fine line distinguishes the Woman's cravings from the romantic longing for love characterizing male characters—the narrator as well as Emmanuel and Silvestre. Following her first appearance, the narrator experiences a peculiar form of solitude, "the torturing solitude of a woman—this solitude of the heart which sees nothing that can fill it and feels itself living and dying for love."[51] The torturing solitude that only women can feel—because of their lack of individuality or their attunement to sexual instincts—adds to the narrator's drama precisely because he is not a woman. Romanticized by association, he reaps the benefits of this added intensity by being a perfect lover and a perfect musician. In the queerly formalist way described by Brian Glavey, music materializes the uncanny association between (feminine) instinct and (masculine) awareness, between the depth associated with wildness and the hypercivilized sophistication Rostand lends to his male characters.[52] Music is a component of the craving as much as its manifestation: like a siren's song, it is both the expression of a need and the means to fulfill it, and male agency redeems it by turning it into art.

"THE USELESS HORROR OF THE BATTLEFIELD": DYSPHORIC PACIFISM

The dual construction of femininity as both domestic and predatory is symptomatic of the French interwar years. In terms of periodization, the mutually exclusive shaping of modern masculinity and femininity can be better understood through the concept of the "European civil war," naming a period stretching from the beginning of World War I to the end of World War II and describing an era of constant conflicts through which European nations redefined themselves.[53] The end of World War I was marked, in France, by the crystallization of anxieties surrounding masculinity.[54] As Carolyn Dean noted, these anxieties weren't new but were "expressed ... more intensely than ever" and "required that the female body be continually sublimated in the interests of species reproduction."[55] They were accompanied by the French state's growing investment in familialist politics designed to sustain the nuclear white heterosexual family. State propaganda defined gender roles around the coupling of mother/wife and citizen/soldier.[56] The violent divide of gender and the external violence of warfare find in each other their mutual sustenance, binding together, *a contrario*, pacifism, dysphoria, and the refusal of heterosexual familialism. In *La femme qui était en lui*, the reference to World War I, which causes the early death of the narrator's father, anchors dysphoric masculinity in the context of the European civil war and reveals the ties between masculinity, citizenship, and war at work in its gender assemblage.

As it unfolds during the interwar period, the European civil war coincides with the moment when European countries gained their shapes and identities through the renegotiation of their territories. The latter were perceived, fantasmatically and geographically, as the soul and body of the nation, an understanding that was crystallized by the Great War, a "total war" fought by the masses, not by professional armies.[57] This defining moment radically altered the relationship between masculinity, citizenship, and state, bringing a new component to the notions of citizenship *and* masculinity: they both required the qualities of a fighting soldier. The (male) citizens' bodies became, metaphorically but also literally, the nation's body: citizens had to be ready to sacrifice their lives for the motherland. As George Mosse noted, modern masculinity literally "emerged from the trenches": "the First World War put nationalism's aggressiveness into sharp focus, and made man as warrior the center of its quest for a national character."[58] The sovereign nation-state, with its clearly defined borders, its identity, its "soul," required a redefinition of masculinity not as an attribute but as a binding ideal: "Masculinity became synonymous with strength, courage, virility, energy, will to action and solid nerves, but also with moral uprightness, generosity, beauty, nobility of spirit and idealism. Summarized in this way, the masculine ideal was inevitably opposed ... to all symptoms of 'decadence': weakness, cowardice, immorality, ugliness, monstrosity. The evil and despicable markers were then focused ... on Jewish and homosexual 'outsiders.'"[59] Rostand's series of tender men disrupts this pattern: their nobility of spirit contradicts their sentimentality, which could be qualified as an utter lack of solid nerves. In *Confession d'un demi-siècle* (Confession of half a century), Rostand recalls that "to experience neither school nor barracks ... suited [his] soul."[60] In the same way, his narrator associates school and war in his hatred and refuses the construction of masculinity enforced through school and conscription.[61]

The historian Sandrine Sanos has described how "the crisis in men" of the French interwar years is entangled in a network of anxieties that find their ultimate expression in far-right movements.[62] Crystallized around race, gender, and sexuality, these anxieties expose masculinity as the fragile core holding together the nation's identity. Eschewing war, aggressive masculinity, and heterosexual families is part of the same process, as are antisocial gestures. The narrator's father, characterized by his moral uprightness and his generosity yet utterly devoid of will to action, embodies these dysphoric contradictions. He is at the same time hypercivilized and asocial. For all his parental devotion, he is described as a melancholic, taciturn recluse, solitary to the point of misanthropy.[63] A pacifist by nature, he dies not so much in the war than from the war. When called to arms, he makes a reluctant soldier: a victim, not a warrior, demonstrating by example the vanity of the pursuit. "There wasn't any warlike enthusiasm or futile revenge in his clear gray eyes. He loved . . . German harmonies: why and where could he have found the absurd energy to murder a human heart? He was thirty-nine, he still looked like a sad, somewhat weary, young man, and the old war would make a corpse of him."[64] Music, here again, marks a romantic form of elitism: as opposed to the ready-to-die citizen-soldier emerging from the trenches, the father embodies sophistication and singularity.

The war reverses the heteronormative familial order and reveals the (dead) father as a young man to his son. The trope of the father's death is turned upside down: not only is it utterly unnatural, but it takes the place of the motif of the mother mourning her fallen son and his lost youth.[65] Similarly, *La femme qui était en lui* reverses the pattern of its author's education: Edmond Rostand, the respected author of *Cyrano de Bergerac*, was by all accounts a figure of authority and a womanizer and had nothing but contempt for the visibility of his son's inner woman.[66] In his *Confession*, Maurice recalls Edmond's disappointment that none of his sons fought in the trenches to protect the motherland during World War I.[67] And while Edmond's plays exalted patriotism, Maurice considered his lifelong pacifist commitment to be the most important trait of his literary career, one that gave "meaning to his destiny."[68]

This commitment had begun with Rostand's 1921 novel *L'homme que j'ai tué*, then adapted into a play, and which raised controversies that continued throughout Rostand's life.[69] Its theme and structure announce *La femme qui était en lui*. Also written in the first person, its narrative is framed as a literal confession in which the narrator addresses the priest to whom he confesses two capital sins: the "murder" of a German soldier he killed at the front and his intent to commit suicide in atonement for this. The entire narrative arc is the exact counterpoint of the patriotic rhetoric of the European civil war: the narrator begins by describing an act of war as a murder and ends by announcing his own death in solidarity with the enemy, whom he sees like a brother. As appears in the symmetry of their titles, *L'homme que j'ai tué* and *La femme qui était en lui* are variations on the same theme: the violence of war and of gender. But while both end with the suicide of their narrator, the eponym Woman acts as a true enemy, while the Man only superficially appears as one. The soldier atones for his murder to the point that his victim becomes his "brother," but the musician actually kills his inner Woman twice: first by severing her from him, then by shooting her. The Man is eventually reunited with his murderer, the narrator who learns to know him intimately by living with his family and chooses to join him in death. The Woman, on the other hand, is shunted from the narrator's life. Buried side by side, they remain, in their "twin graves," two different individuals.[70] Whereas the violence of war calls for a dysphoric male bonding and affection, the violence of gender knows no resolution.

La femme qui était en lui completes the symbolic reversal of war and gender started with *L'homme que j'ai tué*. The monstrous alterity characterizing the Woman, a hunter and killer of men, finds its true materialization in the war, depicted in the novel as a feminine force. The French feminine form, *la vieille guerre*, is emphasized through the adjective, which personifies the war as an old woman. "The old war" is making corpses out of young men and fathers alike, and "the useless horror of battlefields" is exerted upon good men by a feminine force. "What hideous love the Earth seems to feel for the masculine race, so that She seems to want to absorb it?" exclaims the narrator in *La femme qui était en lui*.[71] The personification of Earth as the bloody mud of the trenches inverts the relationship between war, masculinity, and femininity: masculinity is on the side of the victims, not of the perpetrators. Instead of the warlike metaphor celebrating the encounter between warriors' blood and fertile matrix, a feminized soil greedily and fruitlessly absorbs masculine forces. In Rostand's dysphoric pacifism, masculine anxiety has come full circle: femininity is ingrained in the very violence supposed to define masculinity.

"THERE AREN'T ANY SINS OF THE FLESH OR OF LOVE"

In his epigraph to *La femme qui était en lui*, Rostand quotes his 1921 novel, *Le pilori* (The pillory): "There aren't any sins of the flesh or of love." [72] *Le pilori* offers a Catholic version of the reverse hypothesis, calling attention to the "sin" in order to argue that it isn't one. In its final scene, a Catholic priest, also named Emmanuel, begs his ward to accept his homosexual proclivity instead of entering the priesthood: one shouldn't wage a "war against one's nature."[73] From the onset, *La femme qui était en lui* appears as a defense of the love that dare not speak its name, positing male homosexuality as a nature.[74] But this assertion rests on ambiguous ground: at the same time an exception and a nature, male homosexuality draws its contours from the violent context it seeks to escape. It is fueled, in other words, by dysphoria, or rather by the dysphoric affect triggered by this background. Again, I am not arguing that homosexuality and gender dysphoria are one and the same or that Rostand or any of his characters were actually transwomen. Rather, I am interested in the circular logic at work in Rostand's description of male homosexual identity *as* an irreconcilable disruption in the gender divide.

In Rostand's an-Oedipean model, paternity doesn't end with the father's death but generates a branching network of queer attachments that give ground to his affirmation of a male homosexual identity. The thread of paternal affections leads to same-sex love: there is a line of continuity from the narrator's biological father to his lover Emmanuel. After losing his father in World War I, the young narrator is entrusted to the care of a tutor, who happens to be the father of his future lover Emmanuel. This unnamed tutor's most salient traits are his love for his son and his benevolence toward his pupil: again, what counts isn't the name of the father but his tenderness. Emmanuel, the narrator's great love, bears the same redemptive qualities as *Le pilori*'s priest. The name's etymology asserts the solar aspect of the characters: the two Emmanuels have enough divine in them to bring salvation to their confused interlocutors. Emmanuel is described as kind, understanding, and generous: "one of the few beings . . . who were good to me . . . who understood, accepted, and loved me."[75] His redemptive nature, his potential queerness, and his unmasculine empathy are one and the same. Eventually, Rostand's queer kinships take the opposite form of Weininger's male bonding: they merge into a male continuum of pacifist lovers unable to serve or to kill for their country but ready to die for love.

The synthesis of gender bending, male same-sex love and pacifism is materialized in the novel through the mention in the narrative of an actual historical figure, Otto Haas-Eye. A fashion designer and publisher, Haas-Eye had likely met Rostand when they worked on Parisian theater stages in the late 1920s.

In *La femme qui était en lui*, he is referred to as "Haas Eye," "this clever aesthetician, the Prince of Eulenburg's son in law," a mention overcoded with queer attributes, from the name Eulenburg and its historical weight to the artistic ring of Haas-Eye's "aestheticism."[76] Haas-Eye, the narrator claims, "spent the entire war in Zürich, playing the fool in order not to carry weapons and not to be an assassin."[77] Thus the pacifist aesthetician defaults from the concomitant assignments of masculinity: war and the homosexual taboo.[78]

Following Ulrichs, Rostand describes male homosexuality as gender inversion, an ambiguous move fraught with tensions that keep surfacing in the novel. On the one hand, a network of references points to male homosexuality as a distinct, ahistorical identity or "nature." The figure of Antinous acts as an identifiable marker of this romanticized identity, surfacing time and again throughout the novel, first as the hero of the narrator's first opera, then as a statue in the doctor's office. Yet the narrator's initial feelings for a man are undistinguishable from the first appearance of the Woman, "whose heart started beating for Silvestre" and who makes the narrator attractive even to "normal men . . . who were never attracted to men."[79] The narrator and/or the Woman only reciprocate in two cases, those of Silvestre and Emmanuel, who share a certain resemblance, a similar "expression," a queer marker that excludes them from the category of normal men. Similarly, heterosexual attachments are denaturalized. Emmanuel's wife escorts him "more like a companion than a mistress," and, when he finds himself passionately in love with the Woman (still ignorant of her true identity), the narrator exclaims: "Ah, how it was more natural to love you . . . how I was then following the laws of my own nature!" The narrator's love for his embodied inner self is indeed hopeless narcissism, literally love of the same, whereas Emmanuel represents his chance at happiness and some sense of futurity. Yet Emmanuel himself acknowledges at the end of the novel that the Woman "played such an important part in [his] life."[80] It would be counterproductive to dismiss this tangle of contradictions as a sign of inner homophobia. The contradictions don't belong to Rostand and aren't his to resolve: they point toward the gender assemblage, the violence at work in gender assignments, and the dysphoria they trigger.

INVISIBLE ATTACHMENTS: THE WAR BEHIND THE WAR

While pushing back against warlike masculinity, Rostand endorses another type of violence. Just as the "total war" happening in the trenches conceals the global war of colonial expansion, the gender divide structuring *La femme qui était en lui* obscures the racial divide. While the former is embodied by the couple formed by the narrator and the Woman, the latter is manifested by the two couples he and she form with their racialized manservants. Alvaro, the narrator's Spanish servant, and the Woman's unnamed Vietnamese houseboy signal, with their unquestioned care and loyalty, a silenced geopolitical truth: the narrator is literally carried, shuttled toward his destiny, by a cast of racialized helpers, just as the heart of the empire is fed by its colonies. But their presence is more than incidental: racialized subjects act as facilitators of gender trouble, contributing to the disruption of the binary. Revealing how, in Elsa Dorlin's words, "the same set of principles ruled over the emergence of sex and race as categories," in Rostand's novel Brown bodies lead into the uncharted territory that lies beyond gender, and the subalterns facilitate the ungendering rebellion of the dominants.[81] While Rostand's novel is set in metropolitan France, at the heart of the empire, its mapping of the gender assemblage also includes, as if in invisible ink, the entirety of France's colonial expansion, with its array of differently settled territories, from the metropolis of Saigon to the poorly charted tributaries of the Congo River.

Two years before the publication of *La femme qui était en lui*, the 1931 Paris Colonial Exposition enabled its eight million visitors to "go around the world in one day" by visiting miniature pavilions showcasing French colonial possessions. Reflecting a hierarchical evolutionary vision of races and cultures, the exhibit included live scenes performed by Indigenous people in the tradition of human zoos. Commissioned by the Marshall Lyautey, whom Rostand greatly admired,[82] the exhibit encouraged French citizens to "become aware of their empire" and to embrace their belonging to "the Greatest France" (*la Plus Grande France*).[83] Ann Laura Stoler has shown how imperial authority and racial distinctions are structured in gendered terms and how the creation of racialized subjects merged with and sustained the gendering of white colonizers.[84] By the end of the nineteenth century, a series of technological and cognitive mutations, following the Darwinian turn, contributed to establishing an operational technological framework to apprehend both sexual difference and race. While biology and genetics were assimilated into the assemblage of sexual difference, contributing to the psychiatric turn and the emergence of *scientia sexualis*, they also contributed to framing a "racial question."[85] Masculinity and femininity emerged as fundamental traits of the civilized, as an organic part of the discriminating process sustaining modern imperialism—as Kyla Schuller wrote, "sex difference stabilizes civilization."[86] Rostand's cast of racialized subjects reflects the evolutionary staging of the Colonial Exhibition but also enlists a hierarchy of Orientalized subalterns in his quest for gender disruption.

The narrator's servant, Alvaro Gonzalès, first appears as an extension of the series of tender lovers and fathers. "No being has loved me so well," the narrator states; Alvaro treats his adult master as a "sick child" and sings to him in Spanish as a devoted nurse. But unlike the other members of the series, Alvaro doesn't display any other feeling than his attachment to the narrator. After his death, Alvaro returns to Spain but seems to remain permanently in service, and is mentioned as bringing flowers to his master's grave. Although he isn't a subject of the French colonial empire, Alvaro's Spanish origin posits him as a racial intermediate, a foil to the truly Oriental Woman's Vietnamese servant. This gradation is important: Alvaro is European enough to remain on the masculine side of the binary. Civilization, here, stabilizes sexual difference. The quasi-white Alvaro is sensitive to the Woman's presence in his master, and his reaction is the first sign of the narrator's transformation after the Woman has been severed from him: "I could notice . . . that I had lost some of the singular bewitchment I exercised upon [Alvaro]." In other words, Alvaro is a "normal man," qualified to share the narrator's intimacy and to assume elements of (queer) paternity, mourning him as he would "a child."[87] This emotional labor plays an ambivalent part, asserting Alvaro's tender masculinity while enforcing racial roles.

The Woman, as can be expected, possesses the most exotic auxiliary. Her unnamed Vietnamese servant, referred to as "the Annamite," make his first appearance when the narrator, bereaved by the loss of his inner woman, finds himself drawn to the mansion where he grew up. The estate has been bought by a mysterious woman—the reader might guess who she is—but her first connection to the narrator happens through the mediation of the Annamite, who leads him around the empty house. Against all odds, since Vietnam is at the time a French colony, Rostand's Annamite doesn't speak French but English. The language barrier adds a level of exoticism and of dehumanization, building on the trope of Oriental inscrutability. The Annamite is nonetheless affected by the Woman, whose beauty "had even some effect on this uneducated being."[88] The word "being," here, doesn't belong to the critique of the gender binary mentioned earlier but indicates that the Annamite is beyond it or, rather, below it: "sweet and smooth as a cat," he is placed closer to animality on the evolutionary scale. Unnamed, ungendered, and inscrutable, the Annamite forms a reverse mirror of the Woman's monstrous femininity. His portrayal reflects the biopolitics of feeling described by Xine Yao: while "racialized peoples are legible only through their affectability," this trait is contingent upon their subaltern position and their submission to white standards.[89] While the Woman is a creature of longing and of extreme affectability, her servant is affectable only through his uncanny attachment to her.

The parts played by Alvaro and the Annamite in the narrative are, in the end, similar to that of Saül Weininger, who completes the racialized cast of *La femme qui était en lui*. The witch doctor's Jewishness is emphasized early on, if only through his first name. As I will discuss later on, antisemitic markers connect the fictional Weininger to the Jewish names of *scientia sexualis*—Freud, Hirschfeld, and Otto Weininger. They also point toward racial difference. Saül Weininger is as Orientalized as the Annamite, though in a opposite way: dwelling in a nearly dark room, he wears "strange rings" ornate with "pale gemstones," and his "strange Israelite face" evokes "a priest, a martyr, and a mystic."[90] While the inscrutable Annamite is cast as primitive, the bewitching Jewish scientist appears as decadent, with the same dehumanizing consequences. Rostand's antisemitism aligns with that of Otto Weininger, who in *Sex and Character* emphasizes the "servility" of Jewish men and the fact that they feel "less desire for freedom" than Aryan males.[91] They are, like colonial subjects, unfit for masculinity. In this regard, they are both genderless, contrary to Alvaro, a distinction that outlines the predominance of white masculinity.

The 1931 Colonial Exposition privileged a culturalist approach, displaying a patchwork of "countries," each contributing with its own colorful flavor to the unifying French civilizing process. But the patchwork hides a binary: the empire constitutes a vast borderland, one within which, as will become obvious with Gide in the following chapter, white masculine subjectivity wanders to test its limits. Throughout the novel, ungendered racialized characters act as mediators guiding the narrator to the edges of the gender assemblage. Alvaro books the tickets for travel to Switzerland. Saül Weininger plays the part of a ferryman to the underworld, guiding the narrator to the other side. The Annamite leads the narrator to the Woman, literally opening doors, switching on lights, giving cues on the house and its inhabitants, which will lead to the final revelation. This character's utter geographical incongruity allows him to open the way towards uncharted territories. *La femme qui était en lui* closes with Emmanuel's departure for the Caribbean: "to remain in France has become impossible for me," he states before announcing that he will from now on lead a nomadic life.[92] The process initiated on Saül Weininger's island leads to an archipelago of gender dissolution. The civilizing project holding together the empire is matched by its opposite: a process of ungendering that gives a symbolic space to dysphoria—an iterative space of wandering.

THE CUT: GENDER DEVIANCE AS SCHIZOPHRENIA

The series of cuts organized around but not limited to gender and racial divides are symbolized in *La femme qui était en lui* by the unmentioned diagnosis of schizophrenia looming over the narrator. While the character of Saül Weininger, expert in "questions of sex and of inversion," embodies three decades of sexology and psychiatry, the violent intervention he performs on his patient evokes both the stigmatizing medical discourses on sexual deviance and the split-personality diagnosis associated with schizophrenia.[93] In severing the narrator from his inner woman, the witch doctor exposes the trouble but doesn't cure it, or, rather, his very efficient but simplistic cure has lethal consequences. Out of an unhappy in love but talented musician, the gender surgery performed by *scientia sexualis* creates a murderous woman and a suicidal man. Bringing together *scientia sexualis* and psychiatry, the fictional Weininger offers a troubling synthesis of the part these paradigms played in the modern gender assemblage, creating the crisis as they tend to it.[94]

Through the connotations of his name and his presence in Switzerland, Saül Weininger brings together the continental European nexus of sexology and psychiatry: Germano-Austrian sexology and psychoanalysis and Swiss psychiatry. Besides Otto Weininger's, the doctor's ostensibly Jewish first name evokes Magnus Hirschfeld and Sigmund Freud. As befits a sorcerer, Saül Weininger dwells in a borderland: his clinic is located on an island, which, as Böcklin's Isle of the Dead, can only be reached by rowboat.[95] Here fantasy is carefully intertwined with historical reality: before being rowed to the island, the narrator takes a train to the city of Clarens, on Lake Leman. To Rostand's worldly audience, this location evokes the Swiss "sanatorium society" and more precisely the recently created Prangins Clinique, whose director Oscar Forel had recently acquired international notoriety in treating celebrities such as Zelda Fitzgerald.[96] The island, furthermore, is reminiscent of another Swiss psychiatric hospital, the Rheinau mental asylum, located on an island on the Rhine, whose director, Eugen Bleuler, coined the term "schizophrenia." Bleuler was also in charge of the Zürich University hospital Burghölzi, one of the most influential European centers for psychiatric research from the late 1800s throughout the first half of the twentieth century. Jung, Rohrschach, Ludwig Binswanger, and Lacan all worked or studied at Burghölzi. Its previous director was August Forel, Oscar's father, whose work on neurology and neuroanatomy was influential in shaping the very field where Maurice Rostand's brother Jean was distinguishing himself at the time when *La femme qui était en lui* was written.

Sexology and psychiatry are also intertwined in the unmentioned diagnosis facing the narrator: schizophrenia. While schizophrenia was defined by Bleuler as a "splitting of psychic functions," it was also associated, from the outset, with the idea of "split personality" manifest in the Jekyll-and-Hyde structure of Rostand's novel.[97] From the start, the narrator refers to the Woman as an autonomous and foreign creature, through the capitalized pronoun "She," and pinpoints the moments of her emergence and her influence on him in ways echoing the decadents' motif of haunting and possession. In order to be cured, Saül Weininger says, the narrator has to be anesthetized, so that he cannot resist the treatment; he needs, as Weininger puts it, to be at "his mercy." The process is reminiscent of an exorcism: feeling its end near, the evil being trapped in the patient's body will use all its tricks and strength to avoid its fate. Yet it is also described as a modern surgical procedure, under the aegis of science: asked for his formal consent, the patient wakes up in a hospital room, his doctor at his side. In the preamble to his tale, the narrator cautions his readers against the coming intervention of "science": "I'm not crazy. I know you will find people to argue otherwise, some of them scientists."[98] Whether this potential craziness refers to gender deviance or to the intervention of the witch doctor, readers are warned: scientists won't have the last word. Neither diagnosis nor cure will, in the end, be relevant.

Yet the cure, Weininger claims, is simple enough: the woman will be "deleted": "I use the word 'delete,' rather than 'kill,' because, in a manner of speaking, I won't be killing her, since she hasn't been born." The distinction doesn't convince the narrator, who describes "the extraordinary experiment" to which he has subjected himself as deadly, not only for the Woman but for him as well: "I offered myself to this partial death, I sacrificed a part of my being."[99] Here, the narrator, as in *L'homme que j'ai tué*, mourns the effect of his own cruelty as well as its victim, the Woman. For the narrator, subjecting himself to the diagnosis and the cure amounts to murder, suicide, and the betrayal of his pacifist ideals. Like the war that killed his father, the division that will eventually kill him is as absurd as it is deadly. The cut brings no peace. And, while the mental surgery performed by the fictional Saül Weininger echoes the first cases of MtF sex-reassignment surgery practiced in the previous decade, in *La femme qui était en lui* the part severed from the patient's body is feminine, rather than the male appendix that would be severed in the case of an MtF surgery. In Rostand's world of tender masculinity, there is neither room for castration metaphors nor gender reassignment.

Rostand's schizophrenia metaphor echoes the diagnosis of gender dysphoria as psychosis, an association that persists to this day.[100] Here, the gender binary is read as a form of split personality: the two genders cannot coexist in the same body. Rostand's tale reveals how, with the hypothesis of a wrong development of the kernel, Ulrichs threw the baby out with the bathwater, introducing a divide that would pathologize those whom it sought to protect. Between Ulrichs's and Rostand's time, *scientia sexualis* had popularized "the intertwined conceptions of sexual inversion ... and homosexuality ... as a congenital notion of object choice."[101] The (female) wrong half of the kernel returns to haunt the invert through his (male) object choice: unhappy in love, Rostand's narrator surrenders to the metaphorical knife he knows won't cure him. What is found in the process is the dysphoria at work in the gender assemblage, both a structural dysfunction and the gateway to desire, or as I will discuss in chapter 4, fertility.

IMPOSSIBLE EMBODIMENTS, MUSICAL DYSPHORIA

For all its imperfections and its sentimentality, *La femme qui était en lui* is a musical piece held together by rhythmic patterns. Like *L'homme que j'ai tué*, *La femme qui était en lui* uses music as an allegory and as a narrative relay, echoing the queer ekphrasis described by Glavey, both "sustaining and suspending identity."[102] Like the series of echoing characters, the narrative, despite its dramatic resolution, has a circular shape: none of the contradictions are resolved; instead they keep answering one another. None of the divides are bridged: man/woman, real/supernatural, metropolitan France/colonies, France/Germany, object choice/gender embodiment ... the splits persist, along with the impossibility of taking sides in any of them. Dysphoria functions as a refrain, more like an insistence than a common thread. In this regard, Rostand's attempts to navigate across the splits echo Deleuze and Guattari's notion of schizoanalysis. As Ciara Cremin states, "the object of what Deleuze and Guattari call schizoanalysis is to destroy myths, beliefs and representations [and] to break apart ... blockages that territorialize desire for the purpose of capitalist and patriarchal reproduction."[103]

Deleuze and Guattari conceptualized schizophrenia as a response to the compartmentalizing governing processes of the capitalist state.[104] Dysphoria, as an affect circulating, or rather circling through Rostand's echoing narrative patterns, shares similarity with the schizophrenic circulation of desires described by Deleuze and Guattari. The effects of schizophrenic divides faced by Rostand's narrator find themselves reversed: if read through their serial resurgences rather than their dramatic narrative outcome, they capture the attempts to circulate back and forth across the cut as much as skirt the blockages that trigger them. Like with Hirschfeld's theory of the intermediates, a dual structure bears the ability to morph into a fractal structure, not a binary but an archipelago, where the divide loses its discriminating blocking power. Schizoanalysis, as a method of reading the gender assemblage, maps the dysphoric attempts at bypassing the splits.

Paradoxically, considering the fact that its plot is based on the fantasy account of a dysphoric embodiment, *La femme qui était en lui* keeps erasing or postponing embodiments. The whole cast of male characters appears strangely disembodied: none of them is granted a physical description, and their only distinctive traits are their eyes.[105] Their bodies only manifest themselves through signs of sickness and pain, such as Robert's paleness and his clammy hands. The Woman's body is described in a series of hyperboles that do little to evoke corporeality: "the most beautiful creature that ever walked the Earth," possessing "a beauty both idealist and cruel."[106] Ultimately, the ambiguity at the core of *La femme qui était en lui* isn't the narrator's gender but his ambivalent feelings toward the Woman. This "wonderful stranger" who appears as undesirable as she is unforgettable: both hypervisible and necessarily hidden, she manifests the impossibility of any satisfying form of embodiment—she is, as such, a dysphoric creation.¹⁰⁷ A femininity abstracted from women, which becomes unbearable and deadly because of its pure desirability, she exposes the dysphoric desire of an impossible embodiment, echoing the lure of gender euphoria described by Hil Malatino. In the same way that "transition won't deliver you into some promised land of gender bliss," Rostand's attempts to reach beyond the divides of the gender assemblage are best read as a mapping rather than a self-portrait or a quest for representation.¹⁰⁸

2

GIDE'S FAILED MARRIAGES

Either you haven't listened to what I was saying, or you would have realized that my notions assert nothing contrary to marriage.... And I maintain, precisely, that the peace of the household, the honor of the woman, the respectability of the family, the health of husband and wife were more effectively preserved by Greek morality than by ours.
—André Gide, *Corydon*

Families, I hate you! Closed circles round the hearth; fast shut doors; jealous possession of happiness.
—André Gide, *Fruits of the Earth*

In the 1922 preface to his essay *Corydon*, Gide mentions his "fear of grieving" certain people to explain why he has postponed the book's publication. More specifically, he points out "[the fear] of grieving one soul, in particular, who has always been dear to me above all others."[1] Any reader familiar with Gide will easily identify the dear soul as his wife, Madeleine.[2] Conversely, any reader immersed in *Corydon* and its praise of male homosexuality will find it hard to believe that its author would hold a woman so dear: the entire defense of "Greek love" presented in the essay rests on the idea that men and women have nothing in common and that the latter are lesser creatures. The above-quoted endorsement of marriage does little to convince otherwise, while the famous antifamilialist outburst from *Fruits of the Earth* rings truer to Gide's readers.[3] These two poles nevertheless reveal the contours of Gide's sexual politics: the critique of heteronormativity is voiced within its endorsement.

Gide's sexual politics, as exposed in *Corydon* and put into practice in his literary works, illustrates the dysphoria at work in the gender assemblage, that is, the impossibility for anyone to inhabit (to make room for themselves in) the gender binary. But this sexual politics also relies on an endorsement of the assemblage, crystallized in the thematic of marriage as the socially mandated form of compulsive heterosexuality. Ironically enough, in Gide, the only perfect marriages are the ones depicted in *Corydon*. He may refer to his wife as his "dear soul," but in his fictions, marriage is the soul killer, and the memoir he wrote on his marriage, *Madeleine*, does little to convince us otherwise.[4] Gide's critique of the gender assemblage is never definitive: in spite of *Fruits of the Earth*'s injunction, the heterosexual familial model keeps returning and insisting within every rebellion. But marriage crushes its subjects and brings them again to rebellion in an endless loop, revealing itself as a process of subjectification.

As a socially sanctioned relationship, marriage cannot provide fulfillment, yet it acts as a coalescing element: it is the bond tying the (male) individual to the social order, a trap reducing the individual to social functions and animal reproduction, which, since it seems to take place in women's bodies, is blamed on women. They are the ones who bear the guilt of enforcing the heteropatriarchy that weighs on men's freedom and sensuality.

But while male-assigned individuals can find in same-sex practices ways of inhabiting the world, there isn't any escape for women. In Gide's marriages, men suffocate, and women die: their only way out is to leave behind these female bodies that sentence them to an animality they must refuse. Whereas men can outgrow the limited territory assigned to them thanks to homoerotic sensuality and relationships, women are sentenced to abstinence, isolation, and death. In the same way, Gide's definitions of masculinity and femininity—or, rather, the good man and the good woman—are framed by a racial divide, as the spatial and political construction of the Orient affirms their contours and escapes them.

This is Gide's paradox: queer critique has portrayed him as a "gay outlaw" figure (Bersani) and as a sexual dissident (Dollimore), but reading him confronts us with the fact that he "finds in sexuality [the] confirmation of conservative ideologies."[5] Jonathan Dollimore asserts that, thanks to his own sexual dissidence, Gide was able to "see the connections between sexual and other kinds of repression."[6] Yet it is clear that Gide is only able to veer away from the gender assemblage by reinvesting the binary in the form of misogyny and racism. Gide's dissidence isn't a deconstruction or even a critique; it is a circular move, a repetitive motion within systems of oppression. What if it doesn't work? Should we see in queer theory's endorsement of Gide a proof that queer theory itself is rooted in misogyny?[7] And how can we read Gide today? There isn't any room, here, to articulate a compromise, a "but"—"*but* Gide's racism and sexism only reflect the assemblage of his time." The fact that Gide operates inside of a collective ideology doesn't mean that its blind spots aren't his own. Moving beyond the stances of denial or rejection, this chapter articulates an "and" that pertains not only to Gide's works but to a large part of the modernist canon: to queer readers in particular, such texts are part of a collective field of empowering knowledge, *and* they more often than not enforce regimes of discrimination. Setting aside any individual ethical assessment, how do we deal with their limits, how do we address their blind spots: gender, race, and class? This question is not so much about the success of their disruptive strategies but about the mapping that we have inherited from them.

I choose to read Gide's circular pattern not as a failure but as an effective strategy, one that maps the assemblage well enough for us to see it, to touch upon its main axis and its porous borders. As Lucey states, "Gide and Bersani are . . . interested in trying to answer the question: 'which comes first, sex or politics?'"[8] Applied to the gender assemblage, this question exposes the gender binary as a process of subjectification, not one that can be undone but one that must be constantly negotiated, dealt with, hijacked, and tricked whenever possible. As Foucault has shown, ideological formations have no outside. They do, however, have limits, fault lines, and loopholes. In this sense, Gide and the modernist canon need to be read both historically—tracing the contours of the gender binary of the time—and genealogically, as the history of the present, as a series of inconsistent and persistent attempts to account for, or to undo, the classificatory process that is making us.

What can Gide do? To answer this question, I simultaneously endorse and question Bersani's and Dollimore's assertions of Gide's social dissidence. Sexual dissidence operates by channeling masculinity's opposite, a nonmasculinity, which isn't femininity, either. Gide's "shattering of the self" subverts masculinity and the Western domineering subject in its wake. Gide's mapping of gender both exposes dysphoria and relies on it: socially sanctioned masculinity and femininity aren't sustainable positions, and they oppress, however differently, the individuals subjected to their assignations. Yet dysphoria consequently traces a way out, or line of flight: undoing gender, however tentatively, leads toward an escape that translates into forms of superior well-being, knowledge, and awareness. This raises a second issue: what room does Gidean social dissidence leave for femininity as a category and for female-assigned individuals as persons? The dysphoria embodied in Gide's male characters only leads toward an outside—a trans of sorts—if femininity is made to be the repository of cisness, as the foil of a self-satisfied gender embodiment. The dysphoria felt by female characters is a death trap that reflects the misogyny of the assemblage.

LOVE, SEX, DESIRE, AND SPIRITUALITY

"Long before Foucault's unmasking of the classificatory processes that reified bodily behavior as psychic essences," Bersani writes, "Gide took one of those essences and rendered it, as a category, incoherent."[9] The temporality here is dubious: if Gide is able to trouble the essences before Foucault did, it might be because the classificatory processes were at a different stage when Gide was writing and therefore the essence in question didn't exist. While *Corydon* argues that homosexuality is a nature, bringing it a step closer to an essence, or an identity, *The Immoralist*, written two decades earlier, makes a more complex case: its narrator's desires remained uncategorized and only asserted through their effects, particularly in regard to gender.[10] The tension between homosexuality as a nature and as a practice traverses Gide's work and divides his readers. Dollimore perceives him as an "essentialist," seeing in Gide's writing the origin of the modern literary quest for authenticity, "embracing transgression . . . with stubborn integrity."[11] Gide's politics, in this case, would stem from an ethical fidelity to an essence, an irreducible internal quality. Bersani, on the other hand, underscores in Gide the lack of any "ideology of profundity":[12] Gidean homosexuality doesn't "define a self."[13] If homosexuality is both what makes the self and what destroys it, then the question becomes what homosexuality does, rather than what it *is*. And what homosexuality does, in Gide, is to open a line of flight in the gender assemblage, that is, a breaking point or an elusive moment of change.[14] In Gide, as in Deleuze and Guattari, lines of flight are brought about by or associated to desire. Desire evades the tension between nature and practice because it refuses to be assigned to any social function or possess any individual or social productivity; rather, it becomes a means to its own end, rerouting and channeling any element—bodies, beliefs, cultural productions, etc. it feeds upon. As Deleuze writes, "desire is never a natural or spontaneous determination" but "is one with a determinate assemblage, a co-function."[15]

While mapping the gender assemblage of his time and finding ways to navigate it, Gide creates his own assemblage. Its main axes, aligned with the polarity of gender binarism but complicating it, are love and desire, on the one hand, and spirituality and sexuality, on the other. In his coming of age memoir *If It Die*, Gide carefully disentangles love from desire.[16] Love is felt toward women, and particularly to his cousin Madeleine, whom he marries at the end of the memoir. Desire, on the other hand, he discovers in North Africa with Arab teenagers; it is associated to joy, an intense joy of a Spinozan quality, whereas love is the personal (individual) equivalent of marriage, a socially sanctioned affect. Desire, in this perspective, is the line of flight associated with love—an outside that can only exist fleetingly. The polarity between spirituality and religion functions in a similar tension. I use the term "spirituality" in its broad meaning, as a state of being associated to intense individual affects rather than to any type of dogmatic content. Spirituality is to religion, and, in this case, Gide's puritanism, what desire is to love: the rerouting of a socially sanctioned affect into a self-sufficient, quasi-autonomous intensity. Spirituality is not desire, but it is desire's twin, allowing Gide to move beyond the "discordant duality" of his religious upbringing.[17]

THE MARRIAGE PARADOX

As a heavily gendered construction and one rendered impossible precisely by gender, modern marriage is a dysphoric assemblage. It is, like gender, at the same time a requirement and an impossibility. This tension is expressed in the modernist "marriage paradox" articulated by Davida Pines: modernist literature "reaffirms marriage convention even as the novels would appear to subvert it."[18] As a literary trope, marriage allows for an ambiguous mapping of the gender assemblage, which finds itself maintained but eroded. Gide's novels are no exceptions. Operating in the context of the Third Republic, *The Immoralist* and *Strait Is the Gate* expose the contours of this social order's model of model of state-sanctioned conjugality, in which citizenship, gender, sexuality, and moral values are tied together in the institution of marriage: "The Third Republic ... bound together gender ideals—proper masculinity and femininity—with a specifically social and moral account of sexuality.... Conjugality, according to this model, was based ideally on neither financial nor social advancement, but on sexual desire. As an expression and extension of this heterosexual desire, marriage consolidated the citizen's masculinity."[19] Although Gide's notion of love is modeled on this model of conjugality, it simultaneously betrays it: a moral account of sexuality, and a proper form of attachment, it prevents de facto sexual desire. As intense as it may appear, Gidean love is nothing but an empty shell, at once representing and annihilating the conjugal model.

Masculinity is defined as much in relationship to marriage as it is via citizenship. "The distinctive trait of the active citizen," it granted privileges and came with a set of duties "for which married love often served as a metonym."[20] A good husband, a good citizen, and a good man are one and the same. This continuum finds itself constantly taken up and questioned in Gide's texts: while *Corydon* argues that a "normal homosexual" is all three of these, *The Immoralist* shows a narrator proving to be neither. The continuum virtue–citizenship–masculinity also explains why "sexual deviance was identified as one of the main threats against the nation's integrity."[21] *The Immoralist* plays with the reality of this threat; *Corydon* aims to refute it. In both cases, marriage plays an instrumental part in the argument, which wouldn't make sense without it.

GIDE'S DYSPHORIC ASSEMBLAGE

This chapter deals with failed marriages, one of them real (Gide's own), one ending in death (*The Immoralist*), and one that never happens (*Strait Is the Gate*), in order to articulate a trans critique of compulsive heterosexuality.[22] I begin with a reading of Gide's essay *Corydon*, followed by his memoir *Madeleine*, before looking into two of his early works of fiction, *The Immoralist* and *Strait Is the Gate*. This mapping strategy follows neither the order nor the various dates at which the texts were written. I do not mean to imply that Gide's thought didn't evolve over the years or that the world around him didn't change between 1902 (*The Immoralist*) and 1938 (*Madeleine*). What I am suggesting, however, is that the pattern emerging in reading these texts together reveals a consistent aspect of the Gidean gender assemblage in particular and of the modernist gender assemblage in general.

This chapter opens with a discussion of *Corydon* and its erotic of misogyny. Gide considered *Corydon* to be his most important work, while everyone else seems to agree that it is his worst. With the help of evolutionary biology and its understanding of sexual dimorphism, *Corydon* rearranges the dysphoric assemblage of gender in order to make it bearable for the male side of the binary, at the expense of the female side. Describing male homosexuality as natural and socially functional, Gide's essay appears as a "phobic response" merging misogyny and internalized homophobia.[23] But it also provides us with a blueprint with which to read Gide's own work, as well as an entry point into the politics of sexual dissidence that we have inherited. Reading *Corydon* reveals how, in Gide, misogyny fuels the erotic.

Gide, both in his fiction and in the autobiographical accounts of his own life, thoroughly failed to put *Corydon*'s theory into practice. This is particularly obvious in *Madeleine*, the memoir he devoted to his own marriage and to his relationship with his wife. The two Madeleines, the memoir and the actual person, have been overlooked by Gide's queer readers. Yet a careful reading of *Madeleine* confirms the importance for Gide of marriage as a gendering anchor: Gide's account of his own arrangement between his love for Madeleine and his desires for men shows how, far from being neatly compartmentalized, these two dimensions fuel each other. Here, Gide's spiritual polarity between heaven (marriage) and hell (homosexual sex) becomes strangely inverted: heaven is nothing but the fertile ground for the thriving of hell, which is its ultimate raison d'être.

Before looking at Gide's fiction, this chapter takes a detour through the heart of Africa. In the late 1920s, Gide spent several months touring the Congo basin with his nephew and lover Marc Allégret, where he observed the cruelty of the French colonial system. Gide's *Travel in the Congo*, which records this experience, has been read as a proof of his political clairvoyance.[24] Yet here I turn away from Gide's critique of colonialism in order to use the Congo trip as a reality check. Literally a world away from his spiritualized yet bourgeois marriage with Madeleine, Gide's and Allégret's actual practice of sex tourism in the colonized borderlands serves as a useful reminder of the racialized misogyny structuring the gender assemblage. A glimpse into the sheer violence of Allégret's abuse of colonized women and girls, specifically, should serve as a dire warning against the temptation to romanticize Gide's own Orientalism.

The following parts of this chapter focus on two of Gide's early works of fiction: *The Immoralist* and *Strait Is the Gate*. Extensively discussed by queer critique, *The Immoralist* has acquired newfound fame at the turn of the twentieth century thanks to queer theory, and it offers a perfect example of what Kadji Amin has called "the idealizing engine of queer studies."[25] Its narrator, Gide's alter ego Michel, has become the figure of the "gay outlaw," inspiring Bersani's famous question: "should a homosexual be a good citizen?" *The Immoralist* led Bersani to articulate the interactions between sex and politics in the form of a "shattering of the self" that makes it possible to escape both masculinity and citizenship.[26] Following Bersani's argument, I explore how the deidentification process he describes is entangled with the privileges of masculinity and whiteness. The dysphoric line of flight opened in *The Immoralist* radically contradicts *Corydon*'s argument and disrupts its neat alignment of male homosexuality, masculinity, and citizenship. The mapping of gender remains the same, creating a white masculine exception through the erasure and fetishization of other types of bodies. But this masculine position reveals itself as a dysphoria-triggering subjectification process.

Strait Is the Gate was conceived by Gide as *The Immoralist*'s complement. Yet the novel, focusing on a heterosexual couple too devout to even get married, let alone consummate their marriage or look elsewhere for queer pleasures, has been, like *Madeleine*, overlooked by queer critique. *Strait Is the Gate* gives a voice to its female heroine, Alissa, whom Gide saw as Michel's twin. But Alissa is also Madeleine's twin and keeps refusing her cousin's marriage proposal in a scenario very similar to Gide's courting of Madeleine. But the fictional Alissa never bends, preferring to sacrifice her own body to spirituality rather than engage in an alienating process. The impossible marriage of Alissa and Jérôme forms the missing piece of the puzzle of Gide's dysphoric gender assemblage. Echoing *Madeleine* like *Corydon* echoes *The Immoralist*, it exposes what is really at stake in the missed heterosexual encounter: another line of flight, opened by spirituality, not by desire, whose agent is a woman.

CORYDON: THE EROTIC OF MISOGYNY

Gide's decision to publish *Corydon* in 1924 was far from spontaneous. A first version of the book had been written more than a decade earlier and published in unsigned limited editions distributed among Gide's friends. As I discussed in this book's introduction, *Corydon* shouldn't be read as a unique attempt to confront an unquestioned taboo but as a targeted intervention in an existing debate. With *Corydon*, Gide aims to take position in public discussions on male homosexuality by refuting Hirschfeld's theory of sexual intermediaries. In an obvious reference to Proust's recently published *Sodom and Gomorrah*,

Corydon's preface asserts that "Greek love" doesn't refer to "cases of inversion, of effeminacy, of sodomy."[27] *Corydon* intends to do justice to those whom its eponymous character refers to as "normal pederasts," as opposed to "inverts" misrepresenting them.[28] In so doing, the essay defines masculinity and femininity in terms that are not only mutually exclusive but that erase any potential for reciprocity. Far from Hirschfeld's perception of gender as degrees on a scale ranging from the "total man" to the "total woman" with various intermediate combinations in between, *Corydon* asserts a strongly partitioned gender binary in which white masculinity becomes a self-assertive norm.[29] "Normal pederasts" don't digress from this norm—on the contrary, they are its most perfect embodiment. Women-identified individuals are not excluded from this mapping: they are needed to produce *a contrario* the line of flight of male desire. Femininity exists, or insists, as masculinity's foil: a personified enticement to compulsive heterosexuality, from which a healthy and accomplished man wants to distance himself. *Corydon*'s aim of normalizing homosexuality is achieved through an erotic of misogyny.[30]

Written in the form of four Socratic dialogues, *Corydon* casts a bigot narrator in conversation with the eponymous character, a supposedly renowned scientist and unapologetic "Uranist."[31] To make his case, Corydon defends contrary positions relying on the combination of two different tropes, both of them recurring obsessions of Gide's: an aestheticized version of ancient Greece, on the one hand, and evolutionary biology, on the other.[32] These tropes are used in a counterintuitive manner: instead of aligning heterosexual sex with biology and homosexuality with culture, Corydon takes the opposite approach. With admirable bad faith, he relies on evolutionary biology to argue that male homosexuality derives from sexual selection: the imperative of sexed reproduction has given the males a surplus of energy, whereas female bodies are designed for pregnancy and childcare. Females are "captured by the race"—utterly monopolized by fecundation and gestation—while "the male remains unoccupied, endowed with a strength he will soon enjoy." Furthermore, and this is where Greek civilization comes into play, the male's higher sexual needs grant him a fundamental aesthetic disposition, of which females are, again, deprived. "Sexual dimorphism . . . makes the male into a creature of show, of song, of art, of sport, or of intelligence—a creature of play."[33]

Homosexuality, therefore, is spontaneous, and it is heterosexuality that is acquired and needs to be enforced by a complex social apparatus: the institution of marriage. In this regard, ancient Greece offers a perfect model, more satisfying than twentieth-century Christianity: "the peace of the household, the honor of the women, the respectability of the family . . . were more effectively preserved by Greek morality than ours." Socially approved homosexuality protects women from "debauchery" and fosters a sense of moral and sexual honesty. Modern Christianity actively encourages a hypersexualization of women, which is morally wrong because of its promiscuous consequences and biologically aberrant because sensuality is against feminine nature. Christian society, in denying male homosexuality, forces women to make themselves "*constantly* desirable" and to "skillfully apply [themselves] to that end, with the assent, the encouragement, and the cooperation . . . of laws, conventions, etc." [34]

Conversely, Corydon emphatically states his approval of the familialist politics of its time. In order to assert the moral superiority of the Greek social model, he laments the "depopulation of France" resulting from a quintessentially corrupt heterosexual state of affairs. Greek love, on the other hand, safeguards chastity and virtue and ensures that adolescents are properly educated and advised: "a friend, even in the fullest Greek sense of the word, is of better counsel to an adolescent boy than a mistress."[35] In a strange echo of *Fruits of the Earth*, Corydon enlists pederasty in the service of patriarchy. If we take his theory at face value, the only solution allowing for the maintenance of heterosexual familial structure would be to remove any pretense of desire from the equation. How these virtuous and well-advised young men will impregnate their modest wives seems to be a scenario better left for a dystopian novel.

But *Corydon*, unlike a "Wild Boys" utopia, doesn't discard women so much as it fetishizes them. Desire is detached from female bodies, deemed undesirable and unfit to feel desire themselves, but it is never entirely severed from them. Aesthetically displeasing, so much so that "it suits them to be veiled," female bodies serve as a constant reminder that nature, or animality, can be, and ought to be, escaped. Since males find themselves in surplus, both in numbers and in (sexual and otherwise) energy, while females are fully occupied by the species' needs, males' desire is *naturally* oriented toward gratuity and aimed toward an escape from biological imperatives.[36] In this regard, homosexual sex and sensuality are akin to spirituality, an aspect I will pursued in my discussions of *The Immoralist* and *Strait Is the Gate*. Desire can only arise when detached from reproductive and familial contingencies, that is, between men. Women aren't absent but present in absentia, an absence that must be realized over and over again to open the line of flight of manly love. To reach for this sublime exteriority is possible only through a fragile and unsatisfactory balance: familial contingencies must remain in sight, under the guise of female bodies, as a horizon that can only temporarily be foreclosed. Embodied in women, the institution of marriage and the legal enforcement of heterosexuality finds a hidden raison d'être—not the reproduction of the species but free-flowing male desire.

Gide's fiction and the memoir he wrote about his marriage confirm that heterosexual marriage *and* the sacrifice of women are undistinguishable from his conception of (male) desire. In a deeply ambiguous way, women embody both an ideal of purity to which men cannot aspire and an animality from which men are unabashedly free. Simultaneously too pure and too impure, undesirable and undesiring, Gide's female characters both foreclose and fuel desire—toward an exteriority to which they themselves can only aspire in death. Pleasure is taken away from women and stems from the sheer joy of escaping them, a victory over the species *and* over puritanism. In *Corydon*, Gide disrupts the gender assemblage not by modifying its contours but by playing with intensities: masculinity ceases to be a term in the equation, or a functioning organ in the productive social body, to become its own desiring machine. Male desire is turned toward masculinity itself.

MADELEINE: A MARRIAGE OF HEAVEN AND HELL

Married at age twenty-six to his cousin Madeleine Rondeaux, Gide remained in a lifelong relationship with her, though they avowedly never had sex and lived apart for most of their lives. Although his memoir *Madeleine*, written a few months after her death in 1938, is framed as an attempt to come to terms with his loss, it reads more like an accusation than a eulogy. James Baldwin devoted a short essay, "The Male Prison," to *Madeleine*, which he introduces by saying that the memoir confirms Gide's "exasperating egocentricity."[37] Indeed, Gide's writing on Madeleine displays a circular pattern of gaslighting. Every time its narrator expresses regrets, these are somehow blamed on Madeleine's peculiar personality, which in turn is described as the epitome of virtue and self-sacrifice, a sacrifice the narrator then claims was uncalled for or even ridiculous—but sublime nonetheless, which brings him back to self-deprecation and excuses. Circling through this suffocating process, the reader is made to understand that Gide's constant dishonesty toward Madeleine is as perfectly legitimate as his deep satisfaction at having acquired such an exemplary wife. In this regard, *Madeleine* significantly echoes *Corydon*, not so much because marriage does not, unsurprisingly, work as well in real life as in an imaginary ancient Greece but because of the importance that marriage continues to have as a gendering anchor. Beneath the apparent contradiction between a pamphlet advocating for same-sex love and a memoir devoted to a beloved wife, a revelatory thread of similarities exposes the dysphoria traversing Gide's gender assemblage.

Gide's portrayal of the woman he professes to love so deeply mirrors the interpretation of evolutionary theory exposed in *Corydon*. As the memoir's French title suggests, Gide is now the sole repository of Madeleine's life and soul.[38] But indeed Madeleine is never shown to possess any individual existence outside that of her husband. Matching *Corydon*'s description of women as biologically programmed caregivers, Madeleine seems to possess no inner life except for her religious devotion, no interest except for charitable endeavors, and no impulse besides that of self-sacrifice. Each of her actions is skillfully interpreted as a consequence of her devotion to André. If Madeleine doesn't read his books, it is with the purpose of granting him more freedom and to spare him the sorrows of shocking her. If she takes some distance from him, then, "the truth is she believed I had ceased to love her." Madeleine is also blamed for not expressing any desire (one cannot help but wonder about André's listening skills), leaving him to speculate and conclude that every poor decision he made only resulted from the intensity of his love.[39]

The topic of heterosexual sex, or lack thereof, is broached early on in the memoir. Mentioning his lack of "carnal desires" for Madeleine, Gide confesses that he was "so naïve as neither to wonder whether or not she would be satisfied with an utterly disincarnate love."[40] Homosexuality, here, as in *Corydon*, is described in terms of preferences, not of identity or limitations: Gide never seems to envision the fact that an Uranist could not have heterosexual sex if they chose to do so.[41] What seems to stand in the way of desire is love itself. "It so happened that the spiritual force of my love inhibited all carnal desire." Yet love is conditional upon the nature of its object—Madeleine inspires love because of her virtue, which keeps her away from desire: "That my carnal desires should be addressed to other objects scarcely worried me at all. . . . Desires, I thought, belonged to man; it reassured me not to admit that woman could experience similar ones unless she were a woman of 'easy virtue.'"[42]

Gide attributes this lack of insight to "those wonderful feminine figures solicitously watching over [his] childhood: my mother, first, Miss Shackelton. . . . models of decorum, respectability and reserve."[43] In other words, young André doesn't think Madeleine wants to have sex because he sees her as his mother, and if the older narrator now realizes his mistake, this awareness doesn't extend to his mother. Lucey has commented on Gide's ambivalence toward his mother and her lifelong companion, Anna Shackelton: jealousy and hostility toward his mother's companion are mixed with his intuition that Anna Shackelton and his mother might embody "a potential form of desire outside normative expectations, a desire to which he might pay some anti-oedipal allegiance."[44] But Gide disrupts Oedipus in the same way that he disrupts the evolutionary narrative of sexual selection: by pushing it to the extremes, the desexualization of the mother conveniently leading to that of the wife.

Yet Madeleine's body occupies a central place in the memoir as a cause of scrutiny and fascination. André deplores Madeleine's fragile health and laments how little care she takes of herself. In this circular pattern, which, again, makes Madeleine both the victim and the culprit, André pictures himself as the guardian of Madeleine's body and health. Madeleine's hands, for instance, are a cause of sorrow and disappointment: "In her youth she had had the most delicate, the prettiest hands one could see; they were expressive.... It seemed as if she soon enjoyed deforming them. There was no coarse work she did not impose on them, seeming to enjoy mistreating them in tasks at which, furthermore, she revealed herself to be very clumsy."[45]

The divide between Madeleine and her hands, referred to as an accessory separated from her person and that she maliciously damages, fragments her body and turns it into a common good. Madeleine's hands are the property of her husband as much as her own—more so, even, because the husband knows what is best for "them." Gide explains Madeleine's willful desecration by her will to "lop off from herself everything that made [him] love her." Madeleine engages in manual labor with the deliberate intent of making herself unattractive, in the "effort to detach [André] from her after detaching herself from [him]."[46] In a paradoxical move, Gide interprets that Madeleine ruins her own beauty to punish her husband for being attracted to men. The natural feminine lack of beauty mentioned in *Corydon* finds its remedy in careful maintenance (i.e., inaction) and in a religious aesthetic in which bodily attributes express virtue and piety. The male gaze, in Gide, is directed toward an ambiguous object: the spiritualized female body. Prettiness and expressivity are valued, while manual labor and agency are discouraged and perceived as acts of useless rebellion: Madeleine's rightful path is spirituality, not action; her body is a shrine.

Madeleine is also blamed for her aging body, attributed to the same neglectful attitude. "She was two years older than I; but the difference in age, from her appearance on certain days, seemed to be that between two generations." To make his points, Gide evokes a hotel attendant telling him, referring to Madeleine, that "[his] mother is waiting for [him] in the carriage." Husband and wife exist on two different planes of reality, each with its own temporality: the latter caught in the biological clock of the succession of generations and the former attuned to a wandering and carefree present. Although Madeleine's body hasn't been subjected to reproductive functions, reproductive temporality has caught up with her through her own willfulness. Gide mentions that his biggest remorse is the fact that Madeleine "might have liked to be a mother."[47] Yet a reading of *Corydon* reveals how the perception of femininity as nature severs the possibility of engaging in heterosexual sex. Its counterpart, which supports *Corydon*'s dubious praise of marriage, is the portrayal of women as spiritual beings: in Gide's mapping of gender and desire, religious ethics overlaps with scientific misogyny. Desire is denied to women, except for the desire of maternity, and allowing for its existence would lead to the loss of the spiritual bond of love. Madeleine is not allowed to use her reproductive organs any more than have access to her own hands: to be an object of love, she has to disengage her own body from the sole desire that would be in her nature.

Baldwin interprets Gide's investment in Madeleine's chastity as a moral foil, allowing him to see himself as a sinner worthy of redemption. "He had entrusted . . . to her his purity, that part of him that was not carnal; and it is quite clear that, though he suspected it, he could not face the fact that it was only when her purity ended that her life could begin, that the key to her liberation was in his hands." But had Gide used that key, "his world would have turned completely dark": he would have lost the possibility of discriminating between the spiritual and the sexual, from which, according to Baldwin, stems his conception of male homosexuality.[48] Baldwin's words echo Gide's explanation of his decision to marry Madeleine in *If It Die*: "It was the marriage of Heaven with my insatiable Hell."[49] This analysis sheds a different light on how misogyny fuels erotic attractions. If we reverse the terms "Heaven" and "Hell"—Madeleine, being, according to Baldwin, the "Heaven who would forgive him for his Hell"—then the Hell of married life opens toward the Heaven of sensuality and intimacy found in the company of (unweddable) boys and men.

REALITY CHECK: STRAIGHT SEX IN THE HEART OF AFRICA

Before looking into Gide's fictions, I want to offer a reality check on the sheer violence of the colonial context in which Gide was writing, thinking, having sex, and falling in love. From 1926 to 1927, Gide traveled in French Equatorial Africa, touring from the Congo basin to the Chad region with his nephew and lover Marc Allégret. Their trip is recounted in *Travel in the Congo*, which offers, among traditional travel-narrative tropes, an account of the corruption and absurdities of the French colonial system in West Africa.[50] Many have seen in it a turning point in Gide's literary career, marking the beginning of his political involvement. My purpose here is not to dwell on the ambiguities of *Voyage to the Congo*, which, as Lucey has analyzed, exposes Gide's frustration at both "witnessing and furthering" the corruption of the colonial empire he had erstwhile lyricized.[51] Rather, I want to draw attention to its blind spots by referring to an unpublicized aspect of Gide and Allegret's travels, which offers a glimpse into the sheer violence of white male supremacy. What follows is a quotation from a conversation with Gide reported by the French-American writer Julien Green in his *Journal*.[52] Even though it concerns the trip to the Congo, the conversation reported took place ten years later, in 1936, on an unmentioned date, and was erased from the curated first publication of Green's *Journal*. Yet its presence between the lines, so to speak, as the third-party account of banter heard years after the fact, makes it more significant as a glimpse into a history erased in the texts intended for publication: "Gide was speaking to me about Allégret's sexual demands during their trip across Africa. Marc had to have young girls, virgins, not whores, in each village. And it took place in the tent they shared, at Gide's feet, since Marc was fucking on the ground for practical purposes. 'And, Gide told me, you can't imagine the complications of supposedly normal love. It is exactly as if you were trying to open a tin can after losing its key. Whereas it is all so simple for us!'"[53]

The banalized occurrence of rape, prostitution, and pedophilia in the French colonial empire is well documented and constitutes a glass closet of collective racialized abuse.[54] Allégret's acts are no secret: they are unmentioned because they are obvious. They are confirmed by the unpublished version of Gide's travel notes[55] and Allégret's *Carnets*.[56] To this day, a reproduction of Allégret's photograph of fourteen-year-old Hamra, depicted in the *Carnets* as one of his mistresses, can be purchased online from the state-approved institution Réunion des Musées Nationaux.[57] The legitimacy of Allégret's practices and "demands" is taken for granted by Gide and by Green, so much so that the punch line is Gide's critique of vaginal penetration.[58] Yet

Allégret's virginity fetish starkly contrasts with the image evoked in *Corydon* of sexually demanding women tricking innocent men toward their vaginas. What subsides from the contradiction between the fantasy of the man-eater and the reality of violent rapes of young girls on the floor of the colonial tent is racialized misogyny. As will become apparent in *The Immoralist* and *Strait Is the Gate*, the reality of colonized disposable female bodies enables the construction of disembodied feminine personae supposed to be protected from disgrace by the sacred institution of marriage. Colonized and racialized feminine bodies are dehumanized whereas white women are disembodied to the point of erasure, made into pure souls, deprived of earthly life.

THE IMMORALIST: THE GREAT PROBLEM

The Immoralist, published in 1902, is, according to Gide, among the most autobiographical of his fictions.[59] The novella is preceded by an introduction in the form of a letter, supposedly sent by a friend of the narrator's to another, announcing the confession that follows, in which a first-person narrator, Michel, describes his inability to fulfill his role as a husband, landowner, and scholar. The recipient of the letter is asked to assess the confession in view of a specific question: "How can a man like Michel [the narrator] serve the state?"[60] Through a contemporary lens, Michel's troubles could be superficially untangled: his sexual attraction toward boys and men, which forms the obvious kernel of his "immoralism," would explain his failure to perform as a husband, which in turn would explain his detachment from other duties. Michel could serve the state well enough if only the state would recognize same-sex marriage or followed the principles argued for in *Corydon*.⁶¹ But Michel's transgression destabilizes a whole array of gendered and racialized, spatial and temporal arrangements. In *The Immoralist*, the map of marriage drawn in *Corydon* and *Madeleine* finds itself complicated, steering away from patronizing demonstration or posthumous self-justification. There, marriage doesn't act as a safeguard, neither for the protagonist nor for his wife, Marceline, who goes through a miscarriage and dies of tuberculosis after months of suffering.

"The great problem," Baldwin writes about *Madeleine*, "is how to be . . . a man." Baldwin explains Gide's misogyny by the fact that he "found no way to escape the prison of masculinity."⁶² Yet the prison of masculinity is also that of the gendered process of citizen-making, which Michel fails to undergo. Does Michel's bent prevent him from escaping the prison of masculinity, or does it help him escape, and how? To answer that question, we need another question, the one asked by Bersani, paraphrasing *The Immoralist*'s opening question: "Should a homosexual be a good citizen?" Should Michel seek normality, as some of his friends seem to be doing and as *Corydon* argues?⁶³ The gendered production of subjectivity requires a type of masculinity in which husbandly duties are performed because they are a manifestation of masculinity itself, as are the vitality and creativity portrayed in *Corydon*. *Corydon*'s strategy is to force the assemblage against itself and to argue that following male desires makes one more of a man—that is, a better husband, albeit one trapped in the prison of masculinity. But Michel's desires are, in practice, out of control; through his sensual pursuits, he becomes less of a man.

As Bersani underscores, Michel "doesn't know what he is in being a pederast," and this is precisely what makes his position subversive. His uncanny attractions initiate a process rather than reveal an identity: contrary to Dollimore's vision of Gide as an essentialist, Bersani emphasizes that Michel's is "a sexual preference without sex." In *The Immoralist*, Bersani states, all behavior "that can unproblematically be characterized as sexual . . . is heterosexual."[64] Michel's fascination for Arab boys, on the other hand, appears fluid, playful, and elusive. Most of their interactions are conversations, games, and most of all Michel's fascinated observations of each of their activities.[65] Michel's desire for the boys is in fact channeled toward his own body: "he reaches for their bodies—in *his* body." In their presence, Michel opens himself to the pleasure of nude sunbathing and swimming and becomes a "*desiring skin*."[66] Gide has made clear elsewhere that he hasn't much interest in anal penetration.[67] *The Immoralist* substitutes sodomy, an inversion, with a line of flight: it isn't Michel's rectum that is a grave; it is his entire body. In this regard, sex with men is the exact opposite of the vulgar and tedious opening of the tin can: a pure form of desire, nonrelational, and uncompromisingly devoid of "any sexual ideology of profundity."[68]

Yet as Lawrence Schehr has noted, *The Immoralist* is from the outset "placed under the aegis and within the structure of heterosexuality."[69] Michel begins his confession by reminding his friends that they last met at his wedding and that he got married to comfort his dying father. "The structures of paternity and those of church and state . . . mark the space in which Michel . . . is placed."[70] Marriage is a necessary step to maintain one's place in the family circle: a bond, not so much to an individual, but to social order itself. In Foucauldian terms, marriage is a line of subjectification. Escaping it requires a process of deidentification, a form of "psychic denudation,"[71] and this freedom doesn't have any existence in itself, without the "aegis of heterosexuality." Michel's bent leads him toward the borders of the gender assemblage, and only so far: desire only matters when it works against love.

METAMORPHOSES IN THE ORIENT

Meanwhile, women and femininity have disappeared from the picture, replaced by a racialized otherness that contributes to defining white masculinity. Baldwin underscores how the Arab boys Gide is attracted to are categorized as inferior precisely because they "appear to relish . . . their sensuality."[72] In more modern terms, Heaney notes that *Corydon* establishes "the health and value of white masculine homosexuals through contrast with the sick and obsessed effeminates" by using Oriental cultures as a counterpoint.[73] This is the paradox of Gide's sexual and political awareness: to what extent does sexual dissidence disrupt racial oppression—if at all? "The problem for Michel—and, by the same token, for Gide—is that he could not see that identity is a product, not an origin," Farid Laroussi claims.[74] In his fetishization of Arab boys, Gide ignores colonization as a political process. Even at the time of his Congo travel narrative, when the French colonial institutions cease to be a blind spot, Gide doesn't seem to connect this historical process to his own attachments to racialized colonial subjects. Laroussi sees in Michel "the alienated French figure."[75] The tension between Michel's alienation and his ability to overcome masculine subjectification sheds light on the racial dynamics at work in the gender assemblage.

"Africa! I repeated the mysterious word over and over again; in my imagination it was big with terrors, with alluring horrors, with hopes and expectations; and throughout the hot night I turned my longing eyes towards the sultry promise of the lightning-swathed horizon." Evoking his night on the boat crossing the Mediterranean, Gide recalls how his traveling companion Paul Laurens firmly believed that their travel was going to change them: most significantly, it would be the moment when they lost their virginity, a crossing of sorts that would deliver them to their complete selves.[76] The Orient, or the colonies, for them, as for generations of white European young men, is both a spiritual and sexual quest, whose primary aim, as Laroussi points out, was to "generate self-dialogue."[77] Here, the Orient is a necessary part of the quest for authenticity praised by Dollimore.[78] As Laroussi shows, *The Immoralist* departs from traditional French Orientalist narratives because, even though his works "deliberately disregard the colonial condition," they "foster interracial desire" and don't endorse French nationalism in any way. The geographical descriptions in *The Immoralist* nourish, as in any Orientalist narrative, "the ideological dream of an outside world," but, contrary to his peers, Michel "feels at home in Algeria."[79] In other words, Michel experiences disorientation, as described by Sara Ahmed: "a way of inhabiting space by registering what is not familiar."[80] Michel revels in the labor of inhabiting an unfamiliar space, where he ceases to be "oriented" and becomes able to literally live in his own skin. As Gide's literary alter ego, Michel is a figure of disorientation. Like the narrator of *Fruits of the Earth*, he is "born again with a new self, in a new country, and amongst things which were absolutely fresh."[81]

The geographical space of the Orient is associated with the physical state of illness, which marks the crossing of the threshold of disorientation. Michel suffers of tuberculosis upon his arrival in North Africa, as Gide did. For both of them, the first symptoms appear right before crossing the Mediterranean. Michel begins to feel tired as soon as he steps on the boat;[82] the narrator of *If It Die* "catches a cold" during his stay in Toulon.[83]

As they reach the African coast and travel inland, their condition worsens, paralleled by an enthusiasm that leads them to the verge of collapse. Only then are they able to let go of the assignment of social life, with its normative set of orienting activities. Forced into inaction, they surrender to their own gazing desires, drawn toward the "distraction" of the boys who suddenly seem to crowd around them, servants and village kids whose "friendship can be bought for half a franc."[84] Illness and disorientation provoke the mental and physical metamorphosis that makes room for the breaking down of the ego.

Feminine selves, however, cannot be shattered. When, in *The Immoralist*, Marceline contracts tuberculosis, Michel convinces her to travel south, through Switzerland and Italy, chasing an elusive spring. They finally reach North Africa again, where she dies near the place where her husband had been reborn a few months earlier. As Laroussi states, Marceline dies from displacement: "her life has become non-place-specific."[85] She cannot cross the African threshold of disorientation because she was only ever oriented through her husband—his disorientation kills her. Women's selves cannot become undone because they don't seem to have access to desire. The evolutionary argument exposed in *Corydon* finds here a paradoxical development: because women's embodiment is attuned to reproductive functions and deprived of any surplus of energy—of any intensity—women are condemned to be either on the side of pure materiality or to be virtuous social creatures. In Gide's assemblage, women are forever on the side of love.

In *Madeleine*, Gide constantly uses the word "fragile" to describe Madeleine: "she was afraid of everything . . . that fear was increased by the awareness of her fragility."[86] André, on the other hand, is characterized by the surplus of energy attributed to masculinity in *Corydon*.[87] But in *If It Die*, the terms are reversed: fragility becomes a main attribute of Gide, but it has the opposite purpose in the narrative.[88] Whereas Madeleine's fragility explained her fear of any type of change, Michel's is the source of his process of metamorphosis, the reason why he is able to be fully subjected to disorientation. For men, fragility is a becoming; for women, it is a stasis. They are the cement holding the assemblage together, along with the third term of the binary: the colonized, forever at the edge, the quasi-others, restricted to a not-full humanity, seemingly immune to fever and forever healthy.[89] Like women, Arab boys are reduced to an essence, also trapped in a stasis. When puberty and years of prostitution have taken their toll, they become a source of disappointment.[90] Desiring skins have no gender, but this ungendering process is a privilege of the white male.

STRAIT IS THE GATE: MARRIAGE = DEATH

Published in 1909, seven years after *The Immoralist*, *Strait Is the Gate* offers a curious example of Pines's marriage paradox: a perfect marriage—one that doesn't happen. This is, again, a matter of intensity: if the wedding never takes place, it is not because the protagonists are dubious of the institution but because they take it too seriously. *Strait Is the Gate* has mostly been read as part of Gide's religious works and has not been examined with regard to Gide's sexual dissidence.[91] Yet Gide insisted that the novel be read as a complement to *The Immoralist*.[92] He also considered that the novel's female character, Alissa, was Michel's twin, and not Jérôme, its male narrator. These three aspects—a religious focus, a dominant feminine character, and a kinship with *The Immoralist*—are interconnected. The impossible marriage of Alissa and Jérôme is a reverse image of Michel and Marceline's failed union: the missed heterosexual encounter, the line of flight in the gender assemblage, is not opened by desire but by spirituality, and its agent is a woman. Yet the two novels end in a similar manner: Alissa and Marceline die, while Jérôme and Michel find themselves, "still quite young," in the benevolent care of family or friends, blessed and cursed with the freedom of a marriage-less future.[93] Again, the enforcement of heterosexist traditions runs disturbingly close to their undermining, and, again, this undermining happens at the expense of female bodies and desires.

Gide insisted that the character of Alissa hadn't been modeled after Madeleine and that his wife was "merely a starting point for [his] heroine."[94] Yet the autobiographical aspect of *Strait Is the Gate* is obvious from the first pages on, as are the similarities with Michel's story. Both *The Immoralist* and *Strait Is the Gate* open with the death of their narrator's father, their plots blending elements from coming-of-age narratives and those depicting the quest for masculinity. In *Strait Is the Gate*, Jérôme mentions that his father passed when he was twelve—Gide lost his father at eleven—and recalls spending his childhood in the company of his mother and her "governess," Miss Ashburton—a transparent alias for Anna Shackleton. Like the young Gide, Jérôme spends his summers with his cousins in a Normandy estate, where he falls in love with his older cousin Alissa. Most of the novella's plot focuses on Jérôme's and Alissa's coming of age and Jérôme's unsuccessful attempts to marry Alissa—some of them very similar to those recalled in *If It Die*.[95] But Alissa never accepts Jérôme: to her, marrying him would be a sin, for she would stand between him and God. She resolves to disappear from Jérôme's life. He only hears from her after her death, which comes after years of living as a recluse, through the diary she has left him. The similarities between Marceline, Alissa, and Madeleine are also strong and are characterized by unquestioned love for the male narrators, whose happiness always comes before theirs. But whereas Madeleine is shown to age and wither while her husband doesn't, Marceline and Alissa seem to die of their own accord, their bodies simply giving in to their emotional burden.

As with *The Immoralist*, the narrative is inscribed in heteronormative familialism. The narrator's intention of marrying Alissa is triggered by the death of his mother; Alissa herself is a "reminder" of the mother. Like Michel, the fatherless Jérôme wanders in search of a home, never allowed to settle anywhere for long. Their coming of age involves overcoming a brush with marriage and heterosexual love, resolved by the conveniently premature deaths of their love objects. *Strait Is the Gate* ends with Jérôme agreeing to be the godfather of a newborn Alissa, his niece. The last sentence of the novel sparks an ambiguous network of associations: "A servant came in, bringing the lamp." The lamp evokes love, hope, and faith but also generational continuity and family life; the servant is a ghostly echo of Alissa, serving God, Jérôme, or their family. As generational continuity is ensured, Jérôme again finds his place in the family tree through his avuncular position. The niece is a substitute for the daughter whom Alissa wished for Jérôme to have with someone else.[96] A spiritual transaction has taken place: as the new Alissa's godfather, Jérôme is now responsible for her soul, after the former Alissa sacrificed herself to save his. In the end, the circle has to close for Jérôme to escape marital life and heteronormativity—strait is the gate.

As Emily Apter has shown, ellipses and unspoken truths are an essential key to the understanding of *The Immoralist* and *Strait Is the Gate*.[97] One of these truths is hidden in plain sight in a seemingly insignificant character of *Strait Is the Gate*: Alissa's mother, Lucile. Lucile is only present in the first pages and literally disappears from her family's life after leaving her husband.[98] Her defection sets in motion a series of consequences that ripple through the entire novel, but the reader is only meant to see her as an absence. Yet Lucile is the only truly embodied character in *Strait Is the Gate*. When she first appears in the narrator's recollections of his childhood, Lucile is immediately granted a physical description, a rare occurrence in Gide's writing. This portrayal introduces Lucile by ascribing to her the traits of a stereotypically promiscuous Creole woman: all bare shoulders and lascivious poses, Lucile wears "a large meshed net [confining] the masses of her curly hair" and "a loosely tied black velvet ribbon."[99] This portrait closely matches Baudelaire's famous drawing of his lover Jeanne Duval.[100] Whether intentionally referring to Baudelaire or stemming from a common imaginary, the "mass of curly hair" and the visual cue of the hair net place Lucile in the category of what Robin Mitchell describes as the aesthetic trope of the "*Vénus noire*," "sexually available and uncivilized, in direct opposition to French self-identity."[101]

Lucile's description serves three overlapping purposes: racialization, sexualization, and the underscoring, *a contrario*, of her daughter's spiritualization. Lucile's *is* the body that Alissa wants to erase. Like Jeanne Duval, Lucile assumes the traits of "a sexual vampire of biblical proportion."[102] Vain, "languid," she never appears in any other position than lying down: "stretched on the sofa" or in a hammock, holding poetry books she never reads and waving a handkerchief that "filled [Jérôme] with wonder, because of its scent . . . more like the perfume of a fruit than of a flower."[103] In other words, Lucile is ripe: Lucile's scent renders perceptible the "natural" femininity so despised in *Corydon*. She represents a form of embodiment inconceivable in white women, not because

Alissa's, Marceline's, or Madeleine's body would be different from hers but because Lucile *is* her body, whereas Gide's female characters are divorced from theirs. Lucile finds herself on the other side of the threshold between spiritual and embodied femininity: the hypervisibility of a Brown body allows for the blind spots of white female bodies.

Lucile is the Eve to Alissa's Marie, a figure of original sin. In the narrative, the description of Lucile is quickly followed by that of her betrayal, in which a fourteen-year-old Jérôme espies her with her lover, before having to face a mortified Alissa: "I remained standing beside her, while she remained on her knees. . . . Drunk with love, with pity, with an undistinguishable mixture of enthusiasm, of self-sacrifice, of virtue, I appealed to God with all my strength—I offered myself up to Him, unable to conceive that existence could have any other object than to shelter this child from fear, from evil, from life."[104] Alissa bears the burden of her mother's sin, a burden the narrator immediately feels the need to share with her. As opposed to what happens in *The Immoralist*, heterosexual love and the wish to marry aren't born out of a sense of convention but out of a spiritual communion—which is why they won't happen. But, as in *Corydon*, the horror of heterosexual sex triggers intellectual freedom and creative imagination. Lucile's sin opens the door to Alissa's atonement and Jérôme's spiritual life. Desire, here, takes the form of "enthusiasm, self-sacrifice, and virtue," and becomes a co-function in an assemblage where feminine bodies and sexuality are to be erased. Behind Alissa's own sacrifice to ensure Jérôme's fulfillment lies yet another discarded feminine body—her mother's.

Lucile's adultery and betrayal of heteronormative familialism is paralleled by another incident that occurs a few pages earlier, in which she sexually assaults the twelve-year-old narrator:

"'Sailor collars are worn much more open,' said she, undoing a button of my shirt . . . and taking out her little mirror, she drew my face down to hers, passed my bare arm around her neck, put her hand into my shirt, asked me laughingly if I was ticklish— went on—further . . . I started so violently that my shirt tore across and with a flaming face I fled, as she called after me."[105]

As opposed to Lucile's adultery, this incident is never even discussed in the novel. Still, the two moments are symmetrical: Lucile's assault has effects on Jérôme similar to those that her adultery has on Alissa. In the same way that Lucile is the only character whose embodiment is materialized in the narrative, the abuse constitutes the sole mention of Jérôme's body, which is not discussed anywhere else in the novel. Lucile's hand effectively performs a castration, which makes Jérôme a suitable soulmate for her daughter. In an inverted birthing process, Lucile deprives both Jérôme and Alissa of their social heterosexual future, barring them effectively from sex as a practice and from sex as sexual difference. Lucile's unwomanly sexuality ungenders Jérôme and Alissa.[106]

Jérôme, whose "flabby character" annoyed Gide, is divorced from masculinity. This is made obvious through the character of Abel, Jérôme's friend, who, posing as experienced and knowledgeable about women, fills him with misogynistic advice. Abel convinces Jérôme to impose himself upon Alissa and not to take her refusal to get engaged seriously—"a woman should never be given time to go back on herself." Of course, his intervention has the opposite effect: not only does Jérôme fail to convince Alissa, but she ends up being the one who convinces him. Abel's gender rules don't apply to Jérôme and Alissa: Jérôme's powerlessness and Alissa's lack of coquetry depart from the assemblage that was legible to Abel. In this regard, Jérôme couldn't serve the state any more than Michel: his attitude toward Alissa displays a lack of husbandly quality, which in turn reveals a lack of masculinity. While *Corydon* argues for normal homosexuality, Jérôme demonstrates the existence of abnormal heterosexuality, one that ruptures the gender assemblage instead of cementing it. In the end, the "pure hatred" Jérôme feels toward Lucile is not a hatred of sin but a hatred of heterosexuality.[107]

Here again, it is a matter of intensity. In *If It Die*, Gide recalls how his "puritan education" led him to obsess about his desires and the seeming impossibility of following them. Comparing himself to a Prometheus "who could not understand how it was possible to live without an eagle, or without being devoured by it," he states that his mental suffering and moral misgivings wouldn't have been much different had his desires been more "usual." What is at stake here aren't religious beliefs—a content or an essence—but the "importance [attached] to certain things."[108] Similarly to Bersani's assertion that Michel's was "a sexual preference without sex," Alissa's spirituality exceeds religion.[109] The question of "which comes first, sex or politics?" isn't about temporality but intensity: coming first is about taking over, which in itself is at once political and sexual; it is a desiring move with political consequences. In *Strait Is the Gate*, intensity deprives spirituality of its social and psychological functions: it becomes, as masculinity in *Corydon*, a self-sufficient desiring machine that hijacks mental and physical investments instead of redistributing them toward individual and society. Alissa is a Promethean figure, loving the eagle more than her own body—or soul.

Here lies the true kinship between Alissa and Michel: they undergo a similar process of deidentification, Alissa's is channeled through spirituality, and Michel's through desire. Just as Michel "demands nothing from" the Tunisian boys, Alissa does not want anything from Jérôme.[110] To her as well, the shattering of the self is a self-sufficient and self-fulfilling process. Alissa's journal sometimes addresses Jérôme in a tone that is reminiscent of the injunctions to Nathaniel, the young disciple in *Fruits of the Earth*: "Jérôme, I wish I could teach you perfect joy," Alissa writes,[111] echoing "Nathaniel, I should like to bestow on you a joy no-one else has ever bestowed."[112] Alissa's joy, like Michel's, is absolute, untarnished by any relationality, any social assignment, brought about by a shattering of the self. In a letter to Jérôme, she writes: "I think of other lands, vaster, more radiant still, more desert-like."[113] Like Michel, Alissa yearns for a disorienting space, a space outside of society and gender assignment, a space making possible the "psychic denudation" described by Bersani.

But unlike Michel, Alissa cannot actually travel to the desert or invest the actual Orient to let go of her social assignment and become a desiring-skin. Alissa is deprived of her feminine embodiment because of the intensity of her mother's hyperembodiment, but because of her assignment as a woman, she is also deprived of desire. Alissa's line of flight is a line of death: she becomes spiritual because she cannot become a woman, but refusing womanhood, she dies. In the gender assemblage, Michel and Alissa's selves aren't symmetrical—or, more precisely, Alissa has no self to explore or to discard if choosing so: she only has a body. To her, the shattering of the self amounts to the shattering of the body: all she can wish for herself is a disappearance not from society but from her own body, which is all that the gender binary mapped in *Corydon* allows her. Like André and Madeleine, Michel and Alissa form another pair of heaven and hell—though Michel the sinner is in heaven while saintly Alissa is in hell.

3

CROSS-POLLINATION

A Trans Reading of Marcel Proust

An orchid, a bumblebee, an aging aristocrat, an introvert shopkeeper, a teenage boy fascinated by Darwin: these are the main actors in one of the most famous accounts of gender variance in modernist literature. The opening scene of Marcel Proust's *Sodom and Gomorrah* has, for better or worse, served as a reference for how the literary canon might touch upon the taboos of same-sex love and gender incongruence.[1] As I discussed in chapter 1, the influence of evolutionary biology is crucial to understanding modernist accounts of gender and sexuality. Proust's inverts, who at first glance seem to embody the trope of female beings trapped in the wrong body, are no exceptions. But in Proust's botanical references, as in his descriptions of social interactions, the gender binary doesn't work. Or, more accurately, what doesn't work, or barely works, are sexual reproduction and heterosexuality. Like Gide, Proust dwells upon the findings of evolutionary biology and uses them to complicate the naturalizing narratives of heteronormativity. Unlike Gide, he embraces the conflation of gender with sexuality: in depicting homosexuality as inversion, he displays a strategy that simultaneously acknowledges and undermines the gender assemblage. Gender, in Proust, is a missed encounter: even while his conception of male homosexuality is ensconced in a constant flow of references to sexual difference, in his narrative universe, the gender binary never works. Proust's men-women literally hack into the gender binary and become free agents, both orchids and bumblebees, initiating a process of cross-pollination that traverses social categories. Inversion, not heterosexual reproduction, is the real source of change and evolution in Proust's textual landscape.

The title of this chapter also refers to the conceptual divergences between the critical perspectives that I have attempted to merge in this book. Reading Proust, and reading how Proust has been read, reveals the gaps between Deleuzian philosophy, queer theory, and trans studies. While Gilles Deleuze analyzed *In Search of Lost Time* in *Proust and Signs* (published in French in 1964 and augmented in 1970), Eve Sedgwick dedicated an entire chapter to it in her 1990 *Epistemology of the Closet*.[2] Written two decades apart, on two different continents, these books expose both the kinship and the discrepancies between what is now known as "poststructuralism" and its American offspring, queer theory. It is all the more important to consider these because their offspring's evil twin, or estranged child, trans studies, blames the latter for endorsing the former, a judgment possibly based on a series of misconceptions (or productive betrayals). As a matter of fact, Deleuze's and Sedgwick's readings of Proust are fundamentally divergent. While they both apprehend *In Search of Lost Time* as a site of production of meaning, Sedgwick reads *Sodom and Gomorrah* as an epistemological moment, while Deleuze exposes how Proust's use of signs eventually challenges linguistic knowledge. Deleuze's works on Proust mark a turning point in his conception of interpretation, a notion that he refused altogether in his later works.[3] Sedgwick's epistemological approach, in which the economy of secret and disclosure that she describes as "the relations of the closet" exposes "relations of the known and the unknown," diverges from Deleuze and even Foucault's arguments.[4] Eventually, Deleuze's perspective, though seemingly suffering from gender blindness, provides us with better tools than Sedgwick to account for how forms of embodiment at the same time defy and define the gender assemblage.

I should also clarify that my intent is not to read Proust's inverts as transwomen. My use of trans is an analytical method, not a diagnosis. As I explained in this book's introduction, I understand dysphoria as a constitutive trait of the modern gender binary *and* as a concept enabling us to analyze this binary. This chapter addresses inversion as the embodiment of dysphoria. More precisely, I argue that Proust's inverts are what Deleuze and Guattari describe as conceptual personae—or figures—who embody dysphoria.[5] They shouldn't be considered as *representations* of trans or of dysphoric people but rather as agents enacting the traits, the consequences, and the potential of dysphoria in itself. Emma Heaney has pointed out how modernist literature, as well as Foucauldian analyses and queer theory, has used transwomen as an allegory and instrumentalized them in order to promote a critique of gender that nevertheless ignores the lives of actual trans individuals.[6] Proust is no exception: the relationship between his clusters of female and feminine-inclined characters and nonfictional trans- and ciswomen is certainly one of instrumentalization. As I will develop, *In Search of Lost Time* uses lesbians to create a paradigm of male desire, and it doesn't even mention, in any way, actual transwomen. The description of inverts as female beings trapped in male bodies—a reading that I intend to complicate—is only intended to refer to male homosexuality. How, then, does understanding Proust's inverts as conceptual figures differ from seeing them as allegories?

First, a conceptual use of dysphoria shifts the focus from trans individuals toward what trans and gender incongruence can teach us about mechanisms of gender assignment and how to escape them. And then, second, even though I do agree with Heaney's analysis of transmisogyny, I do not believe that a trans analysis should have as its sole objects self-proclaimed transgender individuals and works. As will become apparent in this chapter and the next, one of the most important contributions trans can make to critical theory is nonrepresentative and noninterpretive.

The fact that I don't understand the object of trans studies as the representation of trans individuals, past or present, doesn't mean that this chapter doesn't concern itself with bodies. Dysphoria, as I understand it in this book, and inversion, as it manifests itself in Proust, refer to practices of embodiment. Much has been said about meta-uses and analyses of language in *In Search of Lost Time*. Yet in Proust, bodies are where change happens. Even while they are a constant locus for the manifestation of signs calling for interpretation, they are also the place where the prescriptive codes of the gender assemblage are defeated. The bodies of inverts bring interpretation to its own limits, and because they cannot be interpreted, they let free flows of desire circulate, inducing a process of contamination that traverses the various social circles they populate. Eventually, in Proust, inverts are everywhere and touch upon every character's life. As free floaters inside of the assemblage, the "men-women" are the agents of change, of variation, similar, not opposed, to the bumblebee and the orchid that the young narrator observes in his Darwinian quest.

This chapter follows a series of threads, each exploring one of the many alleys where a trans reading of *Sodom and Gomorrah* might take us. Writing about Proust is an ambitious endeavor, if only because of the considerable amount of research and analysis that his work has inspired over the years. Indebted to many of these previous readers, among whom Sedgwick and Deleuze but also Elisabeth Ladenson, Michael Lucey, and Simon Porzak, mine is but a short incursion in the Proustian pluriverse.[7] My ambition is to offer new critical tools coming from a trans perspective: I approach Proust more as a guide and a reference than as an object of analysis.

Titled "Missed Encounters," the first section examines some of the frustrations created by Proust's description of male homosexuality as inversion. Engaging with previous readings of *In Search of Lost Time*, such as those of Leo Bersani and Didier Eribon, I suggest that looking at Proust's men-women as representations, either of gay men or of trans women, is a dead end.[8] Understanding Proust's inverts as conceptual figures, on the other hand, reveals how dysphoria circulates across the whole social body and gives us an entry point into Proust's mapping of the gender assemblage. "The Cursed Race" delves into Proust's description of male homosexuality as a curse, a process whose effects Proust analyzes in comparing them to antisemitism. The members of the race aren't defined through a common identity; they rather connect with one another through their own exclusion from normative structures. Inversion, in *In Search of Lost Time*, then becomes similar to contagion: it replicates through a process of recognition until it pervades the very norms that created it in the first place.

"Masculinity as Mask, Femininity as Fugue" describes inversion as an embodiment of the gender binary that traverses both individual characters and social groups. It doesn't picture masculinity and femininity as identities but as a subjectification mode based on mutually exclusive polarities. Proust's description, or, rather, his use of lesbianism, focuses on the exploration of affects, in which femininity appears as the locus of blissful sex and reciprocated feelings. On the other hand, the aspect of *In Search of Lost Time* dedicated to male homosexuality constitutes a critique of masculinity, whose constraints the inverts cannot sustain and because of which they escape into feminine oblivion. The inverts are at the same time blessed and cursed with the ability to not belong and to slip away from the heteropatriarchal male assignation.

"Near Impossible Crossings" addresses Proust's Darwinian references in order to discuss his understanding of fertilization in relation to gender incongruence. As Simon Porzak has argued, heterosexuality in Proust is always queer, as it is in Darwin, because of the rarity and the improbability of the phenomenon occurring in nature.[9] The men-women aren't sterile, quite the opposite: they form the fertilizing strength of the Proustian world. "Conceptual Abysses" then compares Sedgwick's and Deleuze's readings of Proust and examines both their kinship and their incompatibilities. In my conclusion, "Shimmering Bodies," I use Deleuze's later concept of line of flight to pursue this noninterpretive perspective. Taking up Eliza Steinbock's idea of a "shimmering" trans ontology, I argue for an antiontology of dysphoria.[10]

MISSED ENCOUNTERS

Often read incorrectly as the first discussion of male homosexuality in French literature, Proust's *Sodom and Gomorrah* has in turn been praised for being ahead of its time or blamed for its latent homophobia. Gide, whose *Corydon* had just been released to a general audience when he read it, thought that it was bound to "confirm the error of public opinion" and "justify heterosexual prejudices."[11] Years later, Leo Bersani still criticizes its "profound heterosexual bias," and Didier Eribon claims that Proust's description of homosexuality is "marked by homophobic representations and often imprisoned in the very structures of the heterocentrist unconscious."[12] Indeed, Proust's evocation of homosexuality might be described as a series of missed encounters: between gay men themselves, since as we shall see they can never be in love with someone who reciprocates their feelings; between Proust's unnamed narrator and his elusive lesbian lover, Albertine, who can never reciprocate his feelings; and between Proust and his queer readers, alienated by his inner homophobia even when they are strongly drawn to his work. I will argue in what follows that these missed encounters are but a lure masking a network of successful interactions. In order to see past a dysfunctional portrayal of gay and trans individuals, we need to shift our attention toward what the tangle of misplaced attractions and identifications reveals about the gender assemblage. Not only do Proust's inverts and their constant dysphoria shed light on the flaws in the assemblage, but they are the only agent capable of circulating in it to their own satisfaction.

The first explicit encounter between two gay men in Proust's work occurs at the opening of *Sodom and Gomorrah*, the fourth volume of *In Search of Lost Time*. This much-discussed overture features a short scene espied by the teenage narrator. Embarked on a naturalist quest, young Marcel has stationed himself behind a window where he is hoping to witness the fertilizing of an orchid placed in the courtyard, should the unique bumblebee suited to this task make an appearance. He is distracted from his watch by the arrival of the famous Baron Charlus, a recurring character in *In Search of Lost Time*. Charlus is soon accosted by the neighborhood tailor, Jupien, who after a short negotiation leads him into his shop, where they noisily make love. In the meantime, a bumblebee has flown across the yard, but we will never know if the orchid has received the pollen it needed. The two superimposed plots, the narrator and his botanical quest and the interaction between Charlus and Jupien, are themselves intertwined with the author's reflections on the "cursed race" and what was first thought of as a sociological essay about inverts, Proust's "men-women."[13] The section constitutes a rare interruption in the overarching chronological narrative of *In Search of Lost Time*. Having introduced his readers to the men-women, the adult narrator resumes his explorations of various Parisian social circles. But exposing Charlus has exposed everyone: from this moment on, the cursed race takes over the narrative.

Sodom and Gomorrah's evocation of the cursed race raises two dead ends, which commentators either dismiss as homophobic or take pains to resolve. The first one is that Charlus, and ultimately every homosexual man, is characterized as a woman. Upon finding out that the latter is attracted to men, the narrator exclaims: "I now understood ... how ... I had managed to arrive at the conclusion that M. de Charlus looked like a woman: he was one!"[14] The second and related issue is that the description of the "cursed race" is based on Proust's assertion that it is impossible for gay men to engage in satisfying relationships. Drawn to men, the "men-women" cannot attract any of them successfully without feeling that they have been bitterly cheated: the fact that their love objects are interested in homosexual affairs excludes them from the realm of virility—if they were men enough, they would only pursue women. Members of the cursed race need to be loved by real men, but real men love real women. In this regard, Bersani's provocative summary rings true: "physical desire is always heterosexual in Proust."[15] Somewhat similarly, Eribon argues that homosexuality and homosexuals don't exist in *In Search of Lost Time*, where "the homosexual believes he is a man who loves other men, whereas he is a woman who loves other men." Eribon traces this understanding of gay sex back to the influence of Heinrich Ulrichs, who argued that homosexuality was the result of an innate condition: a female soul trapped in a male body or vice versa.[16]

But as I discussed in chapter 1, Ulrichs's theory describes gender more than sexuality. For him as well as for Proust, accounts of same-sex love rely on the assumption that the individual prone to it suffers from what can be described as gender dysphoria. As Heaney has shown, Ulrichs exerted a direct influence on modernist portrayals of gay men as transfeminine women. Through Ulrichs's writings, "trans femininity emerged in sexological understanding as an extreme expression of [an] inverted condition."[17] As a consequence, trans femininity became "a critical figure for the construction of sex and gender, rather than a category with its own history and theoretical insights."[18] Proust's men-women fall into Heaney's description of transfemininity's allegoric instrumentalization. Proust's inverts are unsatisfying whether we understand them as gay men or as trans women. They are, indeed, deeply unsatisfying as long as we understand them as representing an ontological category: they do not play any representational part, in either meaning of the term, as they are neither portraying nor speaking for anyone (Gide, for that matter, felt deeply misrepresented by Proust in both ways). They constitute what Deleuze and Guattari have described as conceptual figures, who "carry out the movements that describe the author's plane of immanence . . . indicate the dangers specific to this plane, the bad perceptions, bad feelings, and even negative movements that emerge from it."[19] In this case, the "plane[s] of immanence" are the gender assemblage and its ramifications: inverts are tracers enabling us to take notice of otherwise invisible forces at work in the social and personal dynamics of gender assignment.

Sodom and Gomorrah's men-women, as Maurice Rostand's narrator, are not transwomen but personas displaying male femininity, to reverse Jack Halberstam's expression of "female masculinity." But while Halberstam describes a type of masculinity that strives to exist outside of male bodies and relationships of power and sexism, the femininity manifest in Proust's men-women and, in another way, in his lesbian characters don't have any existence outside of sexist power relationships.[20] What Charlus displays when he appears to the narrator as a woman is the dysphoria underlying the gender assemblage. But it is a type of dysphoria that only affects male-assigned individuals—as I will discuss later, female-assigned individuals occupy a different place in the Proustian landscape. Understood as conceptual figures rather than representations of ontological categories, Proust's men-women open the door to an understanding of the mutually exclusive definition of the two genders and its consequences. Transness is at the core of Proust's work; it is present under the guise of dysphoria and not because any of his characters would be (representing) trans people. It is, in fact, another missed encounter: dysphoria, here, isn't anybody's dysphoria; it circulates through the whole social body. Proust isn't portraying the dysphoria of an individual but that of a collective, a "race," a term on which I will elaborate in what follows.

THE CURSED RACE: INVERSION, CONTAGION

Proust's evocation of male homosexuality as a "cursed race" describes a self-fulfilling prophecy: race and curse are only defining insofar as they point toward a position attributed to some members of a social group that are thus apprehended as a single, though never entirely distinct, subgroup. The curse is about a process, not an essence: what makes the race is not a common trait possessed by its members but the exclusionary mechanism that singles them out. The race is never defined by positive attributes—that is, distinctive traits that could be qualified, in contemporary vocabulary, as an identity or a culture. *Sodom and Gomorrah*'s initial description of the cursed race evokes a process of dissociation similar to antisemitism:[21] its members "must live in falsehood and perjury," are forced to "deny [their] God," and are friendless because their relationships "flourish only by virtue of a lie" because it is not their nature that they have to hide but their allegiances.[22] The constant state of denial forced upon them doesn't attach them to one another as much as it detaches them from the circles to which they still superficially belong (social class, trades, biological families, institutional marriage, etc.).

Race, then, doesn't refer to a distinct, preestablished group but to a spreading, ever-expanding, disseminated collective. It isn't an innate condition but a social process. Proust plays on antisemitic and homophobic fears: he unveils an entire population of double agents who multiply by mutual recognition. Relying on his memories of the Dreyfus affair, Proust reverses the trope of an invisible threat disseminating itself through a process of social contamination.[23] As soon as they start appearing in the novel, members of the cursed race suddenly find themselves everywhere, all the more so since, as the Proustian learning process constantly exposes, it takes one to know one. The curse is introduced in the narrative as "a discovery which concerned M. de Charlus." But this discovery couldn't have happened without Charlus's encounter with Jupien. Their couple almost immediately becomes a collective: their first conversation evokes other gay men from the neighborhood—what of the delivery boy and of the "man who sells chestnuts round the corner?" Then, as he is watching them, the narrator suddenly remembers a previous moment in which he espied the young Mlle Vinteuil with her female lover. Thus the significance of the discovery is already undermined: the members of the tribe were always already there. Coincidentally, Jupien and Charlus's conversation also mentions the young Duc de Chatellerault, who will be the first character encountered by the narrator in the following chapter.[24] Over the course of a few pages, the curse has spread from invisibility, or dormancy, to the narrator's entire universe. From now on, not only will the reader step into a queer world; they will also be forced to retroactively question every relationship or personality encountered in the previous volumes. First a couple, then a neighborhood, then a world: the curse operates not by casting aside dysfunctional individuals but by shaping the dynamic affecting any social sphere. In the last volume of *In Search of Lost Time*, Charlus comments on male homosexuality and claims that only "three or four" out of ten men are true heterosexuals.[25] That proportion is certainly true in Proust's world, where the number of inverts keeps growing, one revelation after the other.[26]

Proust's use of the term "invert" isn't merely a reflection of the vocabulary of his time but a careful choice, one that intentionally focuses on a certain understanding of male homosexuality (which is precisely what Gide blames him for). Proust used the term "homosexuality" in other instances: it is found recurrently in his letters and notebooks. He also used Ulrichs's term of "Uranism" in his conversations with Gide.[27] As we will see, the designation and portrayal of all gay men as inverts is a deliberate strategy. In *La loi du genre*, Murat argues that "the entire structure of *In Search of Lost Time* relies on the concept of inversion." First, of course, because it affects a great many characters. More remarkably, inversion, or its narrative counterpart, reversal (*renversement*), constitutes the temporal framework of the novel: the novel ends with the narrator discovering the relationship between memory, time, and writing and deciding to revisit his entire life—that is, to start writing the book that the reader just finished reading. Last but not least, inversion/reversal becomes a method of reading. Since most of the characters seem to be embarked on what Murat calls "a vast endeavor of denial," the meaning of what they say needs to be, literally, inverted. The energy spent by Albertine to swear to the truth indicates that she is a compulsive liar; Charlus's vocal hatred of effeminacy shows his true preferences; Legrandin's avowed contempt for social events reveals his deep interest in them.[28] Inversion is woven into the structure, the themes, the philosophy, and the characters of the novel.

Proust creates an inverted world as well as a world of inverts, one that reveals the chaotic forces traversing the apparently well-divided gender assemblage. In playing with the antisemitic trope of a population of traitors hiding among normal people, Proust exposes how inversion and contamination go hand in hand: inversion is, by nature, contagious. Contamination, as a trope, feeds the opposition between nature and culture: it is at the same time perceived as an antinatural mode of propagation and considered as an intrusion of an indomitable nature in humane societies. Fear of contagion did, and still does, tap into the obsessive motif of the enemy within: as, for instance, the deeply rooted idea that homosexuality spreads simply by being visible. As Deleuze and Guattari have described, contagion blurs the regulated hierarchy of filiation and generational reproduction. Inversion operates in a similar mode: it empties the naturalized division between sexes that structures the gender assemblage, replacing it with a free flow of contagious desires: "Like hybrids, which are in themselves sterile, born of a sexual union that will not reproduce itself, but which begins over again every time.... Unnatural participations or nuptials are the true Nature spanning the kingdoms of nature."[29] I will examine later on how the unnatural nuptials of the men-women are fecund in more ways than one. But first, I want to dwell on the ways in which *Sodom and Gomorrah* assimilates and disrupts modernist understandings of masculinity and femininity.

MASCULINITY AS MASK, FEMININITY AS FUGUE

The seminal moment in *Sodom and Gomorrah* is not the realization that Charlus belongs to the cursed race but the moment when he appears, to the eyes of the narrator, *as* a woman: "what was suggested to me by the sight of this man ... was a woman."[30] And Charlus, who had been described, until that time, as a haughty, arrogant, and mostly dissatisfied man, is suddenly revealed as a blissful woman. When the curse manifests itself, it is as a blessing, in the form of untainted joy. The reason why Charlus looks like a woman isn't that he could pass as one, nor that he appears, in this moment, effeminate—as quoted earlier, Charlus, as a woman, is still very much a man—but because, unobserved, he is happy:

> At this moment, when he did not suspect that anyone was watching him, his eyelids lowered as a screen against the sun, M. de Charlus had relaxed the artificial tension, softened that artificial vigour in his face which were ordinarily sustained by the animation of his talk and the force of his will.... Blinking his eyes in the sunlight, he seemed almost to be smiling, and I found in his face seen thus in repose and as it were in its natural state something so affectionate, so defenseless.[31]

Masculinity disappears as Charlus lowers his mask, a mask created by means of an "artificial tension," a sheer act of will, aggressively enforced by Charlus's dominating conversation. In contrast, the dominant physical trait of Charlus-as-a-woman is "the kindness ... so innocently displayed upon his face."[32] Is Charlus's benevolence attributable to the fact that, unobserved, he is free to be himself and to let his feminine nature transpire, or are these two modes of being, freedom from masculinity and carefree femininity, one and the same? Forced into masculinity, Charlus produces a forced masculinity; seeking freedom toward femininity, he embodies a carefree, blossoming version of it. Yet the polarity embodied in Charlus, masculinity as a mask, femininity as a fugue, is only a small-scale example of how genders are divided in *In Search of Lost Time*.

Sodom and Gomorrah's epigraph, "The women shall have Gomorrah and the men shall have Sodom," is a verse from *La colère de Samson* (Samson's anger), an epic poem by Alfred de Vigny.[33] The poem is quoted again, a few pages later, to describe the curse: "The two sexes shall die, each in a place apart!"[34] But Proust is inverting the meaning of Vigny's poem. Picturing Samson's anger at Delilah's betrayal, *La colère de Samson* originally gives a horrified description of heterosexual love in which men, because of the kindness of their hearts, are doomed to suffer from women's venality and hypocrisy. Same-sex love doesn't play any part in it, except to connote feminine, deceitful lust. To some extent, *Sodom and Gomorrah*'s reference to the poem might even be considered ironic. But the most fascinating aspect of it is that in order to introduce his account of homosexual love, Proust relies on a trope belonging to a very conservative vision of the (heteronormative) gender assemblage. His characters do not possess any of the gendered traits described by Vigny, but they are subjected to the same radical estrangement as Samson and Delilah. The two sexes shall die apart, in Proust's world as in

Gide's and, in that example, Vigny's because their definitions are incompatible and mutually exclusive. But, and this is one of the reasons why Proust chose to focus on the inverts rather than discussing a more acceptable category of male Uranians, the two sexes don't always characterize and encompass the individuals to whom they are assigned. As a matter of fact, in Proust's world, they mostly don't. Furthermore, their mutually exclusive positions in the gender assemblage make it likely that they can appeal to the same person. As part of a system, the two sexes shall die apart, but dysphoria-induced inversion will allow for a constant stream of circulation between them.

In Proust's inverted world, only male-assigned individuals seem to suffer from dysphoria. As Elisabeth Ladenson underscores, there aren't any female inverts in *In Search of Lost Time*: "Proust's Gomorrheans differ from their Sodomite cohorts in that, in contrast to the men . . . the women are not characterized by . . . gender dysphoria; they are never truly 'masculine,' and they desire their like rather than their opposite."[35] While Proust's initial mention of Sodom and Gomorrah gives the impression that they will be addressed in symmetry, exploration of male and female same-sex love operate in different modes and don't fulfill the same function: the description of Sodom has been conceived as a sociological investigation, whereas Gomorrah's purpose is to expose affects.[36] As the object of the narrator's love and fascination, lesbians, dominated by the figure of Albertine, constitute "the quintessential object of erotic desire, and the narrator's obsession with lesbianism . . . is always assimilated into his jealousy of Albertine."[37] Proust aligns here with a misogynist and heterocentrist tradition in French literature that, from Balzac to Pierre Louÿs, instrumentalizes lesbians as objects of the male gaze. The resulting paradox is that the real site of homosexuality in *In Search of Lost Time* is, in fact,

Gomorrah. Male homosexuality, according to Proust, precludes mutual feelings, but its female counterpart is pictured as a utopia for same-sex love, which fuels the narrator's jealousy and desire. Like Charlus's, Albertine's appearances in the narrative always trigger the emergence of a series of homosexual characters (or the revelation of homosexual proclivities in others). But instead of unlucky inverts pursuing elusive love objects, lesbians are always successful and satisfied: instead of finding out whom they are pursuing, the narrator usually learns with whom they have already had sex—and the numbers keep rising.

Some critics have understood the narrator's love for Albertine as a transposition: Albertine would be a male character camouflaged as female, a hypothesis powerfully rejected by Ladenson.[38] In a conversation with Gide, dismayed by his representation of male homosexuality as inversion, Proust answered that he had transposed in *Within a Budding Grove*, the section of the novel describing the narrator's first encounter and romance with Albertine, everything that was "gracious, tender and charming" from his own homosexual experience. In consequence, all that was left for *Sodom and Gomorrah* was "the grotesque and the abject."[39] Although this suggestion looks like a made-up excuse, it nonetheless sheds an interesting light on the way in which Proust constantly shifts his focus from sexuality to gender. This constant ambiguity, far from indicating Proust's naivety on the matter, stems from an elaborate strategy. What heterosexuality stands for is the intimate, the literary exploration of desire, love, and jealousy—which, for Proust, might be one and the same. When it comes to homosexuality itself, the reader will very well be able to see the tenderness in Jupien's care for the aging and demented Charlus, decades after their first encounter, or the abject in Albertine's deceptions. Lesbians are the perfect object of Proustian love: entirely out of reach for the male narrator, they provide the epitome of the triangular affect of desire, love, and jealousy. But the same gendered polarity also applies to (male) inversion. As Sedgwick noted, in *In Search of Lost Time* femininity and desire are always associated: "all that the two versions of homosexual desire seem to have in common may be said to be a sort of asymmetrical list towards the feminine: Charlus is feminized by his homosexual desire, but so . . . is Albertine most often feminized by hers."[40] Unseen by his peers, Charlus loses his masculine mask and becomes physically desirable and attractive, even as the narrator sees him before Jupien's arrival. "I found in his face seen thus in repose and as it were in its natural state something so affectionate, so defenseless," the narrator exclaims.[41]

But Albertine, the epitome of femininity, is also a "garçonne," which constitutes a strange reversal of Charlus's appearance as a woman. Ladenson underscores how, once again, the symmetry is only superficial: as "garçonnes" Albertine and her friends appear "boyish"—not "mannish"—which doesn't indicate any gender ambiguity and only suggests "liberation from conventional gender restraints." In the same way, far from Gide's chaste and virtuous women, Proust's female characters all are, at some point or another, said to have "mauvais genre," an expression playing on the ambiguity between gender and sexuality.[42] Albertine and her friends, along with, progressively, virtually every female-assigned individual encountered by the narrator, are said to disrupt both gender norms and decency and thus are hypersexualized like Vigny's Delilah. Female sexuality is, in the end, as contagious as male inversion. Slipping away from her very gender, Albertine's hyperfemininity cancels itself out and can be best characterized as a state of fugue. As the narrator eventually describes her, she is "l'être de fuite"—"being of flight,"[43] or as Murat puts it, "Albertine is innumerable."[44]

Lesbians don't need inversion, because their very nature as "être[s] de fuite" allows them to be in constant motion. Femininity, as a gender, cancels itself, whereas masculinity constitutes a rigid disciplinary system of rules and codes. To adopt a Deleuzian terminology, in this perspective, masculinity is the assemblage, whereas femininity is a line of flight. As a male fantasy, femininity is nothing but a fugue: it is what men shouldn't (let themselves) be. Dysphoria, then, is about the unease created by the gender assemblage and the desire for inversion. Dropping the mask of seriousness, Charlus smiles, a blooming, budding "young girl in flowers." Instead of raging like Samson and condemning his characters to a heteronormative hell, Proust allows Samson to be Delilah. The curse of dysphoria becomes the blessing of being able, intermittently, to let go of the sterile mask of masculinity. Charlus is female when he escapes the gaze of his peers. Not that he would suddenly feel free to disclose his true nature, but precisely because freedom is femininity, and the necessity to pass as male is a mask. Dysphoria, here, ceases to be an inability to belong and becomes the ability to not belong, to slip away from the heteropatriarchal male assignation. But to the men-women, the fugue, as we will see, is neither an absence nor a delusion; it is a way of being in the world: it is, indeed, what makes them fertile.

NEAR IMPOSSIBLE CROSSINGS: QUEER FERTILIZATION

Sodom and Gomorrah's opening ends with the mention of a missed encounter: while the narrator was busy spying on Charlus and Jupien, he was cheated of the opportunity to witness "the fertilization of the blossom by the bee."[45] But the reader, by then, knows better. A fertilization of sorts did indeed take place in Jupien's shop, overheard by the teenage narrator and fully understood by the adult reader. As Sedgwick has shown, the narrator's Darwinian endeavor, along with the numerous botanical metaphors present in the narrative, forms a deceptive counterpoint. While these metaphors seem to build a contrast between the (fecund) encounter of a flower and a "rare insect" and a (supposedly barren) sexual intercourse between gay men, they play an ambiguous part in the description of inversion. The two men's encounter is simultaneously described as "a mirror-dance" of identical counterparts and as "a courtship by a *male*-figured Charlus and a *female*-figured Jupien,"[46] even though it occurs shortly after the disclosure of Charlus's quintessential feminine nature.[47] The complex series of sexed botanical metaphors displayed in the chapter simply don't add up. But far from showing a superficial instrumentalization of evolutionary biology, these contradictions reveal how Proust, a keen reader of Darwin, appropriated the latter's description of sexual differentiation to weave his own description of the gender assemblage, one in which fertilization, when it comes to human matters, isn't the same thing as reproduction.

In his comparative reading of Proust and Darwin, Simon Porzak exposes "nature's queer heterosexuality": for Darwin as for Proust, heterosexual reproduction can only happen through the deployment of deceiving and complex strategies. "Darwin insists on the extreme improbability of [a] generalized heterosexuality," and he "denaturalizes the apparent obviousness and efficacy of heterosexual crossing, along with the self-evident limits that appeared to differentiate the 'higher orders' and the invertebrates, the plant and the animal kingdoms, and even sexual and asexual reproduction." In nature, heterosexuality is as unlikely as the perfect match of Charlus and Jupien. But

Darwin's research on barnacles and his discovery of invertebrate crossing came to represent the possibility of evolution and change and the condition for the existence of higher animal forms of life: "Darwin discovers and defines crossing, and thus the variation that is nature as a highly improbable, unlikely, contingent, and nevertheless sustained, aberrance. The sublime scale of nature ensures that the vanishingly rare phenomenon of variation is in fact everywhere visible, but this does not change its fundamental near-impossibility."[48]

Thus, the narrator's quest takes on another meaning: as Darwin's patience with barnacles, his curiosity has been rewarded with another "vanishingly rare phenomenon." Not only was he able to discover Charlus's carefully hidden femininity, but he stumbled upon a crossing as meaningful as that of the barnacle. The successful exchange between Charlus and Jupien, which introduced in his world a "variation ... everywhere visible" but nearly impossible to witness: "M. de Charlus had distracted me from looking to see whether the bumble-bee was bringing to the orchid the pollen it has so long been waiting to receive, and had no chance of receiving save by an accident so unlikely that one might call it a sort of miracle. But it was a miracle also that I had just witnessed, almost of the same order and no less marvelous ... everything about it seemed to me instinct with beauty."[49] It would be misleading to understand the metaphor of plant-insect fertilization as a commentary on the supposed barrenness of gay sex. The orchid and the bumblebee, Charlus and Jupien, the young narrator and his eagerness to discover hidden pockets of meaning in the world surrounding him, are all parts of a secret economy of proliferating yet near-impossible miracles. Nearly missed encounters are vastly different from missed encounters.[50]

Sodom and Gomorrah's evocation of the cursed race is often characterized as a description of the loneliness that plagues its members. A famous passage evokes a disheartened homosexual man strolling along the beach after the departure of his lover, stranded in his loneliness like "a sterile jellyfish." But the story doesn't end there: the jellyfish metaphor is in fact a turning point. After recalling his initial revulsion toward jellyfish, the narrator compares them to flowers—"the mauve orchids of the sea."[51] Jellyfish are the queer flowers of dysphoria—an inverted form of budding femininity. Jellyfish, "méduse," in French, also refers to the Medusa and to a threatening, vengeful version of femininity. Yet orchids bring back the trope of botanical fertilization and, again, the miracle of Charlus and Jupien's encounter. As Porzak underscores, if the jellyfish is a metaphor for sterility, it reveals it as a threat, not as a fate; first and foremost, it reveals the complex and beautiful strategies of attraction characterizing these strange but certainly not unnatural beings: inverts and invertebrates.

Fertilization, in Proust, doesn't have much to do with sexual reproduction (after all, we aren't barnacles) but refers to another type of crossing. A more direct explanation is given by the author himself, appearing, in a typical Proustian strategy, in parentheses: "(and here the word fertilise must be understood in a moral sense, since . . . it is no small matter for a person to be able to encounter the sole pleasure which he is capable of enjoying, and that 'every soul here below' can impart to some other 'its music or its fragrance or its flame.')."[52]

The unattributed quote is from a poem by Victor Hugo adapted to music in 1890 by the composer Reynaldo Hahn, who a few years later became Proust's lover.[53] A quote hidden between parentheses, a souvenir, a love poem, a song composed by a lover . . . the meaning here is as allusive as it is significant. Suddenly, the pessimistic view of male romance displayed in *In Search of Lost Time* seems to be abandoned in favor of the romantic notion of a communion of souls. Of course, the parenthesis and its nostalgic undertones could be dismissed as ironic, and it is indeed ironic that Hugo's poem and its idealistic vision of romance are juxtaposed to what seems a purely sexual transaction between strangers, just as Samson's anger is rerouted toward more transgressive views of sexual difference. But as a matter of fact, Jupien and Charlus's relationship will last for several decades: theirs is the longest and most stable love affair in *In Search of Lost Time*. They are, indeed, a match made in heaven, and the definition of fertilization given here is clear enough: it refers to a "moral" dimension (but by no means ethical), and it is "no small matter." As in Darwin, fertilization constitutes the (extremely rare) possibility of variation that will disrupt the rigidity of the assemblage and allow for new forms of life to emerge.

CONCEPTUAL ABYSSES

Published thirty years apart, Deleuze's *Proust and Signs* and Sedgwick's *Epistemology of the Closet* both read *In Search of Lost Time* as a site of production of meaning. Each author ignored, in all probability, the other's work: Sedgwick's *Epistemology of the Closet* was translated into French after Deleuze's death in 1995, and the only works by Deleuze ever referenced by Sedgwick are his *Dialogues* with Claire Parnet and *Cinema 1* and *Cinema 2*.[54] The first version of Deleuze's essay was written in 1964, but it wouldn't be translated into English until 2000. It is unlikely that Sedgwick read it or had it in mind when she was writing her *Epistemology of the Closet* ten years earlier. Even though they both apprehend Proust's text as an "apprenticeship to signs," they understand signs in ways that are ultimately incompatible.[55] Sedgwick sees them as an opening toward a form of knowledge, and Deleuze's focus is on a temporal, creative, and asignifying process. While Sedgwick's perspective highlights and unfolds how central gender and sexuality are, Deleuze's approach enables us to take Sedgwick's findings further and unravel Proust's mapping of the gender assemblage.

Sedgwick's reading of Proust aims to expose "the spectacle of the closet." In response to Bersani's critique of Proust's homophobia, she shows how the lack of coherence and empathy with which Proust represents male homosexuality is part of an economy of secret and disclosure. In so doing, she points out how Proust uses the gender binary in order to describe same-sex love, and vice versa. This strategy is manifest, for instance, in the incoherence of the orchid-bumblebee metaphor—Charlus-as-a-woman is the bumblebee needed by Jupien-as-an-orchid. What happens here, Sedgwick tells us, is absolutely intentional and deeply meaningful. Proust's accumulation of metaphors "opens gaping conceptual abysses when one tries—as the chapter repeatedly does—to compare any model of same-sex desire with the plight of the virginal orchid."[56] These gaps reveal an excess—or a lack—of meaning: things don't add up, which is precisely how the "epistemology of the closet" works. Same-sex desire produces a constant stream of signs whose contradictory meanings are meant to reveal not what is hidden but the fact that something is hidden. As Porzak summarizes, "Proust and Marcel seize upon [Charlus and Jupien's] encounter to introduce a new narrative code into the novel, finally allowing the reader entry into the blazing hell of same-sex desire . . . that has until now remained an indecipherable secret."[57] Thus, gender binarism and heteronormativity, under the guise of sexed reproduction and gender representation, are apprehended as a coded system that, properly hijacked, leads to the disclosure of a different reality. As always with queer reading, queer signs embedded in narratives act as keys that open doors toward more queerness, until the original appearance of normativity is entirely inverted, queered, contaminated. This is what Proust can teach us about the epistemology of the closet: how to produce and gain access to a hidden knowledge. This is where Sedgwick's reading becomes incompatible with Deleuze's, even though the line between the two is very fine: while the former finds signification calling for interpretation in asignifying practices (the conceptual abysses), the latter rejects interpretation altogether.

In *Proust and Signs*, Deleuze describes *In Search of Lost Time* as a bildungsroman where the narrator is embarked on "a search for truth" and navigates, as he recollects it, a world made of signs that he constantly needs to decipher in order to move on.[58] But Deleuze never uses the term "epistemology." First, because the meaning of the term is narrower in French than in English, but more importantly because what he describes in Proust is not a matter of signification but of production.[59] As Anne Sauvagnargues summarizes, Deleuze's philosophy reveals "a definite trajectory that moves from the discursive toward the nondiscursive," and *Proust and Signs* constitutes a significant step in this trajectory, by opening up a reflection on "the status of the sign and its path from the realm of interpretation to force."[60] The signs offered to (or produced by) the narrator don't refer to a preestablished code. They call for an active interpretation in the form of a realignment, a change of position, but do not contain any meaning as such. They are beacons, not messages, and certainly not guiding rules. This is why, fundamentally, *In Search of Lost Time,* and what is being searched for, "is oriented to the future, not to the past."[61] Instead of looking back to interpret, the text looks forward in order to create and connect. As in Sedgwick's interpretation, signs appear in "conceptual abysses" and lead the narrator between shifting worlds. But the abysses don't offer any interpretive clues. They trigger changes that are nothing less than a changing of worlds; they are, in this regard, the necessary condition for fertilization.

Michael Lucey has exposed how, in Proust, the production and understanding of literature and art, social literacy, and sexual literacy all work together. The narrator's quest for truth and his artistic project cannot be distinguished from his climbing of the social ladder, and his ability to talk about sex is one and the same with his ability to understand intricate social hierarchies.[62] Inversion falls beyond this scope while pervading it. When understood as conceptual figures, the inverts constitute more than a type of literacy: they are the site where literacy and language are overshadowed by embodied practices, giving way to those conceptual abysses from which discourses are changed into desires. This is why Deleuze sees Charlus as the most important vector in the narrator's quest: starting with his voice, which unites "virile content" and "effeminate manner of expression," and his gaze, which "Charlus presents as an enormous flashing indicator . . . a mystery to be penetrated, to be interpreted."[63] Sedgwick also lends to Charlus the traits of a conceptual figure: "the endless, lavish production of M. de Charlus—as . . . the spectacle of the closet—enables the world of the novel to take shape and turn around the steely beam of his distance from the differently structured closet of the narrative."[64] For both Deleuze and Sedgwick, the fact that Charlus is signaling is more important than *what* he is signaling. Deleuze describes him as the "Spider," or the "master of the Logos": "Charlus always has the freshness of a world just created and unceasingly emits primordial signs that the interpreter must decipher."[65] Operating as a conceptual figure, he forces the narrator to establish connections, to weave a web of new variations and crossings that leads him to reconstruct his world anew. He is the master of the Logos not because he makes sense but because he ultimately disrupts given forms of knowledge: dysphoria, here, is what unwrites the codes—of heteronormativity, first, but it ultimately unravels any coding at all. The inversion embodied by Charlus exposes the gender assemblage. But in so doing, it also prevents any other assemblage from operating.

Dysphoria acts as a "flashing indicator," as Deleuze puts it, which disrupts the gender assemblage by manifesting it. When he lays down the mask of masculinity, Charlus unravels the heteronormative vision of two mutually exclusive genders. But this is not, as Sedgwick would have it, an act of enunciation or of representation: it is a process of embodiment, one that has no existence outside of what happens in, with, and to a specific body. Albeit a literary construct and a conceptual figure, Charlus is a being of flesh, always preceded by incongruent but highly visible physical manifestations. His high-pitched voice and the "big bum" praised by Jupien are not acts of language but contingent bodily manifestations.[66] In the same way, Proust's Darwinian references reveal that the orchid learned to trick the bee, just as members of the cursed race evolved into tricking mating partners through a display of misleading attributes. These tricks are about sex, intimacy, and physical coupling, not about meaning or representation.

SHIMMERING BODIES

In *Shimmering Images*, Eliza Steinbock argues that what trans teaches us isn't so much about traversing from one side to the other than about being able to stay in the contradiction: "Trans ontologies deflect the demand for definitive meaning of differences," Steinbock writes.[67] What if, instead of asserting a trans ontology, trans could offer an antiontology, or a glimpse out of ontologies? Not as a utopian undoing of gender, not as a horizon *beyond* gender, but as a trapdoor opening *behind* the (binary) scene. What Charlus's shimmering body offers is the spectacle of the two genders appearing at the same time, which defies the coding of interpretation and even representation. The shimmering signs of inversion maintain an operative contradiction: the interaction is functional, Charlus's encounter with Jupien happens, even though its witnesses are plunged into conceptual abysses. In a reversal of the Vigny quotation, instead of dying separately, the "two sexes" are flashing together, and they are very much alive, feeding, and reproducing themselves in a beautiful tangle. Steinbock's idea of shimmer finds an echo in Deleuze's concept of transversality, which he started formulating in *Proust and Signs*. Transversality as a concept comes from psychoanalysis and was first formulated by Félix Guattari as an antihierarchical account of the forces traversing the unconscious. In *Proust and Signs*, Deleuze uses it to anchor his critique of interpretation and to assert the predominance of relations over structures.[68] Proustian signs, in their overabundance and operative dysfunctionality, can only be accounted for as a decentered, multiplicative, and mobile machine: in Proust, as in the unconscious, "to interpret has no unity other than the transversal."[69]

Paradoxically, transversality operates through the irreconcilable partition manifested in inversion. Forming "sealed vessels," the two genders "are both present and separate in the same individual."[70] Transversality connects what interpretation could not consider jointly—the shimmering effect:

> An aberrant communication occurs in a transversal dimension between partitioned sexes. . . . It may in fact happen that an individual statistically determined as male will seek, in order to

fertilize his female part, with which he cannot himself communicate, an individual statistically of the same sex as himself. ... But in a more profound instance, the individual statistically determined as male will cause his own female parts to be fertilized by objects ... that are just as likely to be found in a woman as in a man. And this is the basis of transsexuality, according to Proust: no longer an *aggregate and specific homosexuality*, in which men relate to men and women ... but a *local and nonspecific homosexuality* in which a man also seeks what is masculine in a woman and a woman what is feminine in a man.[71]

As often when it comes to frontal discussions of gender and sexuality, Deleuze shimmers between fruitful intuition and prodigious ignorance. Blindly following Proust's shift from sexuality to gender without considering what it entails, his analysis paradoxically reasserts the heterosexual mode of reproduction and reterritorializes fertilization as a binary-encoded process. Once confronted with sexual difference, Deleuze reproduces the very pattern his entire thinking teaches us to avoid. Unquestioning gender and sex, whose distinction he never mentions, he follows a very limited understanding of Proust's Darwinian perspective. His denial of homosexual desire and his subsequent fetishization of trans not only fails to do justice to actual desires and embodiments, as Heaney has claimed regarding Foucault, but it also fails to take into account the part played by the gender assemblage in the coding process that he reveals. As I have argued in this book, Deleuzian philosophy is highly relevant for a (nonontological) trans critique, but this isn't thanks to his views on trans matters, which he treats as a black hole. Transversality, as first formulated in *Proust and Signs*, constitutes the beginning of a thread that led to the production of Deleuze and Guattari's most productive concepts regarding trans studies.[72] Regarding Proust and inversion, we need, so to speak, to use Deleuze against Deleuze.

Charlus, as a conceptual figure of inversion, reveals the necessity, the rarity, and the beauty of fertilization. The miracle in which he participates at the opening of *Sodom and Gomorrah* doesn't happen in spite of inversion but because of it. In the same way, Charlus's miracle isn't the opposite of sexed reproduction (as understood by Darwin); it is its nonbiological counterpart: a near-impossible connection, bringing about a radical change in a world that would otherwise be frozen into the rigidity of a mask. It is in fact the opposite of the sterility that appeared at first glance to threaten the cursed race. Inversion fuels fertilization: variation happens through desires that are unaccounted for, not through the coded channels of sexual difference. In Deleuzo-Guattarian terms, inversion is a line of flight. I have described elsewhere how the concept of the line of flight can be applied in trans studies.[73] It is worth recalling that the original term, the French *ligne de fuite*, ambiguously refers both to escape and to leakage: it refers to the point where the rigid codes channeling established social groups cannot be held together and are thus briefly revealed for what they are—an apparatus of control. In this regard, the mapping of an assemblage is always a cartography of its lines of flight, and this is exactly what Proustian inversion accomplishes. Where Gide opposed the two genders in order to rescue one of them from the binary and reclaim male freedom, Proust stays within the contradiction and allows genders to leak or to shimmer in the same body.

Inversion thus enables us to trace the relationship between trans and change, as Steinbock highlights it: "I offer the concept of shimmering images to describe this persistent vision of trans as change, and as a force that continues to achieve change through varying means and ways."[74] In *In Search of Lost Time*, Charlus embodies change not only through his shimmering of genders but by revealing himself a master in metamorphosis and betrayal, evolving through every social circle. In the last volume of *In Search of Lost Time*, set during World War I, he is one of the only characters displaying sympathies for the Germans, which earns him a reputation as a traitor and the nickname "Frau Bosch." The reader is led to believe that this weakness for the enemy stems at the same time from Charlus's kindness, which makes him empathize with the vanquished, and from his masochism, which makes him love his persecutors.[75] Here again inversion blurs all cohesive rules and operates shifts that aren't translatable in any coherent linguistics: Charlus's body, affects, and desires make him occupy an untenable position for two incompatible motives at the same time. Charlus's inversion *and* his sexual practices allow him to be traversed simultaneously by generosity and lust and to draw a line of flight between enemy lines.

Inversion, in Proust, is the textual, or rather conceptual, embodiment of dysphoria: it is the place where the gender assemblage is bursting at the seams, or leaking, into something that is still gender but cannot be deciphered or recoded in terms of gender. This leakage is a temporal process, just as Deleuze opens *Proust and Signs* by stating that "signs are the objects of a temporal apprenticeship, not of an abstract knowledge."[76] The untenable position in which Charlus manages to find himself is also a moment between gender and not gender, inside the assemblage or outside of it. And this is the moment where variation can occur, or change, or take flight: in the brief instant of trans shimmering. Dysphoria makes things happen *because* it escapes representation (as such), which is why the limited understanding of trans studies as representation (of trans individuals and communities) is counterproductive. In the same way, the temporal process I just described renders ontology irrelevant. What Proust, Deleuze, and Sedgwick can teach us about gender is that it doesn't work, or, rather, they can show us the paths through which gender only works when it doesn't work: in the moments where the assemblage is *trans-ed*.

4

ON QUEER CROOKS, ABJECTION, AND MOVING SIDEWAYS

Maurice Sachs's Dysphoric Smuggling

When Maurice was broke, he would stuff toilet paper in his pocket. He would fiddle with it and believe that his pocket was full of bills. This, he used to say, makes me feel self-assured."[1] This is how Jean Cocteau recalls his former protégé Maurice Sachs, the writer, socialite, smuggler, and con artist, who had met an untimely death in Germany at the end of World War II. By all accounts a fascinating figure, Sachs is all the more difficult to portray accurately as, even while he was alive, he was already discussed as a *figure*—a legend—rather than, for instance, a crook or an author. Born in 1906, Sachs began making a name for himself in the Parisian bohemia of the 1920s, associating with the artistic and literary elite of the interwar years, accumulating an impressive list of mentors that included writers like Cocteau and Max Jacob, artists like Soutine, and the Catholic philosopher Jacques Maritain, who became Sachs's godfather when the latter converted to Catholicism—a short-lived but much publicized affair. Unapologetically queer, Sachs never hid his preference for men, even though he married an American heiress and later seduced Violette Leduc, whom, after convincing her to start writing, he abandoned to head for Hamburg and enroll in the Gestapo.

Figure of the crossroads, of the ever-changing compass, wandering Jew and seminarist, art dealer and con artist, Gestapo agent and black-market crook, Sachs's stories are tales of sex and money, of male brothels and diamonds, of narrow escapes and fabulous new beginnings. Although he published only three books while he was alive, Sachs was a prolific writer, and in the years following his death seven more came out.[2] But above all, Sachs was a smuggler: of money and goods, of people, of information, and of gender.

There is obviously a lot to be said about Sachs's relationship to money and gender, but Cocteau's toilet paper anecdote hints at Sachs's relationship to truth and authenticity. In Cocteau's description, the verb *bourrer* (to stuff) suggests the sexual, prosthetic nature of Maurice's sham. The masturbatory gesture of the fiddling hand, the specific choice of toilet paper, the bulging pocket: the act of self-persuasion connects accessories and bodily functions in an assemblage of sexuality, gambling, and gender performance, making no distinction between self and other. Like Gide but in different terms, Sachs is defaulting from masculinity, both as gendered embodiment and as a subjectification process. But where Gide was searching for an authentic form of masculinity, Sachs fakes, counterfeits, and avoids at the same time. His particular type of dysphoria is both willful and imposed, a line of flight and a pitfall, embedded in racial as well as gendered forms of assignation. He embodies, in this regard, the fascist trope of abjection: a simultaneous blurring of the boundaries of the nation and of the masculine individual ego, caused by the interference of foreign elements.[3] A queer crooked Jew, Sachs crystallizes a contaminating potential that makes him the opposite of gentile white masculinity and the values associated with it: honesty, loyalty, strength, and stereotypical physical and mental health.[4]

The line of continuity between masculinity, male homosexuality, and authenticity discussed in chapter 2 finds itself reversed. Whereas Gide's Michel "comes to see his whole life as a hypocritical sham, and in pursuit of what he sees as his true, authentic, homosexual self, abandons everything," for Sachs being a sham is a creative and empowering mode of survival.[5] Sachs saw in Gide a model of authenticity and honesty, "a writer of such rectitude and whose pen . . . is a compass needle," and used him as a sort of moral scale on which to measure his own worthlessness.[6] "You see, it pains me, towards you, to not be as *good* as I would want to."[7] Sachs reveals how morally inclined Michel the "Immoralist" truly is. While he, Sachs, certainly didn't display any aptitude for serving the state, he did serve, and betray, two states: the German one (as a spy) and the French one (as a clandestine purveyor of gold). A mercenary of sorts, neither in nor out, Sachs did the state's dirty work, a task that remains thoroughly invisible in Gide's and Michel's world.

SHAMELESS

Sachs's idea of *good* doesn't include sexuality. While he shares "those inveterate queer tendencies to disassociation and disidentification" associated with gay shame, he appears utterly devoid of this feeling.[8] Sachs's writings are, to use contemporary terms, sex positive, and they validate queerness and male homosexuality in a matter-of-fact tone that few of his contemporaries used. While Genet and Jouhandeau have carried gay shame, under the name of "abjection," to a conceptual and aesthetic level, abjection isn't a term Sachs can reclaim.[9] His defaulting from masculinity, like Gide's, needs to be understood in terms of race as well as gender. Sachs, as a Jew, finds himself on the other side of the binary, where "abjection" retains its fascist meaning of racialized otherness. In spite of his short-lived conversion to Catholicism and his ultimate Gestapo affiliation, Sachs never denied or even belittled his Jewishness.[10] In the same way that he never hid his preference for men, he saw himself as a Jew even while he professed his admiration for Germany, which he praised for its manliness.[11] The paradox is that Sachs, a crook, a queer, and a Jew, precisely because of his lack of shame, came to embody the racist and misogynist abjection fantasies of his time.

Reading Sachs feels like treading in a minefield: while, to this day, many of his commentators are encroached in a complex mixture of antisemitism, class contempt, homophobia, and gender conformity, Sachs's own writing is a constant intervention in these loaded discussions, endorsing, highjacking, denouncing, and confessing.

Sachs acquired his (fading) literary fame through his reputation more than his works. He is a prolific presence in others' texts: a protagonist in Violette Leduc's autobiographically inspired novels *In the Prison of Her Skin* and *La batarde*, the infamous hero of *Le dernier sabbat de Maurice Sachs* (Maurice Sachs's last Sabbath"), an antisemitic account of his last years in Germany, a character in Patrick Modiano's novel *La Place de l'Etoile* . . . [12] Similarly, Sachs is discussed by his contemporaries, and by his critics, as a character more than as an author. More often than not, readings focused on Sachs take on the aspect of an exercise in psychology: they subject Sachs to extensive interpretations, pathologizing and analyzing him. His most thorough biographer, Henri Raczymow, relentlessly returns to the same tautological explanation for Sachs's "misfortune": Sachs doesn't like himself. "What Sachs . . . cannot escape is the tragedy of existence, the tragedy and the shame of being himself."[13] Significantly, these pathologizing interpretations are accompanied by ethical, or, rather, moral, readings of Sachs. The special issue of the very respectable journal *Cahiers de L'Herne* devoted to Sachs opens with a preface wondering about what "we" can and cannot forgive him, a question that would be unthinkable regarding Genet or Céline.[14]

These attempts at moral judgment and diagnosis are problematic in many ways, but their most interesting aspect is that they reveal the efficiency of a strategy devised by Sachs himself. Sachs's books are assertively autobiographical, self-explanatory texts, often written in the first person, sometimes even self-proclaimed confessions. Affecting the apologetic tone of contrition or flaunting sexual adventures in a farcical and self-deprecatory way, Sachs's memoirs rely on the same type of sleights of hand as his schemes. Sachs is, above all, a smuggler. His skills at weaving networks and scheming are at work in his writing and also operate through his writing. Sachs's play with authenticity is, just like the act of stuffing his pocket with banknotes, an arrangement, in both the English and the French meaning of the term, a form of self-creation and self-justification, a way of inhabiting the world, working with and against the assemblage.

Although Sachs does display a sense of guilt in his memoirs, it pertains not to an enforcement of normative masculinity but to a more direct form of cheating. Unlike Gide's Michel, Sachs isn't a gay outlaw but a queer crook.[15] He doesn't aspire to a reclusive (and victimless) isolation but lives off a constant stream of social and affective bonds. Queerness to him is a networking tool: Sachs is Proust's Charlus as a crook. Like him, he exists in the midst of a network of interconnected people and information from which he cannot be distinguished.[16] Dysphoria, on the other hand, merges with guilt in the form of a chicken-egg question. Sachs's avowed feeling of gender incongruence, which doesn't prevent him from articulating the same misogynist endorsement of the gender binary as Gide, is attached to an abstract sense of guilt, taking the form of a thorough and willful impossibility of belonging. Whereas queerness is a transactional tool, dysphoria and crime are part of the same way of engaging with or disengaging from the world while moving through it.

SERIOUSLY CROOKED

Twenty years after the publication of *The Immoralist*, Gide moved sideways and invented the figure of the queer counterfeiter. Sachs was an *authentic* counterfeiter, driven by an urgent need for (actual) money. Yet the strange side effect of Sachs's crookedness is that it prevents him from being acknowledged, whether as a writer or as a criminal. The idealizing process that made Genet's fame, as Kadji Amin has described, doesn't work with Sachs.[17] If Tahar Ben Jelloun, for instance, sees in Genet a "sublime liar," Sachs, by no means sublime, is too good a liar for his own good.[18] Paradoxically, Sachs makes Genet look like a figure of authenticity, something akin to an honest traitor: Genet is at the same time granted more forgiveness for his crimes and taken more seriously as a criminal. Amin has shown how the idealization of Genet persists, particularly in queer communities: the counterfigure of Sachs underscores how these attachments might indeed be disturbing. Genet's association with violent crime seems strangely more acceptable than Sachs's schemes, and this calls attention to the gendered and racial terms of their opposition: the (effeminate) (Jewish) sneaky crook and the (gentile) (manly) bad boy. Describing Sachs as the "anti-Genet," Raczymow explains: "There is good reason for that: he [Sachs] needs to be loved. Everywhere, always, by the first comer. And Genet doesn't care."[19] Pathologized, Sachs falls on the female side of the gender binary: he wants to be loved. The female side is evidently the wrong side, as is the Jewish side.

Gender and race lead us to the third term associated with intersectionality, which is also the most difficult to take into consideration: class. Discussions of Sachs present us with a very interesting case of class ignorance, or, to put it more bluntly, a radical enforcement of capitalist ideology. Strangely, Sachs's crimes are never interpreted as originating in his financial situation. With him, class is about money rather than cultural capital. Sachs was from a well-off bourgeois family, but his divorced mother lost her fortune and had to leave France to avoid being imprisoned for debts when he was still in high school. Even though Sachs was, in fact, ruined, he maintained some connections with bourgeois circles throughout his life but was only able to do so thanks to illegal sources of income and some form or other of leeching. How else would he have found, as an eighteen-year-old hotel clerk, the means to dress appropriately or to pay for his supper? Yet Sachs's bourgeois origin acts like a veil forbidding him from being read in terms of class *while* being taken seriously as a criminal. I want to underscore two things here: first, Sachs engages in criminal activities because he needs the money and doesn't want to engage in the type of labor the capitalist society of his time would deem appropriate for someone lacking a personal fortune. Second, in order to understand Sachs as a writer, we need to take him seriously as a crook.

Sachs made a living through his schemes, which were, rather than failed attempts at finding sustainable ways of generating an income, a series of successful creations, never meant to last because one could always, according to his favorite expression, "se refaire," that is, cover one's losses, literally "make oneself over again."²⁰ The patronizing and pathologizing readings just mentioned seem to operate under the assumption that Sachs could have somehow thrived in a professional activity while having a career as writer. But his position in the class hierarchy of his time makes him an unlikely candidate for comparisons with Gide or Proust. This class-blind assumption ignores the fact that most of the modernist authors of the French canon were benefiting from personal fortunes and didn't have to work for a living. This doesn't mean that I am proposing to read Sachs as a Robin Hood figure. He was only working for himself, or working himself out. His crimes weren't victimless. Not only did he rob his famous friends; he also, among many other schemes, made a lucrative business of smuggling Jewish refugees out of Nazi-occupied France, likely betraying many of them in the process.²¹ While working for the Gestapo in Hamburg, he took part in the arrest of members of the White Rose, an anti-Nazi resistance group, which led to their execution.²²

This chapter explores, through Sachs's autobiographical writings, the dysphoria of the queer crook and the ways in which it exposes and disrupts gender and racial injunctions. The relation between criminality and queerness has been underexamined by critics because most discussions focus, and rightly so, on disengaging sexual and gender deviance from the accusation of crime.²³

SELF-MADE LEGEND AND COLLECTIVE ENUNCIATION

My aim here isn't to deliver the truth of Maurice Sachs, whether psychological, ethical, or historical. On the contrary, I want to describe Sachs as a collective formation traversed by the underlying obsessions of his time, along the lines of what Deleuze and Guattari conceptualize as a "collective assemblage of enunciation."[24] This concept makes it possible to bypass the opposition between subjectivity and subjectification, between the subject and his historical contingencies, between individuality and ideology. Sachs's legend is as much self-made as it is collective: while he actively worked on his own self-promotion (or survival), he was also caught in and modeled into a series of personae: a self-creation as much as invention of his time, "a synthesis of the 20s, 30s, and 40s."[25] Sachs was a socialite with a financial agenda, yet his agenda cannot be distinguished from the series of flows from which he was feeding or to which he was being fed. This type of self-creation occurs collectively, through a network of variable, intertwined narratives. As a collective assemblage, Sachs reflects the sexist and racist gender assemblage of the interwar years in all of its contradictions: cosmopolitan and antisemitic, misogynist and liberal, fascinated by financial speculation yet believing in artistic authenticity. His autobiographical writings, as they claim to reassert his own truth, to come clean, to confess, to convince, and to entertain, are drawing a collective map, exploring the edges, navigating the contradictions.

My reading of Sachs is neither ethical nor historical. I am not interested in reclaiming or validating an identity for him. Nor am I involved in redeeming him, though I am, however, keen on reclaiming his works for contemporary queer and trans readers, a task all the more necessary since most of them have not been translated into English. After describing Sachs as a collective assemblage of enunciation, this chapter follows a series of threads at work in the collective assemblage that is "Maurice Sachs." First, I discuss the concept of abjection, in regard to both queerness and antisemitism. Caught between two contradictory injunctions, Sachs was barred from reclaiming abjection, as opposed to some of his gentile contemporaries, and condemned to embody the shame of others. I then explore the relationship between dysphoria and guilt, asserting the transgressive delight Sachs took in embodying and exploring various social personae.

Analyzing Sachs's misogyny in relation to his defiance of heteronormativity, I assess how gay sex allowed him to skirt social stability and to move across social hierarchies. I then move on to Sachs's crookedness to assess its literary aspect: did Sachs really confess, or is it just a sleight of hand? Yet I argue that, beyond the question of truth and authenticity, his serial confessions are a transactional play with codes not for the sake of communication but as an iterative process. I then examine the connection Sachs establishes between writing and dysphoric embodiment: writing, like being written, is anchored in body and flesh. In way of conclusion, I invoke Sachs as a perpetual runaway: moving sideways and moving fast.

FROM SELF-GENERATIVE LEGEND . . .

Sachs's fame reached its peak at the beginning of the 1950s, in the years following his death. Most of his books were published at that time: his memoirs *Witches' Sabbath* (1946) and *The Hunt* (1949); his novels *Abracadabra* (1952) and *Histoire de John Cooper d'Albany* (1955); and the French translation of his 1933 essay published in the United States, *The Decade of Illusion* (1950).[26] But Sachs's legend wasn't posthumous, nor was it born from the admittedly dramatic events leading to his death. His reputation was already well established by his early twenties, a self-made and self-generative legend, as he made his way through the literary, artistic, and social avant-garde circles of the Parisian roaring 1920s. A self-proclaimed writer, Sachs began working on his reputation before working on his books, and when he did write, these were mostly autobiographical accounts, so much so, that, as his biographer Thomas Clerc puts it, "Sachs neutralizes the alternative between author and character."[27]

Born in 1906 in Paris into a bourgeois Jewish family, Maurice's last name was actually Ettinghausen, from a father who disappeared from his life when he was five years old. Sachs is his mother's maiden name. Yet the decisive event in Maurice's early life wasn't the disappearance of the father but the fall of the mother. In 1923, Andrée Sachs, after having spent her entire fortune and then some, attempted to kill herself in her Deauville hotel room. This is the turning point in Sachs's self-fashioned coming-of-age story: taking the situation in his own hands, the seventeen-year-old Maurice proceeded to ask for financial aid from his extended family (in vain), smuggle his mother into a ferry bound to England, and trade his books and her diamonds in order to provide for them both.[28] He would pursue the same type of activities (asking for money, smuggling, trading) for the rest of his life. In this moment, he was also faced with "the full extent of bourgeois baseness"[29]—his family's disapproval of his mother and refusal to help them financially—an experience that, he claims, "completed the distortion of [his] character."[30] Dropping out of high school, the young Sachs subsequently embarks on a quest for cultural and financial capital and resources, which leads him to develop an impressive career. Love affairs and gay networking land him at the prestigious Vouillemont Hotel, a gathering place for artists and bohemians, where he starts out as the protégé and employee of the owners.[31] Introduced to Cocteau in 1924, Sachs becomes part of his inner circle. Cocteau, in turn, introduces Maurice to Jacques Maritain, the contemporary leader of the French Catholic renewal; Sachs converts to Catholicism, is baptized, and a few months later, at age twenty, becomes a seminarian, only to be expelled six months later.

The two decades that follow are packed with a series of adventures that have led many to affirm that Sachs's life "was more interesting than his works."[32] After serving in the military, Sachs makes a living as an art dealer, publisher, and dealer of rare books, all the while engaging in spectacular schemes, the most famous being his forging of Cocteau's signature in a letter allowing him (Sachs) to sell his possessions.[33] Mandated to open an art gallery in New York City, Sachs "borrows" paintings from his friends and settles in the United States, where he embarks on a conference tour as "Maurice Sachs, distinguished young Frenchman, well known for his brilliant forecasts and observations on European Politics." This is how he meets Gladys Matthews, the daughter of an influent Presbyterian pastor. They get married a few months later, after Sachs undergoes yet another religious conversion—only to reappear in Paris the following spring, having left the marital household and with a young Californian lover in tow.[34] Toward the end of the 1930s, Sachs works for the prestigious Gallimard publishing house as a series editor, translator, and biographer, all the while still trading stolen goods. A radio host at the time of France's defeat against Germany, he remains in occupied Paris until 1942, fully engaged in black-market schemes, dealing in diamonds and gold and smuggling Jewish refugees to unoccupied France. In November 1942, he travels to Hamburg, in a still unexplained move, where he enrolls as a volunteer worker. After living for several months in a workers' camp and working as a docker, he approaches the Gestapo and becomes an informant. This comfortable position allows him to again engage in the black market. He is eventually sentenced to jail for double-crossing the Gestapo and is killed as the Allied armies approach.

...TO SELF-MADE COLLECTIVE ASSEMBLAGE

Reading Sachs as a collective assemblage of enunciation amounts to letting go of all attempts to gauge the porous boundaries between the ways in which he was working on his own persona and the ways in which the persona was working through him. Sachs's readers tend to marvel at his "protean" personality. Reading the table of contents of the special issue of *L'Herne* dedicated to him confronts us with a monotonous list of adjectives that document precisely such an attempt: Sachs is "uncategorizable," "inauthentic," "elusive."[35] When the authors aren't insisting on his versatility, they are cataloguing him as a barometer of his time, who informs on "the atmosphere of an era." The contradiction between the avowed impossibility of describing Sachs and the tendency to reduce his trajectory to historical contingencies leads his critics to embark on pathologizing and patronizing accounts of his life and works. *The Hunt*'s 1948 preface, still reproduced in the 2014 edition, acknowledges the author's "abject personality";[36] a doctoral thesis on Sachs argues that he writes in order to keep at bay "the depths of quicksand in which his innermost being is engulfed."[37] Apprehending Sachs as a collective assemblage, on the other hand, allows us to shift from this psychological and moral quicksand toward a political reading and to analyze how Sachs both recreates the series of ideological constraints weighing on him and diffracts them, rerouting them for his own benefit.

Referring to Kafka, Deleuze and Guattari define literature as both "individual enunciation" and "collective enunciation": "a statement is literary when it is 'taken up' by a bachelor who precedes the collective conditions of enunciation."[38] This definition doesn't include Sachs. Sachs isn't a bachelor but a serial concubine. He doesn't precede; he is caught in a web of intensities that are enunciating him. Sachs's thousand stories are traversed by the manifold obsessions of his time: modern arts, the American business model, Catholic renaissance, Judaism, communism, Germanophilia, fascism. His social agenda associates him with the places and people that are emblematic of his time: the bohemian cabaret Le Boeuf sur le toit, Juan-les-Pins and the French Riviera, Paris, London, New York City. Featured in his writings as badges of honor are names whose celebrity endures decades later: Cocteau, Coco Chanel, André Gide, Max Jacob, Pierre Fresnay, Soutine, Gallimard . . .

By a process of concatenation, Sachs embodies a series of contiguous terms: Jewish, homosexual, criminal, effeminate, sentimental, perverse, amoral, seducer, cunning, bookish, snob, traitor, dandy, socialite . . . The list has no limits, since its terms are related by intensity—as insults—rather than by meaning. As Jeffery Dennis recalls, the association between homosexuality and crime emerged in the late nineteenth century with a pattern similar to the figure of the "Wandering Jew," popularized at the time by Eugène Sue's novel of the same title. Both promote the idea of "conscious pariahs" who reproduce their own alienation from a productive, modern society.[39] As collective statements of enunciation, they are bound to embody contradictory terms in a tautological process of pathologizing the undefined array of outcasts they produce.

"MAURICE IS A CHAMELEON . . ."

Sachs-as-a-Jew is at the core of Sachs's legend, a fundamental trait associated with his very name, and made visible through a constant rewriting of Sachs's body as ostensibly Jewish. Sachs's physical appearance is crystallized in the archetypal figure of the ugly seducer—without any distinctions, for instance, between the eighteen-year-old Maurice dancing at the Boeuf sur le toit and his balding, middle-aged counterpart. He is consistently described, even by his biographers, in doubly negative oxymorons, such as "physically unappealing yet highly seductive." David J. Jacobson has discussed how this portrayal stems from the antisemitic double bind of hypervisibility and invisibility.[40] Cocteau's description of Sachs, for instance, shows how this double bind prevents the latter from being acknowledged: to be visible is to be ostentatious, which in turn reveals a lack of individuality. "Maurice is a chameleon. He is addicted to mimicry. Set him down on white, and he turns white," Cocteau writes.[41] As Jacobson analyzes, the recurring mention of "Sachs's adaptability" is "a euphemism or corollary of what was often called Jewish 'rootlessness.'" In the same letter, Cocteau insists: "Maurice imitates and will always imitate, with this Jewish need to impress. . . . But he is wrong . . . when he writes 'us' instead of 'I.'" Cocteau can't articulate a "we" with Sachs because, "as Jews do," he is overdoing it.[42]

As Jacobson underscores, Sachs actively contributes to the antisemitic narrative constituting his persona.[43] Referring to his family as a noisy and dishonest "tribe," Sachs adopts the narrative of a corrupted and corrupting lineage: "It wasn't only against myself that I struggled but against an entire tribe who threw its hateful rags on my shoulders."[44] But he complicates the trope by adding to it a new set of tainted ancestry. Erasing his father's Jewishness and replacing it with Blackness, he claims that his father's mother was "a mixed-race Martinican, lavish and carefree, as are all people of color."[45] Underlining the fantasmatic connection between Blackness and Jewishness, he sets a multiplicity of impure tribes against the standard of whiteness. Being racialized, here, is turned into surplus: not a lack but a proliferation. As with Cocteau's chameleon metaphor, the problem isn't so much Sachs's talent for mimicry but the excess of it, the fact that it is out of control ("set him down on white . . ."). In what follows, I want to introduce two examples of animal metaphors highlighting the antisemitic collective assemblage that shapes portrayals of Sachs.

My first example is taken from *Maurice Sachs's Last Sabbath* and offers a sinister counterpart to the chameleon metaphor.[46] Philippe Monceau, one of the book's coauthors, had worked alongside Sachs for the Gestapo and turns out to be the only witness of Sachs's German years. By the time he told his version of Sachs's story to the conservative and gay writer André Du Dognon, his coauthor, Monceau had "graciously atoned" for his war crimes—he was, unlike Sachs, a convinced Nazi.[47] While some of Monceau's account of Sachs's life in Hamburg has been verified, the book's description of his death is entirely made up.[48] According to it, Sachs had been killed in prison by his fellow inmates after the arrival of Allied forces in Hamburg. After finding out that the Germans are gone and have left "Maurice the Queen" behind, the inmates, who hate him because he is responsible for their incarceration, smash his cell's door open and rush in to beat him up. "Shaking and afraid, the narrator comments, Sachs reminded me of a pig I saw being butchered in a farm."[49] After being beaten by the crowd, Monceau's Sachs is first lynched, and then his body his fed to the dogs, as a final proof of his animality. Nowhere in this scene is any indication given of Sachs's actual moment of death, which contributes to further dehumanizing him. This sadistic account reduces Sachs to a literal scapegoat. Pure flesh, reduced as meat, but still embodying cowardice, he is meant to be absorbed by a crowd (inmates, dogs) to which he is inferior but from which he still stands out.

Another fiction drawing on Sachs, Patrick Modiano's *La Place de l'Etoile*, reclaims antisemitic animal metaphors. Sachs, here, embodies both the insult and its queer reversal: animality becomes a way out or, as in Sedgwick's definition of queerness, a way "across."[50] An anti–coming of age narrative, *La Place de l'Etoile* explores French antisemitism by taking up historical events, characters, and obsessions from the past decades. Its young narrator, a French Jew haunted by the war, evolves in a parallel universe made of antisemitic tropes and resuscitated historical figures, the first of which is Maurice Sachs. Having survived the war, Modiano's Sachs introduces himself as the owner of a bookstore in Geneva. Under the double aegis of Europe's neutral zone and of literature, Sachs the survivor provides the narrator with an inexhaustible number of anecdotes and reading material on French antisemitism and supervises his writing (that is, his constant rewriting of history) before disappearing for an unknown destination. Modiano's meandering quest around the truth of race takes on Proust's argument that oppression creates race yet refutes it through the never-ending narrative of this very oppression. Modiano's Sachs passes on the French Jewish archive of the 1930s and 1940s, but with the archive comes the transmission of queer survival skills based on versatility. Explaining to the narrator why he didn't die, Modiano's Sachs exclaims: "I'm a Jew, I have the survival instincts of a rat." Through Modiano, Sachs reclaims the chameleon's versatility. As a cure for the narrator's melancholy, he advises "flexibility": "People quickly forget their origins, you know! A little flexibility and you can change your skin at will! Change your color! Long live the chameleon!" In Modiano's wandering quest, Sachs the chameleon is key: the chameleon will live, still lives, being no one and nowhere to be seen and answering the question of the truth of race with his constant unreliability.[51]

SUBLIME ABJECTION (OTHERNESS)

In a 1936 article titled "How I Became Antisemitic" and published in the far-right newspaper *L'Action Française*, the writer Marcel Jouhandeau names Sachs as the cause of his racist commitment. The article delivers a dramatized account of Jouhandeau and Sachs's encounter, in which Sachs assumes the quintessential traits of the hated Jew. Having supposedly invited himself at friends of Jouhandeau's with the sole motive of pursuing his favors in spite of earlier rebuffs, Sachs first "flatters [him] (they excel at it)," soon then becoming the center of attention: "Mr. Sachs . . . makes himself at home . . . and there he is, in the foreground, revealing the tattered bottom of his trousers to the ladies. Soon, his feet on the table, with ham on his knees and all the way into his hair, he talks: Sachs has a lot to say, since he makes a living of exaggeration and scandal."[52] Devouring (food, attention), spoiling (morality, clothing, furniture), Sachs is characterized by his excess, an excess that proliferates and spoils everything around him. His admiration for Jouhandeau is interpreted as flattery, and his eating of ham, instead of being read as a sign of integration, appears as gluttony and excess, in keeping with the pig metaphor. In Jouhandeau's account, Sachs embodies an obsession of French fascism: he is the very figure of abjection.

The historian Sandrine Sanos has shown how the concept of abjection is a "*historical* product" of the interwar years, one that "translated a larger concern with the relation of the self, bodies, and nation and . . . the very condition of the individual." Abjection represents a deadly loosening of individual contours, amounting to a process of deindividuation: "abjection . . . was a horrifying state, for it undid the possibility of . . . plenitude." This process appears in Jouhandeau's description of Sachs's animality: Sachs knows no boundaries, be they social or physical (intimate body parts are revealed by his disheveled clothing, and he has food in his hair). As Sanos shows, abjection is a gendered concept. The individuality threatened by abjection is always understood as male, and the boundaries that need to be secured in order to allow for a proper individuation coincide with "the boundaries of normative masculinity."[53] Abjection is a threat to masculinity, and its definition always contains some elements associated with femininity. Offending the ladies with his gossip and showing them his rear parts, Sachs embodies the association of Judaism with effeminacy, homosexuality, and moral decadence.

Yet abjection is a volatile concept, marked by its intensity, which, as such, can be reversed. At the time when he published the article just quoted, Jouhandeau was working on a book titled *De l'abjection* (On abjection), anonymously published in 1939.[54] As Didier Eribon notes, the essay not only discloses its author's homosexuality but also offers a striking analysis of homophobia and its self-perpetuating process of discrimination.[55] This raises the question of the "abjectifying abjected" ("abjecté abjecteur"): how would someone so attuned to "the process by which a category of individuals is 'abjected' reproduce a similar process on another category of people?"[56] Fascinated by abjection, Jouhandeau sees in it, ultimately, the very mark of humanity.[57] Yet this is about a masculine humanity, one characterized by the "ideology of a manly order."[58] Jouhandeau's Sachs assumes the gendered and racial traits of abjection, while gay sex, cast aside, is crystallized and sublimated.[59] Yet the two faces of abjection cannot be split from each other.

David Halperin has shown how abjection has come to signify queer transgression. Referring to Jouhandeau and Genet, he describes "the alchemical transmutation of social humiliation into erotico-religious glorification." But Sachs's transgressions are elsewhere: a true criminal, Sachs isn't a gay outlaw. In this regard, he is as much an anti-Genet as he is an anti-Jouhandeau. Jouhandeau is obsessed with his own abjection; Sachs isn't. Genet redeems sexual abjection; Sachs doesn't need sexual redemption. As I will discuss later, he is a stranger to gay shame. But precisely because he is, so to speak, beyond (gay) shame, he embodies abjection; he can be not a figure of abjection but abjection itself. If, as Halperin claims, "we need to admit our pleasure in being the lowest of the low," Sachs gives this pleasure to others: Du Dognon, Jouhandeau, or maybe Cocteau.[60] Abjection isn't Sachs's truth, but it nonetheless constitutes his modus operandi. Embodying and appropriating the obsessions of his time, he is the abject Other to the gay outlaw.

FEELING GUILTY AND ARRANGING FLOWERS (DYSPHORIA)

Sachs knows no shame, but guilt is one of his most familiar affects. "From earliest childhood, I was dishonest," he reports in his first memoir, *Witches' Sabbath*. The story of his life, Sachs asserts, begins with guilt: the guilt of being born "into the most disorderly family imaginable" and, most importantly, the guilt of being himself, a circular process.[61] "My life has been nothing but one long complicity with the guilty. . . . But certainly my greatest fault has always been to believe myself guilty a priori."[62] This is the memoir's entry point: Sachs is doubly guilty, by heredity and by essence. These two guilts, instead of canceling each other out, create an all-encompassing and self-generative guilt that thwarts any moral resolution—or any redemption or punishment, for that matter. Sachs's untraceable guilt is beyond absolution. It is also dysphoric because it is indistinguishable from bodily and social assignations and the refusal they trigger. Crime, gender incongruence, social incongruence, and sexual deviance find themselves intertwined in a common origin that is at the same time obvious and beyond interpretation.

Framed as a traditional memoir, *Witches' Sabbath* opens with a first chapter devoted to lineage, followed by a second that recalls the author's early childhood. But in the midst of this double assertion of guilt an additional element is inserted. At the beginning of the chapter on his childhood, after opening on the conventional first memory of being smiled upon by a loving woman, Sachs adds a twist. The woman in question, he tells us, was his nurse, Suze. Suze, he continues, is "the first person [he] ever scandalized, for [he] passionately longed to be a girl . . . to the point of insisting on urinating in a seated position."[63] From the evocation of an affectionate mother figure, Sachs abruptly moves on to scandal, dysphoria, and gendered bodily functions.[64] Recalling how he made Suze promise that he would become a girl, Sachs concludes that he was "predisposed toward homosexuality." Yet, he insists, he doesn't associate homosexuality or sexual activity with the sense of guilt mentioned earlier. "As far back as I can recall, I have never had any particular shame in this regard [sexuality] nor in that of the special nature of my physical inclinations." What the guilt is about is "a deviation which has been very difficult . . . to correct: from earliest childhood, I was dishonest."[65] In the space of a few pages, guilt, dysphoria, homosexuality, and criminality superpose themselves. The narrative of a dysphoric first memory, placed as an obscured link between Sachs's two dramatic admissions of guilt, raises two sets of questions: that of the articulation between sexuality and gender and that of the connection between crime and dysphoria. Which comes first, guilt or gender incongruence?

An earlier version of *Witches' Sabbath*, the posthumously published *Mémoire moral* (Moral memoirs), evokes the same memory but offers a different perspective. The four-year-old Maurice forces Suze to promise him that, if he is good, he will become a girl; the next morning, he wakes up "fearful to be male," an expression that associates cowardice and the refusal of masculinity. The memories that follow explore this thread further: Sachs portrays his young self as a fearful and lazy child, "deterred by the idea of effort," "dreaming too much," and victim of an "obvious cowardice." Moving on to his teenage years, he expands this description to a series of related traits such as "lack of scruple" and "a taste for scheming." Bored by his classes, young Maurice only wants to be left alone to enjoy his true passions: reading Bibliothèque rose books, "arranging flowers in a vase," and remodeling his bedroom.[66] From this portrayal, *Witches' Sabbath* only retains one element: theft. The coincidence between tastes coded as feminine and Sachs's guilty nature is erased, with the exception of the conflict with Suze, channeled into "homosexual predisposition." If Sachs's "sense of guilt preceded [his] first fault" yet has nothing to do with sexual preferences, are we also to assume that it is also distinct from his inclination toward femininity?[67]

To be clear, I am not proposing that Sachs's guilt stems from dysphoria, in the sense that, had he been reassigned as female, he would have been freed from it. Neither am I reading Sachs as a transwoman. Just as Proust's men-women are neither actual cis nor trans women, Sachs's dysphoria doesn't translate into trans femininity. It is, however, a refusal to inhabit masculinity. Dysphoria, here, is another name for Sachs's untraceable guilt—a negative but compelling distancing from the norm even before that norm has taken shape. If guilt is not related to sexuality, this is because Sachs has defaulted from masculinity and its associations with courage, strength, and moral rectitude—all qualities he describes himself as lacking. Sachs isn't engaged in a critique of gender, as will become obvious later on, or in asserting alternative femininities or masculinities. Gender incongruity is only valued because of its transitory aspect, its smuggling properties. Dysphoria, in this context, is akin to a moral shortcut: the refusal of male assignation, far from taking the fascist path of the abjected/abjectifying, leads toward a complete defaulting from citizenship and the law—no distinction is made here between the law of the father and the law of the state.

A CASSOCK LINED IN PINK (DELIGHT)

Recalling his time at the seminary, Sachs mentions how he obtained a special authorization to wear a cassock as soon as he joined (instead of having to wait until his fourth year as was the rule).

> When, after having kissed it [the cassock] as is customary before dressing, I put it on for the first time, I felt a mixed delight that was not entirely pious. The black was becoming, and made me look slender; I even suspected I was handsome. . . . And when the reader recalls that even as a child I dreamed of being a girl, it is easy to imagine what strange and dissimulated dissatisfactions, concealed even from my own mind, were suddenly gratified when with both hands, like a young woman, I gradually raised the skirts of my robe to climb the stairs.[68]

The term "delight" brings to mind Marquis Bey's question regarding gender politics: "can we extract the portions of the corrosive regime of gender that delight us and affirm us without upholding the entire empire?"[69] As Bey points out, this question cannot be answered without thinking about the gendered and racial binaries that sustain "the notions of a proper person and a proper embodiment."[70] In acknowledging his own delight, Sachs is already channeling the regime of gender, steering it away from proper persons and embodiments—a perfectly *abject* move tainted by a mischievous, blissful joy. Yet this delight stems from racial and gender assignations: as a man, he has to uphold standards of masculinity that, as a Jew, are denied to him. The cassock is at once transgressive *and* inclusive: welcomed in the gentile church, Sachs gains racial invisibility; clad in religious clothes, he can reclaim his "slender," "handsome" body to climb the stairs as a Hollywood diva.

What *Witches' Sabbath* doesn't mention is that Sachs chose his cassock with the help of his friend Marie delle Donne, the daughter of the wealthy owner of the Vouillemont Hotel, who paid for the garment before dropping him off at the seminary with her chauffeur. Marie's friend, recalling the transaction, adds that "a few months later the cassock had been lined with pink silk."[71] My point here isn't to contradict Sachs's protestations of sincerity regarding his religious calling but to show that this calling cannot be understood outside of the gender assemblage. The cassock reveals how the image of priesthood taps into other images, opening the door toward different types of embodiments, and the color pink takes its full significance in the following chapter of *Witches' Sabbath*. There, Sachs the seminarian, who has been once again granted a special authorization, visits his grandmother on the Riviera, reconnects with the glamorous circles of the Vouillemont Hotel (they were never far apart), and falls in love with a man (in less than a week). A mastermind at spreading his own legend, Sachs insists on denying the "absurd rumor" claiming that he "came to the beach in [his] soutane and unbuttoned it in front of everyone to reveal a pink bathing suit."[72] True or not, the anecdote is followed by the portrayal of the poet

Max Jacob, which suggests that the pink bathing suit is a reference to Jacob's poetry volume *Les pénitents en maillots roses* (Penitents in pink tights).[73] The critic Lucienne Cantaloube-Ferrieu emphasizes how the volume associates opposites in order to create an impossible balance, a contradiction not denied but sought and relished.[74] The pink/black opposition in *Witches' Sabbath* fosters a similarly rich network of oppositions, describing two types of transgressions across genders: one dignified, virtuous, and religious, the other frivolous, promiscuous, and provocative. These two forms of cross-dressing explorations are not exclusive but cumulative: each of them bears its own delight, and each of them also carries Sachs not only across gender but across race.

A change of clothing concludes the story of Sachs's life as a seminarian: as he welcomes his new lover into his room, he has "taken off [his] soutane and put on a bathrobe."[75] The robe is still there, a delightful transitional device. Yet what it creates goes beyond cross-dressing or gendered role-playing. Clerc compares Sachs to the impersonator Fregoli, whose use of costumes and impersonations makes him a figure of constant metamorphoses.[76] Sachs's passion for clothes is everywhere: pieces of clothing and accessories constantly circulate in his writing, as currencies, gifts, tools for social climbing, or items to be traded. In his last memoir, *The Hunt*, the narrator is greeted by his friends with neckties as a welcoming gift before having to sell his watch and waistcoat a few lines later. Stuck in a workers' camp in Germany, Sachs writes that he has "been living in clogs, [his] feet wrapped up in rags, Polish fashion," and concludes that he is "*very* happy."[77] Regardless of the circumstances, clothing carries a delight of its own: pieces of clothes are acquired and disposed of so deftly that they come to signify a process of constant mutation. The clogs serve him just as well as a cassock lined with silk: they enable a self-reinvention that is at the same time a joy and an escape.

"THE WOMAN BESIDE YOU IS AN INSURANCE COMPANY" (GAMBLING)

Sachs interprets his avowedly feminine traits as signs of homosexuality and associates them with a sophisticated subversion. But when it comes to actual women, there is no ambiguity in his misogyny. From the Gidean double construction of women as spiritual creatures deprived of desires and as physical beings devoid of higher abilities, Sachs only retains the latter, which he articulates without ambiguity: "three months spent in the company of a woman . . . has confirmed me in many of my opinions about women—they have such cowardly minds, are so hardened in their materialism, so devouring by nature. They are life, if you like, but nothing to do with the higher sort of life."[78] This description embraces the very language associated with antisemitism and conveniently erases the distinction between materiality and materialism. It is worth noting that the woman mentioned here is Violette Leduc, who, from her own and Sachs's account, has been in love with him for several years and has rescued him, emotionally and financially, on several occasions.[79] Like Gide, Sachs uses misogyny to navigate his way across a gender assemblage that he both disrupts and reinforces, conveniently confusing women and compulsive heterosexuality and valuing queer sex as a countermove. While heterosexual relationships signify stability and immobility, queer sex allows for an endless flux of moves.

Sachs's account of the social enforcement of heterosexuality is at the same time more cynical and honest than Gide's. The narrator of *Witches' Sabbath* relates how, after having been forced to have sex with a prostitute during his military service, he finds out that she and he can actually be "good friends." He moves into her room, to the satisfaction of his fellow soldiers and superiors:

"Indeed I never understood so clearly these wells of calm, those tunnels of sweetness, when the soul sinks into the order established by nature and society. . . . The woman beside you is an insurance company: security of the body, of time, of posterity, an organized home. . . . You belong to her; this gradually effaces the anxiety of being a man."[80] The paradox, of course, is that this well-organized home is a prostitute's bedroom in the attic of an army barrack. But, as is often the case, Sachs's statement isn't only provocative: from a gambler's perspective, heterosexuality feels like a remarkably safe investment. "The woman beside you" proves itself an invaluable pawn in the social game: not merely an insurance policy but the entire company, guaranteeing an all-encompassing safety.

Compared to the safe investment of straight sex, homosexuality is a high-stakes game. Like Gide, Sachs doesn't understand homosexual desire as limiting: to him, having sex with women is always a possibility, sometimes even a pleasing one. Sexual preferences aren't interpreted in terms or identity or nature but tempered in terms of viable options or bad choices. Following the army episode, Sachs expresses regret for his lack of interest in women's bodies, mentioning how he "longed for this absolute and concrete devotion one meets only in women."[81] Yet he sought, and obtained, this comfort time and again, when he married Gladys Matthews or when he moved in with Violette Leduc.[82] Homosexuality, for Sachs, translates into a series of options, of games. Men or boys are always referred to in the plural, whereas woman, "la femme," remains a singular abstraction, as dull as an insurance policy, guaranteeing comfort and rest but forcing one into immobility.

Gay sex is omnipresent in Sachs's memoirs, evoked in detail with an unabashed sense of humor and associated with a sense of joy and of playfulness, often at the expense of the narrator.

While it is often used to introduce farcical elements and picaresque narrative twists, Sachs's writing is always, in modern terms, body positive. A memorable scene in *Witches' Sabbath* pictures Sachs the seminarian's vain efforts to abstain from masturbating, rushing back and forth to the chapel in the hopes of getting rid of "that extreme turgescence that preceded [him] like a lantern and sent abominable gleams of light through [his] body." Evoking images of satanic monks in gothic castles, the lantern metaphor is as evocative and ironic as the image of the robed Sachs going up the stairs like a Hollywood queen. Yet the following sentences offer an earnest discussion of masturbation. In a rare parenthesis interrupting the narrative, Sachs argues that "education has stupidly made it a crime. . . . Onanism [is] a suitable release from harmful moods, from isolation . . . giving a certain freedom to action."[83] Unlike the dramatic masturbation scenes in Jouhandeau's meditations on abjection, Sachs demystifies gay sex—and all sex, for that matter.

Sex is also used to introduce a queer temporality into the narratives. As sex scenes break away from normative chronology in the "rapid bursts" described by Jack Halberstam, they bring about a sense of transience and contingency.[84] Trapped in the madness of Bordeaux during the Exodus, the narrator of *The Hunt* struggles in his search for lodging while trying to host his radio show. Finding out in the evening that the show will air at 2 AM, he announces that this "gave him some time for philandering."[85] The scene that follows is a matter-of-fact lesson on queer life: in less than a paragraph, the narrator finds a cruising spot, meets not one but two consenting partners, negotiates terms, and embarks on a quest for a room, which he ends up renting from a female prostitute. This episode is at the same time a narrative break, a comic interlude, and an accelerated vignette in which the narrator travels between places, people, social circles, and emotional states in under a couple of hours. Throughout all of Sachs's works, sex scenes pace the narratives and facilitate transitions: Sachs's readers know that "after the dining room comes the bedroom."[86] Sex is as transitional as it is transactional.

As opposed to the immobility associated to "woman," sexual encounters and love affairs with men enable a multiplicity of countermoves, a constant circulation up and down the social ladder. *The Hunt*'s narrator quotes the famous Maréchal Lyautey, claiming that he "can only work with people [he has] made love to."[87] Over the course of the memoir, we see him have sex with male prostitutes, actors, black-market crooks, smugglers, and students. As we witness him recruiting and becoming acquainted with customers and providers while he trades in gold, jewels, and financial portfolios, we never know if the "friends" that connect them to one another are crooks or queers—or both. Queer sex, rather than gay identity, offers a transversal path across social classes, a shortcut through the vertical hierarchies: sex makes it possible to move sideways.

CROOK AND QUEER: A GAME OF INTERMEDIARIES (PASSING)

Even though *Alias*, Sachs's first published book, is framed as a novel, it features not one but two characters transparently inspired by their author. While its narrator Blaise Alias is Sachs's obvious alter ego, the novel has him mentored by his older avatar: by a sleight of hand typical of Sachs, Adelair is as much Sachs's alias as Alias himself. What Adelair embodies and the narrative enacts is a game of intermediaries, the very game Sachs has played all his life. Adelair introduces the narrator to the world of schemes and parasitizing, playing the same initiating role as Modiano's fictional Sachs. And like Modiano, Sachs operates from inside out, inhabiting the hostile tropes assigned to him and using them to his own benefit. Adelair describes himself as a "middleman" (*intermédiaire*), yet he is also a *passeur* (the French word for smuggler). Like Sachs, he is a social smuggler, passing from one world to the next. Adelair compares himself to Proust's Charlus, citing his ability to navigate across social circles.[88] The ability to pass goods and information isn't distinct from the ability to pass—to move from one space to the other and to be perceived as someone who belongs there. Sachs/Adelair is a diplomat, as described by Baptiste Morizot: etymologically "folded in two," twofold, the diplomat "finds herself at the border" and masters a "hybrid code."[89] The image of the fold, here, operates similarly to the transversality of queerness: a form of circulation of self and information (or of self as information, or of a deformed and reformed self), through borders otherwise impermeable.

The figure of the queer criminal takes on a deeper meaning here: Sachs operates literally as a queer crook. Here again, Sachs is the opposite of Genet. His schemes, compared to the manly, physically demanding "crimes" associated with Genet, don't evoke the glorious isolation of the dark criminal but the mastermind at connections and web weaving. Sachs goes back and forth across social barriers while Genet forces actual house locks. The two of them bring forth opposite economies of invisibility: while in *The Thief's Journal* Genet wanders unseen in strangers' homes, Sachs labors to be admitted at their table, to eat their food, to be seen with them in order to be introduced into more circles, and to relieve them of a couple of valuables on the way out.[90] The only romanticization Sachs can aspire to is that of abjection, such as Jouhandeau's description of him as the abject, uninvited guest, which attributes to him an unspeakable crime instead of a very concrete one. Today, as in Sachs's time, most of what is known of his actual criminal activities is based on what he revealed about them. What keeps emerging are his most spectacular schemes, which are also the easiest to verify because they involve celebrities: the forgery of Cocteau's signature, the money Sachs embezzled from Coco Chanel while pretending to acquire rare books for her. Treated as practical jokes by their victims, these scams are the glamorous trees hiding Sachs's forest of criminal activities, playing the part of a decoy leading critics to either tone down or pathologize Sachs's criminal activities.[91] This is but a reflection of the strategy Sachs adopted in his memoirs.

The memoirs obscure as much as they reveal: they loudly confess schemes that are already known, expose failed plans, elaborate on betrayals and subsequent guilty feelings, but give no explanation whatsoever of the actual process of converting stolen goods into money or of Sachs's network and partners in trade. *The Hunt* performs an exemplary display of fake transparency. Finding himself in German-occupied Paris in 1941, the narrator exposes black-market trade through a conversation in which unnamed protagonists sell and buy various items they don't have (tobacco, train locomotives, sugar, etc.). He then comments on the "illusion" of this game of intermediaries, explaining how he himself found a better niche within the gold trade, then disclosing his own role as a successful and efficient go-between.[92] Yet the following accounts of his successive deals simply don't add up. An overabundance of numbers, names, and comings and goings acts as a decoy to let the reader forget that although Sachs claims to have made a consequential benefit during a period of time, what he describes are only losses. The most detailed schemes are also shown to be thoroughly unprofitable. For example, Sachs's interactions with jewelry dealers show him accepting pieces of jewelry at a price he has borrowed from various speculators, then selling them at a loss the next day.[93]

A seemingly minor scheme, on the other hand, provides a valuable insight into Sachs's real modus operandi and also illustrates the way in which it is erased from his confessions. *The Hunt* pictures its narrator, hit by a streak of bad luck, resorting to a desperate measure: "Without thought for the future, I sold all the carpets in the apartment (at a vile price), though they didn't belong to me."[94] Raczymow, however, uncovers a different truth, "a carefully orchestrated scheme, typical of Sachs's method at the time": Sachs didn't sell the carpets once but *twice*, scamming the first buyer and deceiving his landlady (their actual owner) by purportedly sending them for dry-cleaning.[95] This elaborate process, stretching over a few weeks and involving many interlocutors, is the opposite of the careless and unprofitable move described in *The Hunt*. Similarly, Violette Leduc recalls how, when she was about to leave Paris with Sachs, she found him in conversation with a young girl to whom he promised to meet her at a train station the next day.[96] The girl was a Jewish refugee to whom Sachs had promised passage to France's unoccupied zone, only to abandon her after taking her money. Leduc's memory stands in sinister contrast to the farcical accounts given by Sachs of his adventures as a smuggler of refugees, which, as I will discuss later, mostly focus on his encounter with "a pleasant boy called J." and their lovemaking in the hay.[97] But through Leduc, we know that Sachs ran a business-like operation from Paris where he met with potential customers and arranged passage for them—or simply embezzled them.[98] The game of intermediaries is always double, folded in two: entertaining readers with his schemes while hiding their actual depths, Sachs is acting like a seasoned diplomat: a queer crook.

SLEIGHTS OF HAND: SACHS'S SERIAL CONFESSIONS

To Sachs, smuggling is both what Deleuze and Guattari call "form of content" and "form of expression": not only what we are given to perceive but how it is conveyed to us.[99] In a 1944 letter from Hamburg, Sachs hides in plain sight his work for the Gestapo: "I'm employed by an organization where my talent for scheme and machination has particularly proven its value. There I make an honest and sufficient living."[100] While Sachs exposes his sleights of hands, we also are led to forget that he is tricking *us*. This raises, in different terms than in the chapter 2, the question of authenticity: if Sachs knows no shame, does it follow that he is a sham? What are we to make of the confessional style and self-professed sincerity of his memoirs? Recalling his conversion in *Witches' Sabbath*, Sachs declares that he has lost his Catholic faith. Yet he maintains throughout the memoir a rhetoric of confession and self-amendment. Stating that he believes "in the absolution public confession affords," he deplores "his follies" and ostensibly blames himself for every misfortune he incurs. He addresses readers directly, names (or pretends to) every protagonist, and settles accounts with them, expressing that his "heart fills with gratitude" toward them or that he wishes to make a "profound and true act of contrition."[101] Confession, with its display of sentimentality and sex, is Sachs's favorite sleight of hand, hiding technicalities, hard work, skills, and, paradoxically, intentionality. Confession turns Sachs, again, into a collective enunciation: he lets himself be spoken for, casts himself as a narrative, albeit an abject one.

The passage of *The Hunt* mentioning Sachs's activities as *passeur* (smuggler of refugees into France's unoccupied zone) could be summarized in the tale of his encounter with J., who becomes Julien a few pages later. Julien seems to materialize by magic while Sachs is going through a rough patch: "I chanced, very opportunely, to meet up with a pleasant boy . . . extraordinarily attractive sexually." The fact that Julien is a *passeur* and that Sachs finds himself in Angoulême, the gateway to unoccupied France, aren't explicitly connected. Even when they find themselves discussing business together, Sachs claims that he was "less anxious to anticipate [their] gains than to seal [their] association with an act of love." With his "well proportioned" body, "all muscles," and his "smooth and fresh skin," Julien is the (queer) tree hiding the (crooked) forest: by confessing to sex, Sachs hides organized crime.[102] Using sexuality to exonerate himself, he makes the best of the repressive hypothesis. Delight becomes decoy: a fake sin masking the actual crime and a token of authenticity veiling the scheme. In a very Foucauldian marriage, Catholicism works hand in hand here with Sachs's experience of psychoanalysis. The display of sexualized early memories in *Witches' Sabbath* and their interpretation as signs of homosexuality reveal his work with the analyst René Allendy.[103] Similarly, he dramatizes and pathologizes his kleptomania or his alcoholism, precipitating the pathologizing embraced and perpetuated by his commentators.[104] In spite of his own claim, Sachs uses sexuality and gender disruption *as* guilt: not the guilt he feels but the guilt he confesses.

Sachs's confessional writing style orchestrates an economy of visibility and erasure. While Sachs's crimes aren't confessed, they are hidden in plain sight. Guided by Julien to a farm where they spend the night, Sachs find himself sharing a room with a group of Jewish refugees traveling from Poland, who had spent what little money they had in the vain hope of reaching the free zone. The narrator comments: "I don't know who had held out to them the hope that this was possible. The unfortunate creatures were unaware that they would be arrested before Limoges."[105] Once again, the display of sentimentality and honesty (the narrator empathizes with the refugees and acknowledges his awareness of their fate) conceals a dire truth: Sachs is about to engage in the exact same trafficking. Just as visibility enables erasure, authenticity is a mask. Sachs disrupts the Gidean principle that talking about gay sex in the first person warrants authenticity. If he, as he claims, learned from Gide, what Sachs learned is a form of counterfeiting where the nexus of masculinity, homosexuality, and authenticity is hijacked in favor of a more radical form of queerness.

Confession erases the question of sincerity and becomes a writing process that is not dialectic but serial: each individual confession announces a future confession, a future sin, a future need to confess, and so on. Sachs's picaresque style is shaped in a circular narrative mode: a series of adventures paced by recurring tropes (having sex, falling in love, needing money and obtaining it, betraying and being betrayed). Sachs's suggestion that *Witches' Sabbath* was written in search of "a thread of dignity . . . in the labyrinth of my conscience" reflects an ambulatory process: walking around, walking away, walking back.[106] *Witches' Sabbath* ends, or doesn't end, in a series of loops. Sachs describes himself on the deck of the "ship" (actually the ferry from Dover), announces "several new resolutions" born from "a profound self-scrutiny," and evokes "the incessant renewal of the ocean" (the British Channel) as a metaphor for his own. This promise of reform is followed by a postscript announcing, again, "new beginnings" and followed by a second postscript, in the form of a 1942 letter inserted in the 1939 manuscript, in which Sachs confesses that he has "succumbed" again to "the ignominy of civilized peoples, the pleasures of shady neighborhoods and the froth of champagne." Unsurprisingly, he then announces that he will "try once again to tear myself from the infernal round of the *witches' sabbath*."[107] The confession is an endless writing process, forever promising new beginnings. This is how Sachs's moral undertones need to be read: not as a "compass," as he says about Gide, but as an iterative process, unfolding in circular patterns of self-justification, pleading, and bargaining.

A NOISE OF TEARING PARCHMENT: ON WRITING AND BEING WRITTEN

After undergoing a surgical intervention, Sachs exclaims: "How tough man's skin is after all! And what a noise of tearing parchment as it's cut!"[108] The association between human skin and parchment is no coincidence. Just as it is antisemitic and homophobic, Sachs's collective assemblage is a literary one, entangled in tropes and in characters both fictional and real. In the same way as the question of authenticity is erased, the distinction between interiority and exteriority is blurred. Sachs's critics often attribute what they consider his failure to a conflict between life and work: according to them, Sachs would have lived too intensely to be able to write, except when he was in prison.[109] This classist argument—being in prison, in this case, simply amounts to not having to work for a living—also ignores the stream of continuity between life and work not only as inspiration but as process. Sachs writes as much as he is being written and constantly rewrites himself in order to, in his words, "*se refaire*"— literally, "to make oneself over again."[110] The expression originally refers to gambling: Sachs recovers his losses by reinventing himself, which involves the creation of a new scheme but also a new image, a new body, and a new text. Sachs's writing, in spite of its confessional aspect, is oriented toward an exteriority, as part of a constant flux of negotiating, scheming, and smuggling that also involves his own body.

When it comes to bodies, Sachs's seems to have a much easier relationship with those of others than with his own. The critic Adeline Brunschwig argues that Sachs is obsessed with the "threat of materiality," so much so that "owning a body is painful" to him. The cause, according to her, is both pathological and moral: Sachs "ignores the euphoria of good health" and suffers among other things from episodes of chronic sepsis "caused by a chaotic lifestyle for which it seems a punishment."[111] While I don't concur with Brunschwig's interpretation of moral "punishment," I propose to read Sachs's descriptions of bodily distress as dysphoria. Again, I do not argue that Sachs is an ignored transwoman. Rather, I want to point out the nods of resistance to the racialized male assignation imposed on him. Samuel Berlin and Sage Brice have analyzed dysphoria as "the social friction of knocking up against a normative presumption." Gender expectations, they argue, are contingent but unavoidable: "creating a livable body" can only happen within gender normativity.[112] The same goes for race: assigned as Jewish male, a contradiction in terms, Sachs isn't granted any livable space.

Sachs describes himself in *The Hunt* as a "cheerful fatty" who "puts up with his misfortune with a serene face" but "burns his loneliness in a hell of worries." These repressed feelings, he explains, produce "bad blood."[113] The discrepancy between the façade of the easy-going smoothness of the "fatty" and the invisible turmoil, emotional "hell," and rushing of bad blood doesn't endorse a mind/body division but describes a single, unlivable form of embodiment. Sachs then explains how this "bad blood" (a case of sepsis) left him covered in "a leprous rash of boils."[114] Commenting on the frequency of cancer metaphors in his works, Brunschwig sees Sachs's body as a "site of proliferation."[115] The body produces hostile substances that, like the cancer metaphor, reveal another aspect of Sachs's Fregoli-style metamorphoses. In *Witches' Sabbath*, Sachs attributes his bodily changes to a refusal of adulthood, which coincides with a refusal of masculinity: "No sooner did I understand that *I still wanted to be a child* than I began growing old as fast as I could, thereby scrupulously avoiding *man's estate*. I have never wanted to be thirty, I dreamed of being fifty, which I represented to myself as a true youth, the true *beginning* of something. . . . And in this need to diminish myself, to shrink, ultimately to kill myself, I happily watched my hair fall out, my stomach swell, and I began to drink heavily."[116] The "chaotic lifestyle" stigmatized by Brunschwig becomes in Sachs's account a symptom among many rather than a cause. Far from the vaguely moralizing concept of "self-hatred" often assigned to Sachs, dysphoria has its specific triggers and strategies: becoming a man needs to be avoided by a shrinking or by a proliferation of the body. While death sometimes appears as a welcome way out ("To die! The complete, the realistic solution," exclaims *The Hunt*'s narrator), Sachs's unlivable body expands through metamorphoses.[117]

These can be actual physical changes, such as the visible marks of illness (rash, hair loss) or Sachs's spectacular weight variations.[118] Sachs's queer embodiment is also exposed through others' inability to describe him other than in contradictory terms. In Manceau's and Du Dognon's words: "He was so attractive one would forget how ugly he was."[119] Sachs appears both disembodied—mysteriously attractive—and subjected to an excess of materiality—a legendary ugliness. Besides being characteristically antisemitic, this type of statement suggests a form of shimmering instability in which Sachs's body unwrites and rewrites himself according to circumstances. His *Mémoire moral* opens with a strange statement: "I lived four times my flesh and my blood," by which he means that he has lived four decades. Sachs then compares himself to the mythological figure Aristaeus, who "saw new bees being born out of rot."[120] Bad blood is also a flux: body, life, and works follow a similar pattern: what matters is *circulation*.

MOVING SIDEWAYS . . .

In his analysis of abjection, Eribon underscores how, for Jouhandeau and the masculinist far right, cultural transmission doesn't happen "laterally but in a rigorous order of succession, from father to son . . . the slightest interference of intruders corrupts and betrays it."[121] Here again, Sachs is on the side of abjection, as a smuggler and a *passeur*, appropriating and circulating the cultural capital of his time. His lawful occupations are always related to art, literature, or the media: publisher, editor, art dealer, art critic, radio host. Similarly, Sachs insists on claiming his kinship with fictional characters and emphasizes his familial connections to the literary scene. *Witches' Sabbath* opens with mentions of family acquaintances with Anatole France and Proust and is then punctuated by encounters with literary idols: Cocteau, Gide, Jacob. *Alias*'s Adelair compares himself to Charlus, Balzac, and Balzac's Rastignac; the same Rastignac is a constant reference for Sachs himself, as is Stendhal's character Julien Sorel.[122] Literature is writing material: Sachs's first book, *The Decade of Illusion*, was published in the United States and features a series of portraits, from Proust to Coco Chanel. Just like he crossed the ocean with stolen paintings, Sachs smuggled French culture and his personal stash of celebrity gossip into the United States, with his American wife as a translator. The authenticity of the traded goods (Sachs's actual skills as a critic or the truth of the anecdotes he shares) is of no relevance: what counts is to move them and to keep moving.

There isn't any interiority (or integrity) in Sachs's writing, since content and information only serve a transactional purpose. As such, they circulate among a constant stream of heterogeneous currencies: sex, clothes, diamonds, artworks, etc. Money is only one of these, with the same porous proprieties: when Sachs stuffs his pockets with toilet paper, he disrupts the boundaries between currencies, clothes, body, and self.[123] For Deleuze and Guattari, "the strange case of Maurice Sachs" reveals the absence of a clear line separating the two figures of the "deceiver" and the "betrayer."[124] Each of these figures tampers with the regime of truth in which they are operating, but the latter introduces radical change, while the former disrupts the assemblage without changing it. As such, both coincide with the figure of the queer traitor described by Dennis.[125] What deceivers and betrayers are disrupting are codes—not truth or meaning but signifiers that find themselves detached from their anchors. Sachs the chameleon appropriates others' traits, styles, secrets, stories, and valuables and redistributes them laterally. What he exposes or modifies in the process brings to mind Marquis Bey's question regarding the imperialist structure of gender and race: does Sachs's delight in smuggling uphold the empire, or does it contribute to its demise?

. . . AND MOVING FAST

Who takes "Alias" as an alias? Sachs's transparent name-switching is complicated by the double structure of *Alias*, where both Alias and Adelair are Sachs's aliases. His following book, *Au temps du Boeuf sur le toit*, features Alias as a friend of the narrator, "a charming guy," who scandalously dances with him and attracts envious glances from other men.[126] Again, Sachs is hiding in plain sight, and between fiction and reality, or book and life, or signs and bodies, words and flesh, by superposition. A constant alias, navigating beyond alterity, Sachs first claims the name of his mother, then hides under the name of his father,

Ettinghausen, in order to hide his Jewishness while in Germany, but eventually uses other aliases, some transparent, such as "Saxe," the Frenchified spelling of his name, and others that we will never know about.[127] Life and fiction coexist on a fluctuating plane characterized by its urgency. Sachs is, one way or another, constantly on the run.

I stated earlier how Sachs's narratives offer examples of the queer temporality described by Halberstam. But ultimately, speed characterizes all of Sachs's writing. *The Hunt* is conducted at a pace that echoes its title.[128] *Alias*, which unites coming-of-age and travel narratives, features a constant stream of trains, taxis, and Parisian sidewalks. With a rhythm that never slows down, the narrator is shuttled from one end of France to the other, from boarding school to monastery, from elegant salons to shabby hotels. To these actual places correspond social spaces: school, church, bourgeoisie, bohemia ... The same is true in *Witches' Sabbath*: one adventure, or one phase, leads to its opposite: gay nightlife leads to the seminary, which leads to a love affair on the Riviera, which leads to military service ... Sachs is always on the run.

The schemes depicted in *The Hunt* are zero-sum games that follow the same repetitive pattern: contact, exchange of item/information, trade of the acquired item/information with another contact in exchange for another item/information, and so on.

Again, this isn't about content but about an iterative process in which no balance can ever be achieved. Sachs's perpetual flight matches the insatiable hunger of dysphoria.[129] As Sachs mentioned to Leduc: "My dear, I was starving and I couldn't eat since I had to talk, tell a thousand stories, since I had to pay for the dinner they were giving me."[130]

The wins can only be temporary, which makes them all the more glorious. What Sachs accomplishes, as a Jewish socialite in an antisemitic world, as a crook in a bourgeois world, as a counterfeiter in an artistic world obsessed with great names and authenticity, is properly impossible. On April 14, 1945, as he was part of a group of convicts led by SS troops on a forced march away from the Allied forces, Sachs finally refused to keep moving. He was shot in the head. Ultimately the house of cards collapses, like Sachs by the roadside, swept by its own velocity.

5

INTERMITTENT MIRACLES
Queer Time and Temporal Dysphoria

A divorced woman making a living in cabarets, a teenager skipping classes to entertain an affair with a soldier's wife, a convicted felon fantasizing in his cell about pimps and prostitutes, and an outcast bourgeois planning his suicide: these are the four figures guiding this chapter's exploration of temporality. As their lives expand beyond the heteronormative frame imposed by the gender assemblage, they find themselves out of place, out of sync, out of time. Instead of making their way in the temporality that is charted for them (education, marriage, reproductive sex), they wander in the here and now, attuned to the present and to presence, at times establishing queer bonds with themselves and the world, at times avoiding and rejecting any kind of alliance. Breaking the bounds and bond of normative temporal linearity is a dangerous, though sometimes unavoidable, endeavor: by refusing its network of socially given relationships and intimacies, one is also exposed to the risk of utter loneliness. This chapter pursues the exploration of dysphoria and the gender assemblage that guided the previous chapters by examining it in relationship to temporality.

As others have argued before me, the gender assemblage determines acceptable ways of pursuing one's existence through time, centered around the heterosexual institution of marriage and its hold on various stages of life. In looking at queer and dysphoric temporalities, I take up previous descriptions of queer time and add to them the concept of temporal dysphoria. In so doing, my object isn't to create a queer or trans archive; nor do I aim to tell a trans history or to theorize how this history might be created. Rather, I am interested in pointing out how queerness and dysphoria work to disrupt time itself, as well as the stories we tell ourselves about it. The four semiautobiographical texts just evoked, Colette's *The Vagabond* (1910), Raymond Radiguet's *The Devil in the Flesh* (1923), Jean Genet's *Our Lady of the Flowers* (1943), and René Crevel's *My Body and I* (1925),[1] open paths to map the ways in which the gender assemblage weaves its temporality and how queer and dysphoric perceptions and practices tear down this fabric.

My description of queer and trans time is deeply indebted to previous explorations of queer temporality, particularly to Elizabeth Freeman's conceptualization of chrononormativity, Jack Halberstam's description of queer time as attuned to speed and intensity, and Lee Edelman's discussion of reproductive futurity.[2] In spite of their differences, these notions have shed significant light on the heteronormative framing of temporality and have provided invaluable tools to explore alternative ways of relating to time. Temporal dysphoria inscribes itself in continuity with these critical tools. As queer time, temporal dysphoria eludes heteronormative temporality and its linear progress. But whereas queer time manifests itself in the form of "intermittent miracles," in the words of Crevel—a time of connection to self, others, or the world—dysphoric time takes the shape of pure isolation—from self, others, the world, and from time itself.[3] In spite of their difference, queer and dysphoric times need to be understood as a continuum: from escape to vanishing, from intentional desertion to irredeemable severance.

It is no accident that Freeman's description of chrononormativity found its origin in modernist literature. Through Robert Graves's poem "It's a Queer Time" and its queer account of the trench war, Freeman describes "military history's failure to fully organize time toward nationalist ends." Using Graves's example to oppose queer temporality to chrononormativity, Freeman describes the latter as "the use of time to organize individual human bodies toward maximum productivity."[4] Chrononormativity is a linear temporality anchored in an ideology of progress and productivity. Framing individual lives, it stretches as a straight line from one stage to the next, marked by social rites of passage such as schooling, religious rites, marriage, anniversaries, and, even more significantly, war and combat. Chronormativity is above all a time of "service," a service divided along the lines of gender and race. While white men are supposed to invest their lives in the preservation of the nation, like Graves's soldier, white women are subjected to the institution of marriage and to the necessity of heterosexual reproduction. The racialized subjects of the colonial empire, however, are committed to invisible forms of service, or, rather, the services they perform are excluded from this biopolitical organizing of time. The white nuclear family, as the focal point of the gender assemblage, is tied to and conceptualized as a temporal system that controls bodies and time.

In this regard, Freeman's concept of chrononormativity echoes Lee Edelman's discussion of reproductive futurity: they both refer to modes of temporality involved in "preserving . . . the absolute privilege of heteronormativity."[5] The interwar years are an era of social reorganization through work forces and the production of goods, in which the good citizen accumulates wealth, surplus value, and children. While Edelman's analysis of the figure of the "Child" and its reification of futury is anchored in contemporary American society, the tensions it reveals were also prevalent, albeit differently, in the French modernist era. Gide's refusal to serve the state, for instance, doesn't make any distinction between productive and reproductive futurity: families are as worthy of hate for the tangle of heteronormative relationships they foster as for the estates they dedicated themselves to. Sachs's ironical bend toward priestlike celibacy and his delight in short-term scheming show the same contempt for productive futurity and the sabotaging of long-term investments. In the same way, the characters and authors discussed in this chapter engage in futureless behaviors: Colette builds a case against marriage, Radiguet explores ways of "growing sideways," Genet composes a masturbatory ode to crime and prostitution, and Crevel ponders taking his own life.[6] While chrononormativity and reproductive futurity describe a temporality organized around production and accumulation, queerness and dysphoria precipitate a waste and a squandering of time.

Queer time and dysphoric time are stolen time, time appropriated against the rules, and time to serve oneself and not the state. But while queer time might be described as the interstitial time of dream, of joy, of play, of escape, and of nonreproductive sex, temporal dysphoria is time lost, not in the Proustian sense but as a loss of temporality. Queer time may take the form of an escape, but temporal dysphoria is the moment when time itself feels like a trap. It is the ultimate disjunction, the moment when body and time are out of sync, an embodied loss of the sense of self and continuity. Again, my purpose isn't to conceptualize dysphoric temporality as the opposite of queer time but rather as its continuity: dysphoric temporality is queer time taken to its limit. While queer time may appear, in the texts to be discussed in this chapter, as a sense of acute presence, foreclosing chrononormativity through the fleeting ability to live in the moment, dysphoric temporality is time suspended, carrying us beyond the fine line separating here and now from nowhere and never. The difference between queer time and dysphoric time echoes the distinction between feeling and affect: while queer time is felt, sometimes embraced or even sought, temporal dysphoria emerges outside of personal agency. Or, in a Foucauldian terminology, queer temporality is a desubjectifying time, while temporal dysphoria happens beyond subjectivity.

Drawing from Foucault via Carolyn Dinshaw, Heather Love analyzes queer historiography as a series of "failed or interrupted connections," a process that has occurred in each chapter of this book.[7] Queer historiography, Love argues, is contingent on the acknowledgment of its own desire for the past as well as its longing for impossible encounters and synchronicity. Leah Devun and Zeb Tortorici assert a similar trait in trans*historicity. Trans*historicity requires, and enables, weaving together "multiple and interconnected binds—of sameness and difference, presence and absence, 'tradition' and 'modernity.'"[8] In this regard, trans*historicity itself, and the labor it stems from, is already embedded in dysphoric temporality: it materializes a breach, or rather a series of breaches, in linear temporality, which can't be equated to one another yet share the same quality of "presence and absence." In tracking queer time and temporal dysphoria through to the French modernist canon, I am without doubt pursuing my own asynchronous desire. In this book's introduction, I described how dysphoria led me to Proust, or, more precisely, how dysphoria kept me from turning my back on him. Throughout this book, I have been tracking dysphoria as one of these "negative affects . . . that characterize the relation between past and present."[9] As I now trace dysphoric temporality through failed connections not only across time but *with* time, I take the paradoxical chance to rely on dysphoria, that is, to follow an impossibility, a dysfunction. In the same way as it manifests the dysfunction of the gender assemblage, dysphoria tears a hole in its temporal fabric. If, as Devun and Tortorici argue, trans temporalities are akin to "temporal dislocations," what part can dysphoria play in locating the dislocation?[10] "No bridge leads me to others," Crevel writes to relate his experience of utter solitude.[11] Dysphoria is the conceptual equivalent of the absence of a bridge, akin to the failed connections that, according to Love, make queer history.

In his description of queer temporality, Jack Halberstam quotes Baudelaire's description of modernity: queer time, like modernity, is best described as "'the transient, the fleeting, the contingent.'" If queer time escapes the "middle-class logic of reproductive of temporality," it is first and foremost because of its fugacity: queer time manifests itself not so much in opposition to linearity or futurity than to stability. Emerging in "rapid bursts," queer time disrupts these "long periods of stability" that define heteronormative temporality. The sense of motion and speed traced by Halberstam in queer postmodern writers allows him to unfold the relationship between writing, temporality, and forms of embodiment.[12] Queer and dysphoric times are the time of bodies, the moment when the elusive articulation between body and self becomes apparent. Similarly, Devun and Tortorici argue that "trans*historicities . . . [provide] language to describe embodiment across time."[13] Bodies in writing, bodies in time: the texts discussed in this chapter engage in explorations of the relation between selves and bodies, using temporality to question the sense of self and the feeling of continuity allowing us to believe in it. Writing is a time-making practice where both the "intermittent miracle" of queer time and the rupture of temporal dysphoria find room outside of chrononormative temporality.

This chapter is divided into two sections: the first explores queer temporality and chrononormativity in Colette's *The*

Vagabond and Radiguet's *The Devil in the Flesh*; the second draws from the first to expand it toward dysphoric temporality through readings of Genet's *Our Lady of the Flowers* and Crevel's *My Body and I*. The first two of these texts, *The Vagabond* and *The Devil in the Flesh*, follow a chronological timeline, but their plots revolve around their narrators' refusal to walk the straight lines of heteronormative temporality. Colette's novel portrays the dilemma of a divorced woman struggling to make a living as a cabaret performer and weighing the appeal of getting remarried against the toll it would take on her freedom. Her dilemma can be narrowed down as a choice between two types of temporality: the constraining time of reproductive futurity or the empowering immediacy of queer time. The weight of heteronormative futurity and the desire to escape it is also at the core of Radiguet's *The Devil in the Flesh*. While the years of World War I create a suspended time, the teenage narrator "grows sideways" and explores sex and romance with a married woman. As does Colette's protagonist, he damages his own future by living in the now and by enjoying sex, romance, and intimacy outside of wedlock. Ultimately, the "devil in his flesh" corrupts time: by having as a teenager what belongs to adulthood, the narrator rips the fabric of heteronormative futurity.

The second part of this chapter describes temporal dysphoria through Crevel's *My Body and I* and Genet's *Our Lady of the Flowers*. They share the same narrative frame: a narrator confined in a single room for an unknown duration mentally explores alternative temporal threads, past, future, or fictional. In a prison cell, Genet's narrator awaits his sentence. In a hotel room, Crevel's is planning his suicide. Both of them give voice to nonlinear narratives that are loosely connected and defy chronology. In *My Body and I*, the narrator reflects on his own life. His ruminations move from the remembrance of past events to hypothetical considerations of the future, but his stories also include the parallel time of dreams and the unconscious. *Our Lady of the Flowers* intertwines the evocation of the narrator's life with fictional episodes from a "saga" involving imaginary characters. In both novels, the fragmented narration keeps circling back to the space of a single room, which is also an arrested time. Confinement disrupts daily rhythms, blurring the boundaries between sleep and wakefulness, between imagination and dreams. Immobilized in space, both narrators seem to be sitting amid fragments of time swirling around them and find themselves immobilized in temporal dysphoria. Ultimately, the only escape consists of "intermittent miracles," in Crevel's words: queer moments of sensual harmony.

THE EARTH BELONGS TO ANYONE WHO STOPS FOR A MOMENT

When Colette published *The Vagabond* in 1911, she described a situation very close to the one she found herself living in at the time. The narrator, Renée Néré, is recently divorced from a cheating husband and makes an independent living as a dancer, just as Colette began a career at the music hall after she divorced from her wealthy husband, Willy, in 1910. Renée's ex-husband, an arrogant womanizer, bears a strong resemblance to Willy. Over the course of the novel, Renée, in spite of her initial reluctance, engages in a blissful and sensual romance with one of her admirers, Max, just as Colette did with Henry de Jouvenel, whom she married in 1912. But Colette's fictional alter ego parts ways with her: when Max proposes to her in order to stop her going on tour and resuming her wandering life, she ponders her decision and ultimately decides to refuse him and keep her bohemian ways.

While marriage is, from Max's perspective as a well-off bourgeois male and an abiding citizen, the natural outcome of their love affair, it presents Renée with an impossible dilemma: she must choose between loneliness, financial precariousness, and independence, on the one hand, and comfort, emotional and material stability, and submission, on the other. Like Gide, Colette makes a case against marriage. But while Gide's case rests on the impossibility of desire and sensual attachment between heterosexual partners, Colette bases hers on the incompatibility of marriage with sex and desire. While Gide's Michel needs to betray his marriage to discover his own body, Renée knows her own body too well to consent to it. Ultimately, Colette's fictional self chooses the sensual bursts of queer time to chrononormativity's linear preestablished stages and investment in the future.

The Vagabond's plot strives to demonstrate that even the most reciprocated and sensually satisfying relationship between woman and man cannot survive marriage. As the reader is made well aware of, Renée is sexually attracted to Max, "a subtle lover . . . endowed with so much foresight that his caresses seem to be thinking in steps with [her] desires." Similarly, there are no doubts about the authenticity of Max's feelings: Max is vouched for by Renée's most trustworthy friend, who emphasizes how different Max is from her womanizing ex-husband.[14] Nor is Max, whom Renée usually refers to as "Grand-Serin," literally "big canary," a dominating and threatening figure: consistently depicted with attributes generally associated with femininity, Max appears to be relentlessly faithful, patient, and affectionate.[15] But far from making up for the unbalance of power in the gender binary, these traits emphasize it: from the very beginning, the Big Canary displays an entitled belief in the self-imposing power of his desire. He makes his first appearance in the novel as one of the harassing admirers who regularly knock at the door of Renée's dressing room, attracted by her profession and its reputation of sexual freedom. From this moment on, sex and desire are the most ambiguous and volatile components of Renée's and Max's relationship. The narrative seemingly assumes that heterosexual sex is the only kind there is, a strategy that essentializes heteronormativity and makes sex as desirable to women as it is perilous to them.

Max enters Renée's dressing room with a very visible erection. Instead of engaging in small talk, he remains frozen, reduced to the manifestation of his own body: "his burning desire . . . weighs on him like a cumbersome piece of armor."[16] Paradoxically, Renée, who had been exposing her own body on stage moments ago, has the upper hand: female nudity, or body objectification, are the tools through which she ensures her financial and moral independence. Finding herself outside the heteronormative gender assemblage, the divorced Renée isn't afraid of male gazes and erections. But while she has the upper hand in the space she has carved out as a bohemian artist, she never forgets that this advantage is of very little significance in the bigger picture. Once she abandons this queer position, she will lose at every turn. Her first kiss with Max triggers a complex web of contradictory feelings and sensations. "From my lips down to my sides, down to my knees, I feel the rebirth and diffusion of that exigent pain, that swelling of a wound about to reopen and widen—the sensual pleasure I had forgotten."[17] The "wound" and the pain come not so much from the previous trauma of betrayed love but from the knowledge of the betrayal to come, the threat of futurity tainting the delight of her sensations. To men, sex offers two asynchronous rewards: immediate pleasure and familial futurity; to women, the latter turns the former into a "swelling wound," a tangle of worries made flesh.

For Renée, there isn't any distinction between being "caught" by heterosexual love or being caught in the network of social constraints that come with it, outlined in the projected time of chrononormativity. The network of contradictory feelings, impulses, desires, and social imperatives embedded in the word are crystallized around the figure of the Child, which makes a brief and frightening appearance in the novel. Max enthusiastically considers the possibility of having a child, adding that this would prevent Renée from leaving him since she would be "caught." The risk of pregnancy materializes Renée's fear, materially turning the "swelling wound" of her sensuality into the trap she saw in it all along. "Caught.... I had judged him correctly when I laughingly called him a monogamous bourgeois, sit-by-the-fire patriarch." Unlike Gide's heroes, Max is a good citizen: *he* would thrive in a heterosexual marriage. But in spite of her best efforts, Renée is eventually unable to conjure the image of the child she could have with Max: "no matter how I try, I can't see or love the child."[18] The child belongs to futurity. In her present as a divorced and independent woman, Renée has found another type of companionship and of family making: sharing her home with her French bulldog Fossette. The presence of a companion animal, which also echoes Colette's own life, is by no means anecdotal. Fossette is an outrage to chrononormativity: the child's position is already occupied by a beloved adult animal.

As an autobiographical account of a period of Colette's life, *The Vagabond* is strangely lacking: its author's involvement with women is left out of the picture. Here again, Colette resorts to the unintelligibility pointed out by Michael Lucey when it comes to her bisexuality.[19] While Max can be traced to several of her male lovers, his name is also the nickname of Mathilde de Morny, also known as Missy, whose life Colette had been sharing for several years when she wrote *The Vagabond*.[20] The fact that Missy/Max can be perceived, in contemporary terms, as a transman rather than a lesbian, doesn't resolve the issue at stake here: Max, the character, is an embodiment of cis-masculinity, which drives Renée away from him; that said, sex and romance outside of heteronormativity aren't considered as viable options either.

Colette's ambivalent fascination with lesbianism manifests itself throughout her oeuvre and particularly in her 1932 novella *The Pure and the Impure*, with its "textual movements of desiring idealization, energetic purification, and phobic denial."[21] *The Vagabond* follows suit with an evocation of lesbianism as the safe space that comes outside of sexual difference. Its portrayal of lesbian love as a "touching image" acts as a foil confirming the irrepressible attraction of heterosexual sex and romance: "The melancholy and touching image of two weak creatures who have perhaps sought shelter in each other's arms, there to sleep and weep, safe from man who is so often cruel, and there to taste, better than any pleasure, the bitter happiness of feeling themselves akin, frail and forgotten."[22] This homophobic vision of lesbianism bears an achronic dimension, as Amin states: "The text's valorized model of female same-sex love is staked on the ontological claim that there can be no difference, and therefore no temporality, within femaleness."[23] Lesbianism pictured in those terms not only escapes chrononormativity but is ultimately deprived of any kind of temporality. It is, in this way, a negative kind of queer time: a time of absence and not of presence, a time away from time and not in the midst of it. In the end, Renée is incapable of wishing for herself the radical exteriority to the world that she sees in her lesbian friends.

The Vagabond makes room for queer temporality at the expense of queerness, in the same way as *The Pure and the Impure* explores same-sex relationships at the cost of keeping its author out of it. Lucey has described how Colette's strategy of unintelligibility regarding her own (bi)sexuality relies on a form of temporal disjunction: the narrator of *The Pure and the Impure* describes a group of lesbians to whom she belongs but "couldn't share their sexuality because she came from a different time and class."[24] While the first-person narrator of *The Pure and the Impure* situates herself in a different temporality than her subjects, the fictional narrator of *The Vagabond* distinguishes herself from her creator by living in different temporality. The discrepancy between Colette and Renée attests how the act of writing can make room for queer time. Shortly after her book was released, Colette remarried and became pregnant; she gave birth to her daughter in 1913, two years after *The Vagabond*'s publication. But it would be a mistake to consider the novel as Colette's way of experimenting with and weighing out her options, just as it would be to imagine that she first felt like Renée and then had a change of heart. Escapes from chrononormativity, as from any type of normativity, are always elusive and only settled in the queer time of writing. Rather than successive, the two temporalities are simultaneous: the fictional Renée is able to remain in the temporary, as opposed to her alter ego. This isn't, however, a disembodied process: Renée gives over her body to the rapid bursts of queer time in a way that is out of reach to her (actually embodied) alter ego. Paradoxically, the queer time of sensuality is most of all a question of presence to oneself that is only accessible in writing, not because it isn't real but because it eludes futurity.

In the last section of the novel, Renée has gone on tour while Max is making plans for their wedding, and she spends her time in a succession of shabby hotel rooms and train compartments. The discomfort she experiences stands in stark contrast to the cozy walls of the bourgeois apartment Max is already choosing. But her exhaustion is balanced by moments of perfect bliss, such as the glorious spring afternoon she spends wandering in the park of a Provençal town.

> Below me, the lovely garden lies flat.... The approach of the storm has driven away every intruder, and the hail, the hurricane, ascends slowly from the horizon ...
>
> All this is still my kingdom, a small portion of the magnificent wealth that God bestows on passersby, nomads, and the solitary. The earth belongs to whoever stops for a moment, observes, and passes on; all of the sunshine belongs to the naked lizard basking in it.[25]

Solitude in the face of a coming storm: the suspended moment might be read as a metaphor of Renée's situation as a single woman. It also materializes the fragile encounter between two temporalities: the dread of chrononormativity and the bliss of immediacy. Renée belongs in the garden, and the garden belongs to her, because, like the lizard, she finds herself basking in it. The underlying opposition between nature and human society produces an effect similar to that of Graves's poem, where dreaming of lying in the hay allows the narrator to escape the reality of the trenches. Through a feeling of sensual connection to its immediate surroundings, the body escapes a morbid abstraction, regains some agency, and accesses immediacy instead of being trapped in the net of chrononormativity. As in Gide's *Immoralist*, contact with nature allows for a bodily self-discovery (or self-enjoyment, for those moments of sensual escape in nature are essential in Colette's writings since *Claudine*). In the colonial fetishism of *The Immoralist*, the warm North African climate is conflated with its inhabitants, so that the narrator finds his own body through those of teenage boys. In *The Vagabond*, heterosexual sex is intensely fulfilling but tainted by the dread of being caught. Nature, therefore, offers a fuller way to connect with one's body, a unique moment of belonging.

The Vagabond ends when Renée refuses Max and chooses freedom over the predetermined path of normative temporality, marriage, and family. As Renée's tour brings her closer to southern France and springtime, she agonizes more and more over Max's love letters and feels herself disconnected from the things she likes the most. "My torment lords it over me; it comes between me and my pleasure in living, in observing, in drawing deep breaths. . . ."[26] The "torment," here, is a self-perpetuating process, one that can only be escaped once and for all in the limited space of a text: it is caused by the temptation to subject oneself to the imperatives of futurity, losing one's own present in the process. Saying "yes" to Max wouldn't end Renée's anxiety, but it would throw her into the perpetual anguish of possessing a future already written yet never certain. To attain material stability, she would have to become emotionally dependent on her husband. And this emotional dependence would foreclose the kind of connections made in the park: pure bodily enjoyment of the presence of surrounding natural elements, that is, pure enjoyment of the present. The present is, in itself, a queer time: in the logic of the capitalist heteronormative nation-state, living in the now is a theft of time. Renée's decision to renounce marriage, and with it love, intimacy, and companionship, is based on the future, not on the present. She enjoys every minute of her present with Max, and she also enjoys her own time. In the chrononormativity of marriage, she would literally lose herself: she would lose her own present and her presence in the world.

TIME GONE TO HELL

Published twelve years after *The Vagabond*, Radiguet's *The Devil in the Flesh* offers a similar insight into the gender assemblage of its time, but from the perspective of a teenage boy. Like Renée, its unnamed narrator diverts heterosexual love, sex, and intimacy away from chrononormativity. Set during World War I, *The Devil in the Flesh* tells the story of a fifteen-year-old teenager's affair with the young wife of a soldier fighting in the trenches. As the narrator occupies their suburban home, she also is drawn back toward her own teenagerhood. As Stockton describes, the young narrator and his mistress do not grow "up" but "sideways," or, in her case, back.[27] Instead of following the socially sanctioned stages toward adulthood, he remains a child while exploring the adult world of sexuality and conjugality. Meanwhile, she disengages from the path she has already accepted, bending sideways the time of conjugality.

In Radiguet's novel, the war acts as a disruptive force that offers a way out of chrononormativity. Like the pacifist Maurice Rostand, his narrator avoids both schools and barracks, not by choice but because of his young age and middle-class upbringing. While barely older men considered to be adults have left home for the trenches, he is spared by the randomness of calendar years and the queer juxtaposition of historical and personal times: "Is it my fault that I celebrated my twelfth birthday a few months before war was declared? The disturbance I experienced during that extraordinary period was probably of a kind never given to a boy of that age."[28]

If war is supposed to make men out of boys, for the teenage narrator it is but a prolonged childhood, which he describes as "four years of holiday."[29] Like the ambivalence of adolescence referred to by Stockton as "the matter of children's delay," this suspended state is in itself a queer time, marked by an intense feeling of asynchrony. "It's a mistake to take innocence straight," Stockton writes. The expression "growing up," suggesting "a simple thrust toward height and forward time," misses the thickness, the dense complexity of the present and its tendency to reach sideways or even backward.[30] Growing up isn't a straight process, and the assumed innocence of the child creates a web of queer possibilities. It is worth mentioning here, however, that innocence, at the beginning of the twentieth century, does not refer to a lack of sexual intercourse. Teenage boys were expected to lose their virginity at a young age but not, as the narrator did, with a married woman from their own social circle.[31]

Introducing his story, the narrator refers to forbidden sex as something that is for him as real "as cheese to a cat," despite the fact the cheese finds itself behind a glass cover. Yet as the narrator observes, "the glass does exist." To him, the war is the triggering incident that breaks the glass, an opportunity for transgression. We are left to believe that the relentlessness of the teenage cat would have been rewarded by another incident, if it hadn't been for this one. "The cat was still looking at the cheese under the glass. Then the war came—and the glass was broken. The master had other cats to whip and the cat celebrated his good fortune."[32] The war distracts the parents' attention and renders them unable to keep the children under control, thus setting free a whole world of uncontained energy. Growing sideways, the kids—the cats—are free to eat the cheese, which represents here not only the forbidden fruit of sexuality but also the imminence of chaos and ruin—the end of organized chrononormative time. Free, unbinding time is at the center of the novel's plot. Thanks to what he calls the "poetry" of war, the narrator discovers a temporality of pleasure and play. The heteronormative timeline, which attributes play to children and pleasure and reproductive sex to adults, is disrupted. The narrator playfully skips classes and spends hours in bed with Marthe, his mistress.

The narrator's relationship with Marthe relies on the inversion of the life stages announced at the beginning of the novel:

a child, the narrator, steals the grownup's place in his home and in his bed. It no coincidence that the grown man is also a fighting soldier, engaged in serving the nation. The competition between the child and the soldier is manifest in a scene in which the narrator surprises Marthe by entering her bedroom in the middle of a stormy night. Marthe mistakes him for her husband; when she realizes who he is, she insists that the narrator, soaked by the rain, put on pajamas belonging to her husband. "Jacques' pajamas! And I thought how possible it was . . . that he might arrive on the scene at any moment."[33] The French text, instead of the pronoun "he," uses the term "soldier," underscoring the narrator's fear and fascination for Jacques's role not as a husband but as a grown man. It is worth noting here that because of conscription, Jacques's military status is a step into male adulthood and temporality more than a chosen activity. Yet despite the gravitas conferred to him by his status, Jacques remains an abstraction, paradoxically deprived of a body by his commitment to an external temporality: war means life and death, but in *another* time and place. In wearing his pajamas, the narrator literally animates and embodies him, bringing life and flesh to Jacques's bedroom and to his relationship to Marthe, which would have otherwise been the empty shell of chrononormative futurity.

Embodying Marthe's husband, the narrator also allows her to return to her embodied self, but in doing so he brings her back in time. Marthe is in fact barely older than him. As opposed to the modern adolescent described by Stockton, forced to delay her growth toward adulthood, she has been forced into marriage and adulthood. Wedded at the age of eighteen, she lives alone, playing house in a home for which she has no more genuine interest than for her husband—a child seduced by the abstraction of chrononormativity and the empty shell of suburban life.

The war leaves her, as the narrator, unsupervised. As she becomes more and more involved with him, she regresses toward childhood and abandons her duties as a housewife. When her husband joins her during a leave, she sulks and throws tantrums until the unfortunate soldier confides in his mother-in-law, who decides that Marthe should return to the parental home. But the plan backfires: "He accompanied Marthe to her mother's.... She would sleep in the room she had slept in as a girl. Jacques thought that the least they might do was set up a bed for him in the same room. Marthe became hysterical. She would never allow the purity of that room to be sullied by his presence."[34] Subjecting Marthe to parental control is an ambiguous move: taking her home amounts to making her grow back, not up. While she welcomes the narrator's presence in the conjugal bedroom, she refuses Jacques's intrusion into her childhood room. To her, sex is only enjoyable when it leads back.

The lovers in *The Devil in the Flesh* remain children—children having sex. Here heterosexual sex marks not the entrance into adulthood but its playful and stubborn refusal. In the narrator's case, losing his virginity while still a schoolboy isn't in itself a transgression. Rather, the rite of passage required for a member of his social class is supposed to happen in a brothel or with a woman of lower social standing. Marthe isn't a suitable mistress: she and her parents are friends of the family. Her young age makes the idyll even more transgressive, excluding the conventional trope of a young boy seduced by a mature woman. There is no initiating here, no education, no transition into maturity, and no way back toward chrononormativity. The transgression, however, carries a different weight for each of the two protagonists. The narrator will carry on living with the moral burden of his transgression. But to Marthe, sex outside of wedlock means death: social death, first, when the narrator is seen coming out of her house early in the morning; familial death, when she becomes pregnant with his child, breaking the heteronormative links of heredity; and finally, literal death since she dies giving birth to her illegitimate child.

The Devil in the Flesh tells a story of ruin and squander, of dilapidated time. The narrator's transgression disrupts the straight line of chrononormativity by foreclosing the possibility of a future. Learning about Marthe's death, the narrator professes his atheism: "Marthe! My jealousy pursued her to the grave and I hoped that there was nothing after death." Deprived of any kind of future, the love story is a dead end, happening outside of temporality. In terms of chrononormativity, the narrator's transgression seems to amount to a zero-sum game. The widowed Jacques acknowledges paternity of the narrator's child, who is, unsurprisingly, a boy. Marthe's baby will bear the first name of the narrator, but this name will seal her secret, as the narrator finds out while eavesdropping on a conversation. Acting, until the very end, as a child spying on the adults, the narrator overhears Jacques sharing with his father that Marthe "died calling him"—by which he means her baby: "Seeing this widower . . . I realized that in the end order reasserts itself over everything. Had I not just learnt that Marthe had died calling my name, and that my son would have a reasonable life?"[35]

"Order" means that, as far as everyone else is concerned, the narrator's transgression can be forgotten. The breach opened in chrononormativity by two children's transgression has been repaired with a new child. What remains is only a word, the narrator's first name adeptly smuggled into Jacques's family tree, a seed of the devil. This fictional subversion echoes a lived one: a few years after choosing to marry again, Colette, now in her late forties, embarked on a passionate affair with her stepson, the sixteen-year-old Bertrand de Jouvenel, the son of her second (and also cheating) husband. Their affair lasted several years, caused a divorce and a scandal, and disrupted chrononormativity in a messier and probably more radical way than Renée's clean fictional break with married life.

THE QUEER TIME OF WRITING: GENET'S SAGA OF ROSES

Whereas *The Vagabond* and *The Devil in the Flesh* are articulated through a mostly chronological narration, the last two novels I discuss in this chapter are queering temporality in both their form and content. In what follows, I will first examine how Genet's *Our Lady of the Flowers* and Crevel's *My Body and I* make room for queer time. I will then explore the relationship between queer and dysphoric time in these novels in order to elaborate more specifically on the concept of temporal dysphoria. While these two novels have never been read together, they present a number of similarities in their ways of apprehending time and space. The most obvious of these similarities is that their plots are both set in a single room, where a confined narrator gives voice to meditations, memories, daydreams, or dreams. But these rooms—a prison cell in Genet's case, a hotel room for Crevel—are more than mere backgrounds for the stories to be told: they constitute an anchor around which series of narratives uncoil. At once a starting point and an endpoint, the limited space of the room allows for the absence of chronology. In spite of its complexity, Genet's novel relies on the same type of temporality as Crevel's seemingly simplified narrative. In both texts, narrative threads swirl around a narrator arrested in space, stranded in a single room. Temporality isn't a straight line; it spirals toward past, future, or imaginary dimensions before coming back to a bare and fruitless present. The narrative itself becomes, or gives room to, a queer temporality bursting in intensities and blurring boundaries between past, present, and future and also between reality, memory, and fiction.

In his foreword to Genet's *Our Lady of the Flowers*, Sartre recounts that the book was originally written on fragments of brown paper given to its author in prison. "French prison authorities, convinced that 'work is freedom,' give the inmates paper from which they are supposed to make bags. It was on this brown paper that Genet wrote, in pencil, *Our Lady of the Flowers*."[36] The anecdote, reported by Genet to Sartre and seemingly unquestioned by the latter, also includes the punitive burning of the manuscript by a prison guard after which, according to Jean-Paul Sartre, "Genet began again. Why? For whom?" Sartre's point is existentialist freedom, the novel itself being, in his terms, "an act of the rashest optimism."[37] Regardless of its authenticity or the relevance of Sartre's argument, the anecdote points to the fragmentary and proliferating nature of *Our Lady of the Flowers*. Supposedly written on pieces of paper and written again at will after its destruction, the text seems to produce itself and to branch out almost spontaneously. The novel and its many subplots have been compared by Jean Cocteau to "flowers": "Obscene flowers, comic flowers, tragic flowers, nocturnal flowers, field flowers, arabesque of roses spring forth everywhere."[38]

The main narrative line of *Our Lady of the Flowers* follows the imprisoned narrator as he awaits his trial and mentally escapes his condition through masturbation and fantasies. His muses, the "unknown lovers" he summons, will inspire him "to write a story."[39] This imaginary story line follows a series of characters revolving around the incestuous family formed by Divine, a transgender prostitute in Montmartre; Mignon,[40] Divine's pimp and lover; and their lover/child, Our Lady of the Flowers, who is a teenage thief and murderer. This blooming proliferation takes the form of a "saga," a term introduced in the first pages of the novel, along with the first fictional character, Divine. Divine's story opens on her deathbed, as would the eulogy of a royal. "Since Divine is dead, the poet may sing her, may tell her legend, the Saga, the annals of Divine." Divine, as her name states, is of divine nature, worthy of a saga or legend. And, as any mythological hero, Divine is also human, in a very physical way, since the readers soon finds out that she died of consumption in "a pool of her vomited blood."[41]

Proliferating instead of linear, the narrative form of the saga bears a multiplicity of tales, never ending, never closed. Stemming from the narrator's cell, this proliferation gives shape to a dysphoric temporality, which can only expand sideways, not forward, and not even backward, since it cannot reap the fruits of a chrononormative life. Any part of the saga can be subjected to new modifications and additions, as new tales can be added to the whole: characters and stories are growing in clusters, as if they were made of space and not of time. Born from the present of their secluded creator, they belong to this inescapable present. Yet the boundaries between the narrator's presence in his cell and the fictional events he imagines become progressively blurred. As the novel progresses, new bridges keep appearing between the real and the imaginary story lines. Through a complex network of narrative crossovers and parentheses, synchrony and fictionality are both asserted and denied. The narrator and his creations find themselves time and again in the same physical spaces, trapped together in a labyrinthine judicial system: prison cells and commons, courtrooms, police stations. At the end of the novel, the narrator claims to have met Mignon in jail and produces "the letter Mignon wrote to Divine from prison."[42] While the narrator remains locked up, his creatures wander in and out across the walls. But the escape they represent is always temporary and, in that, always a failure.

This ever-growing yet arrested present is mirrored stylistically by the figure of the hyperbaton. The linguist Agnès Fontvieille notices two main types of sentences in *Our Lady of the Flowers*: the "Proustian [sentence], labyrinthine, support for digressions and regressions, and for rhythmic explorations," and a "short format sentence, inherited from the literary tradition, energetic, enunciative, and categorical."[43] In both types of sentences, Genet's style is characterized by a variety of stylistic devices that disrupt word order, among which Fontvieille identifies the hyperbaton as the most emblematic.[44] The hyperbaton, Fontvieille notes, is at the core of Genet's writing strategy, which is to "create a new order of truth." Stylistically, a hyperbaton is meant to lengthen a sentence by adding words where logic or grammar prevents the reader from expecting them. Fontvieille quotes for instance Divine's description of Our Lady: "Our Lady is so proud! And so dumb!"[45] The second sentence, unexpected, undermines the first, changing its meaning from a compliment to an insult.[46] The hyperbaton creates a sudden change of direction, thus imposing constant twists of linearity. Its aims, according to Fontvieille, are to keep the audience alert and in awe, as well as to maintain an idiosyncratic singularity throughout the text. The text itself thus acquires a thickness that increases its materiality. Genet's systematic use of the hyperbaton echoes the form of the saga: new ramifications are possible at every level. Neither the narrative nor its sentences follow straight lines: they can always be interrupted or extended, divided, or contradicted. The text itself grows sideways.

THE TIMING OF GENDERS

As with plot lines, genders tend to multiply in *Our Lady of the Flowers*. The gender binary isn't ignored but pushed toward its limits through both form and content. The Divine-Mignon couple finds itself at the core of a process that undermines gender and is similar to that of the saga and the hyperbaton. The saga keeps adding stories to the story, the hyperbaton disrupts the sentence by adding on new words, and the set of referents dividing the gender binary between male and female is used so constantly that it loses its significance. Stories, sentences, and genders are constantly outgrowing their own limits, overflowing, and shape shifting, yet they remain arrested in time.

After referring to Divine with female pronouns while introducing her, the narrator seems to take a step back. "I shall speak to you about Divine, mixing masculine and feminine as my mood dictates, and if, in the course of the tale, I shall have to refer to a woman, I shall manage, I shall find an expedient, a good device, to avoid any confusion." The term "confusion" is in fact misleading. Over the entire course of the novel, the narrator never "mixes" genders when referring to Divine: Divine is always feminine. Genet saves the masculine for sections about Louis Culafroy, the child and teenager who then becomes Divine. Genet's ironic wish to "avoid any confusion" serves, rather, to make clear that Divine is not a cisgender woman and that she maintains an elusive relationship with Culafroy, whose memories she sometimes shares.[47] Divine and Culafroy, like many characters of the saga, are both synchronous and asynchronous.

Divine's gender fluidity is contagious. Mignon isn't the alpha male that his bulky appearance might suggest: his hypermasculinity is carried to a paroxysm that disrupts the gender binary. Mignon is indeed the perfect male whom everyone (Divine, the narrator, and their intended audiences) is dreaming about, but his perfection binds together the aesthetic tropes associated with masculinity and femininity. Because of his virility, Mignon is an object of worship. When evoking his body, Divine and the narrator constantly resort to religious metaphors. The narrator:

"[He will] penetrate me so deeply that I shall be marked with stigmata"; and Divine: "When I see him lying naked, I feel like saying mass on his chest." The nickname Mignon has a feminine connotation, even though it is in the grammatically masculine form. While he first refuses to let Divine address him with a female pronoun, Mignon finally gives in:

> Divine dared say to him:
> "You're pretty," adding: "like a prick."[48]

The French text uses the feminine form of the adjective *belle* (beautiful), which furthers the contrast. Divine's compliment is one of the hyperbatons mentioned earlier and has the same disrupting effect. By comparing Mignon to a penis, Divine softens the insult to his male ego.[49] Mignon's virility is never questioned; it is, rather, reinforced. What is shaken in the process is the disjunction between genders and their attributes, which can coexist to their extreme in the same sentence.

Genet's biographer Edmund White notes that "Divine exists in historical time . . . but Darling [Mignon] does not," a distinction that requires some nuances.[50] Unlike Mignon, Divine does age, but she remains atemporal through her variations. Genet indicates, when conjuring Mignon for the first time: "He was young . . . and I would like him to remain so to the end of the book." Divine's and Mignon's disjointed temporality reverses the usual gender binary. While Mignon is aestheticized, Divine creates herself time and again and takes charge of her diverse incarnations. When she feels herself changing, she seems to lean toward the virility she admires in her pimps, yet "Divine had not become virile; she had aged. An adolescent now excited her, and that was why she had the feeling of being old."[51] Instead of becoming a loving and self-erasing mother, Divine defies gender roles and becomes a loving and self-effacing pimp who gives away Our Lady to her former lover. Divine's existence in historical time is not told as a linear process but along the semi-mythological conventions of the saga. As always in *Our Lady of the Flowers*, temporality is not a straight line, so that various avatars can coexist. Ernestine, Culafroy's mother, carries throughout the narrative the existence of her son. Culafroy is as alive, or as dead, as Divine. The linear time of secular lives doesn't give enough room for fulfillment. Divine grows old too fast—particularly since she has already met her death when we first meet her; Our Lady is doomed from the moment of his appearance; and whether counted in months or in years, the idylls inevitably meet their end through losses, crimes, punishments, and separations.

Eventually, like the saga, Divine is plural. She is always part of a group, always susceptible to subdivisions and rearrangements. She is part of the Divine/Culafroy couple, made complete by the presence of Ernestine; in the same way, the Divine/Mignon couple is completed and disrupted by Our Lady. Unlike Plato's hermaphrodite, these gendered couples are calling for a threesome. Unbalance, imperfection, and misplaced desires are the rule, not the exception. Divine is also constantly surrounded by multiple lesser incarnations of herself—les "tantes": Mimosa I, Mimosa II, First Communion ... Again, Divine grows sideways, to the point that she doesn't exist as a singular being. Individuals aren't any more singular than genders are clearly attributed. In the same process, individuality and identity cease to signify anything else than flows of desire. Divine's love for Mignon causes her to worship his virility *and* to address him with female pronouns. The love triangle, or holy family, formed by Our Lady, Divine, and Mignon is based on a playful game of interactions: the role of each member stems from their particular position, not their individuality. Divine feels herself turning masculine because of the presence of Our Lady, who after some years in prison could very well become an ageless pimp such as Mignon or reinvent himself as a member of Divine's tribe.

Abstracted from chrononormativity, the gender binary ceases to represent a set of roles and functions, a way to live one's life (the soldier, the wife, the mother-to-be, the provider-husband, the school boy . . .) and becomes a blossoming architecture of desire and play. In *The Devil in the Flesh*, the narrator sins by having now what he should have had later; Renée Néré's impossible wish is to stay involved in a kind of relationship (heterosexual romance) without entering its next stage (marriage). But the boundaries transgressed by Colette and Radiguet are temporal: their characters suffered the consequences of acting out of time. Genet's saga takes an opposite approach: gender-deviant characters evolving outside of time take over the attributes of the gender binary and its temporal dimension and use them to fool around. What is disrupted in the process is not only heteronormativity but also a sense of individuality: without the aim of reproductive futurity, individual lives lose their state-sanctioned purposes and stability.

TEMPORAL DYSPHORIA: NO BRIDGE LEADS ME TO OTHERS

In *In a Queer Time and Place*, Halberstam suggests that queer places need to be understood in relationship to time. Referring to "place-making practices," he underscores how these practices are tied to a different understanding of temporality.[52] In other words, queer places are literally located away from chrononormativity. The opposite is also true: in tracing the contours of queer temporality, space is key. Queer places, such as described by Halberstam, play a crucial part in the novels discussed in this chapter: the transient spaces of hotel rooms, train compartments, cabarets, bars, nightclubs, and prison cells . . . Space is the place, or the moment, where linear time unravels. As with Renée's moment in the park before the storm, awareness of surrounding space grounds temporality in a present that makes its materiality palpable. By closing the door, the confined space of the room opens awareness to alternative modes of temporality.

Like Genet's *Our Lady of the Flowers*, Crevel's *My Body and I* opens with its narrator finding himself alone in a room. But while Genet's narrator is in prison, Crevel's is about to spend his first night in a room in "a small hotel in the mountains" where he has come to experience a complete isolation.

> Here am I, alone in my room.
> Alone.
> I have wanted this adventure so badly and for so long. . . . But tonight, my wish having come true, I find myself available to myself at last. No bridge leads me to others.[53]

At first, this long-awaited adventure might be perceived as a quest for self-discovery. The hotel could be a retreat where the narrator, finally able to avoid external solicitations, explores his true self. The alpine village, whose actual location is never revealed, echoes the literary tradition of romantic retreat and meditation found in Rousseau or Senancour. In *My Body and I*, however, the arrested time of rural confinement doesn't bring about peace, nor was it ever meant to. As the reader progressively finds out, the narrator does not seek wisdom but death: the reason why he has come to this place is to commit suicide. Being master of one's time, "available to oneself," doesn't open doors toward futurity but closes them. The mountain retreat is not a bridge enabling the narrator to travel back to the world after having gained the wisdom he needed. The room is what remains when all bridges are closed.

The room's isolation allows the narrator to sever himself from the chronological line of chrononormativity by cutting any ties that could anchor him in social life. The title of the first chapter, "In the Time of Others," asserts this rupture: the time of others, where one loses oneself in a quest for companionship and intimacy, is over. As the narrator in *Our Lady of the Flowers* doesn't know for how long he is to stay in his cell, the protagonist in *My Body and I* finds himself outside of time. As he has not set a time for the moment of his suicide, past, present, and future emerge indistinctively in the closed space of his room. Memories are getting confused with imaginary conversations; regrets and introspection intertwine with speculation; sleep and dreams blend with reminiscence or anticipation of other dreams. Detached from daily tasks and social obligations, the mind wanders in a timeless abyss. "Travels and surprises. In spite of the nightly terror, the bodiless head feels no joy when at dawn it regains its place on someone's shoulders."[54] The severed head, which recalls Crevel's psychic experiments with the Surrealist Group, suggests that linear time has come to a halt.[55] The cycle between night and day doesn't so much suggest sleep and wakefulness as a haunted nightmare. In the room, time runs in circles instead of moving forward. In escaping the "time of others," the narrator has fallen out of time and finds himself trapped in temporal dysphoria: dysphoric time precludes any type of futurity, and the queer sensuality of the present is inaccessible as well. Temporal dysphoria is stranded time, where one is neither here nor there.

TIME AND THE BODY: A DYSPHORIC ASSEMBLAGE

As I discussed in this book's introduction, dysphoria appears as a pure sense of estrangement, grounded in one's own body. In *Our Lady of the Flowers* as in *My Body and I*, the imprisoned body and the space of its confinement—the room—become the means of exploring a mode of temporality akin to dysphoria or, rather, of exploring dysphoria *as* time. In *My Body and I*, the queer space of the room, both intimate and anonymous, keeps manifesting itself to the narrator through the intrusions of the chambermaid, the roses of the wallpaper, or the vapor of his own breath on the mirror. As opposed to a monastic cell, the hotel room doesn't erase the body but puts it at the foreground through its very function: a refuge for anonymous bodies. Queer time, in all the texts discussed in this chapter, is a time in which bodies find ways of inhabiting, of queering, spaces. The train compartments, dressing rooms, and hotels where Renée escapes from Max, Marthe's marital bedroom desacralized by Radiguet's narrator, Genet's prison cell and Divine's room, are spaces owned by bodies. Dedicated to bodily functions, these rooms bear these bodies' imprints: bodily fluids or beauty accessories, beds and mirrors. Yet dysphoric temporality carries the process to its point of rupture: instead of owning spaces, bodies become pure spatiality.

Alone in his room, Crevel's narrator remembers other hotel rooms in which he shared intimacy with other bodies, male or female, loved or despised, and the inextricable mesh of feelings and sensations he experienced with them. Thus haunted, the room channels recurring reminders that he cannot establish a connection with any other body or with his own, leaving him with a sense of circular claustrophobia that is the reverse echo of Genet's ever-expanding saga. Going from one mental room to another, the narrator laments: "but the rough key of the senses doesn't open any doors. A sexual organ isn't a master key." Far from offering a relief to its feeling of estrangement, sexuality failed to provide any type of connection, leaving the narrator both secluded in his own body and divorced from it. Describing the lives of Parisian male prostitutes reminiscent of Genet's characters, the narrator pictures them as tragic figures, "Saint Sebastian of the Suburbs" or "Ophelia of the Canal Saint-Martin," adding that "their exhibitionism on command signifies neither frankness nor truth."[56] Sexuality appears through the novel as a type of *vanitas*, and the queer time of sex with strangers becomes a dysphoric time: a time of complete estrangement, or a complete estrangement from time.

Each in his room, Crevel's and Genet's narrators draw parallel but opposite accounts of their sexuality. *Our Lady of the Flowers* is a textual exploration of bodies: one's own and its possible connections to others. None of the characters in *Our Lady of the Flowers* are voluntarily secluded, but their confinement has the same consequences of bringing the body to the foreground. Dysphoria, here, takes the form of a divorce between time and space, where bodies are the only space that remains but cannot be fully inhabited. While Crevel's narrator experiences desire as inherently frustrating, desire in Genet appears as an endless and empowering source of enjoyment.

Blurring boundaries between interior and exterior worlds, the narrator of *Our Lady of the Flowers* creates tales to entertain himself, as "a prisoner who plays (who plays for himself) scenes of the inner life." The novel's opening, an ode to crime and masturbation, invokes a list of famous criminals. "Weidmann appeared before you in a five o'clock edition.... His handsome face, multiplied by the presses, swept down upon Paris and all of France." Thus begin the narrator's daydreams as he pleasures himself in his cell. "Beneath the sheet, my right hand stops to caress the absent face, and then the whole body, of the outlaw I have chosen for that evening's delight."[57] The novel, which Sartre has called "the epic of masturbation," relies on a writing method that is transparent enough.[58] Then again, even if we take Genet's, or Sartre's, words at face value, the novel largely exceeds its own masturbatory material. The reader is cyclically brought back to the reality surrounding the narrator's mental activities: "This story may not always be artificial, and in spite of me you may recognize in it the call of the blood: the reason is that within my night, I shall have happened to strike my forehead at some door, freeing an anguished memory that had been haunting me since the world began."[59] A door, not a wall: the free flow of memories, bodily fluids, reveries, affects, thoughts, that take form in writing is not so much an escape as it is an attempt to explore sideways, alternative temporalities. The space of the room is at the same time the door opening toward Crevel's reminiscences and Genet's fantasies and the wall against which they come crashing back. *Our Lady of the Flowers* is an epic of confinement as much as an epic of masturbation. But in neither case does the intellect have the upper hand over the body: they are at all times intertwined in both their limitations and the means of escape they offer.

Our Lady of the Flowers turns seclusion into a self-perpetuating narrative process. The repetitions of trials, police detention, imprisonments ... endured by all the characters, narrator included, reinforce the same trope. At first sight, the narrator is in prison while his creatures, Divine, Mignon, and Our Lady, walk free on the boulevard. But as always, the threads of the narrative are intertwined: Our Lady awaits trial, Mignon is constantly in and out of prison, and Divine, who may have met the narrator in jail, spends most of her time secluded in her beloved "tower," a rented room dominating the Montmartre graveyard. Hence, the text encompasses both sexual arousal and what renders it necessary, both the liberating fantasies and the limitations repeatedly bringing back real and fictional characters to their need for escape.

OUTSIDE OF CHRONONORMATIVITY: SOLITUDE AND INTERMITTENT MIRACLES

Dysphoria carries a particular type of solitude. Crevel's chapter titles repeatedly underscore the narrator's isolation: "Truly Alone," "The Last Presences," "Encounters with Sensuality: Missed Encounters," and lastly, "Solitude, the Pain No One Can Heal." As he faces the impossibility of inhabiting his own body and of connecting with others, Crevel's narrator is left, time and again, with suicide as his only horizon. In the proximity of death, time ceases to bear any meaning, to offer any legibility except that of habit. "The death that has often tempted me exceeded in beauty this fear of dying, vulgar at its core, something I could very well call a petty habit."[60] The end of the novel does not hint toward a resolution—we do not know if the narrator will cross the line, probably because he has already crossed it and has found himself out of time, trapped in the loop of temporal dysphoria.

Attempting to pray, he ends up arguing with himself instead. His endless monologue, cause and consequence of the solitude, is also arrested in time, bringing him repeatedly to the same conclusion.

> When the battle is over, when the curtain has fallen, I am alone, empty-handed, empty-hearted.
> I am alone.[61]

Ten years after the publication of *My Body and I*, on June 18, 1935, René Crevel committed suicide. This decision was made a few days before the opening of the International Writers Congress in Defense of Culture, which Crevel had worked tirelessly to organize. Its purpose was to bring together European intellectuals to oppose the rise of fascism. Crevel killed himself a few hours after he found out that the Surrealist Group, led by Breton, had decided not to attend the Congress. Even if Crevel had been toying with the idea of suicide for years, the betrayal of his former friends probably represented a final disappointment: joint efforts toward a cause seemed impossible. Eventually, no bridges could be built even in the face of imminent disaster. Crevel left a single note: "Please cremate. Disgust."[62] Sometimes, queer time doesn't offer a viable "time out" of the violence of normativity. Crevel spent his adult life seeking ways out of familialism, fascism, and heteronormativity—the latter triggered his rupture with Breton, who didn't accept Crevel's bisexuality. Eventually, the loneliness of temporal dysphoria took over the queer time of sex, love, writing, or revolt. "Nothing overcomes this angst, of which our flesh is molded and which, parching us with the thirst for truth, gently pushes us toward the land of absolute mirrors: death."[63]

While anchored in the present, dysphoric time is a time of dissociation: as opposed to the intensity of sex or of sensuality (Renée's moment in the park), dysphoric time occurs through dissociation, when present and presence are lost, when even a temporary reconciliation with the world is impossible. Time, body, and mind cannot be reconciled. Dysphoric time is a dysfunctional queer time: nothing happens and—again—nothing. For the narrator of *My Body and I*, there is no present. Being present only triggers feelings of dissociations: between body and self, between self and others. Crevel's is a narrative of burned bridges, of severed ties, whereas Genet builds these bridges, sending out textual threads in every direction, in search of connections with himself and the world. But open or closed, queer and dysphoric temporalities expand in their texts, revealing the dysphoric assemblage formed by time and the body.

Queer time and dysphoric time constitute lines of flight out of chrononormativity, whether happy or deathly ones. The violence of chrononormativity spurs the dilemma exposed in *The Vagabond*: a choice between submission and social banishment. It also leads to the misogynist narrative sacrifice of Marthe—in the novel, Marthe conveniently dies during childbirth, but for many flesh-and-blood women, the birth of an illegitimate child meant death in many forms. The same violence imposes itself upon the outcasts brought to life in Genet's and Crevel's texts: sex workers and thieves cruising the boulevards, lost souls wandering from one party to the next. Narrative explorations speak of lives not lived as much as they seek to create viable alternatives. Reaching through time, the dysphoria of the gender assemblage extends beyond individual questions of identity and into the dynamics of history, collective lives, and biopolitical power.

In the penultimate chapter of *My Body and I*, "Encounters with Sensuality: Missed Encounters," the narrator escapes his room and wanders through alpine meadows where, his desire awakened by the presence of a vibrant nature, he strips naked and starts masturbating, but his feelings of lack and loneliness overcome him again. "Naked in the sun and so close to being saved forever, there comes the awakening of the flesh, a flesh to which light and joy can no longer be anything except intermittent miracles."[64] Queer and dysphoric times don't have happy endings, since they are only holes in the fabric or chrononormativity. The best one can hope for are intermittent miracles.

NOTES

INTRODUCTION

1. Marcel Proust, *In Search of Lost Time*, vol. 4: *Sodom and Gomorrah*, trans. C. K. Scott Moncrieff and Terence Kilmartin, revised by D. J. Enright (New York: Random House, 2003), 19.
2. See, for instance, Didier Eribon, *Insult and the Making of the Gay Self*, trans. Michael Lucey (Durham, NC: Duke University Press 2004); and Laure Murat, *La loi du genre. Une histoire culturelle du 'troisième sexe'* (Paris: Fayard, 2006).
3. Gilles Deleuze and Félix Guattari, *Anti-Oedipus: Capitalism and Schizophrenia*, trans. Brian Massumi (Minneapolis: University of Minnesota Press, 1983), 46.
4. Laura Doan, *Disturbing Practices: History, Sexuality, and Women's Experience of Modern War* (Chicago: University of Chicago Press, 2013); Benjamin Kahan, *The Book of Minor Perverts: Sexology, Etiology, and the Emergences of Sexuality* (Chicago: University of Chicago Press, 2019); Michael Lucey, *Someone: The Pragmatics of Misfit Sexualities, from Colette to Hervé Guibert* (Chicago: University of Chicago Press, 2019). These three authors share an emphasis on situated practices, discourses, and knowledge that puts them in an ideal position to apprehend the overlapping gray area between gender and sexuality.
5. Eve Kosofsky Sedgwick, *Between Men: English Literature and Male Homosocial Desire* (New York: Columbia University Press, 1985), 15.

6. For a historical perspective on gender, sexuality, and French imperialism, see, for instance, Elsa Dorlin, *La matrice de la race. Généalogie sexuelle et coloniale de la nation française* (Paris: La Découverte 2009); Françoise Vergès, *The Wombs of Women: Race, Capital, Feminism*, trans. Kaiama L. Glover (Durham, NC: Duke University Press, 2020). For a European perspective, see Ann Laura Stoler, *Carnal Knowledge and Imperial Power: Race and the Intimate in Colonial Rule* (Berkeley: University of California Press, 2002); and Ann Laura Stoler, *Race and the Education of Desire: Foucault's "History of Sexuality" and the Colonial Order of Things* (Durham, NC: Duke University Press, 1995). For an American perspective on race, gender, and sexuality, see Siobhan B. Sommerville, *Queering the Color Line: Race and the Invention of Homosexuality in American Culture* (Durham, NC: Duke University Press, 2000).
7. Christian Gury, *Lyautey-Charlus* (Paris: Kimé, 1998).
8. The tensions created by this double racial divide are still impressed on today's French political landscape. For instance, the Jewish far-right candidate in the 2022 French presidential elections, Eric Zemmour, publicly took a position against Dreyfus's innocence in an effort to align himself with the conservative French right. Jon Henley, "Rise of Far Right Puts Dreyfus Affair Into Spotlight in French Election Race," *The Guardian*, October 30, 2021, https://www.theguardian.com/global/2021/oct/30/rise-of-far-right-puts-dreyfus-affair-into-spotlight-in-french-election-race.
9. Carolyn Dean, *The Frail Social Body: Pornography, Homosexuality, and Other Fantasies in Interwar France* (Berkeley: University of California Press, 2000), 7–8.
10. Eve Kosofsky Sedgwick, *Epistemology of the Closet* (Oakland: University of California Press, 1990); Eve Kosofsky Sedgwick, *The Weather in Proust* (Durham, NC: Duke University Press, 2011).
11. Leo Bersani, *Homos* (Cambridge, MA: Harvard University Press, 1996).
12. Kadji Amin, *Disturbing Attachments: Genet, Modern Pederasty, and Queer History* (Durham, NC: Duke University Press, 2017), 15.
13. Heather Love, *Feeling Backward: Loss and the Politics of Queer History* (Cambridge, MA: Harvard University Press, 2009), 24.

14. Leah Devun and Zeb Tortorici, "Trans, Time, and History," *Transgender Studies Quarterly* 5, no. 4 (November 2018): 522.
15. Love, *Feeling Backward*, 25.
16. Amin's reflections on Colette and Genet are exemplary in this regard. Kadji Amin, "Ghosting Transgender Historicity in Colette's *The Pure and the Impure*," *L'Esprit Créateur* 53, no. 1 (2013): 114–30; and Amin, *Disturbing Attachments*. See also Emma Heaney, *The New Woman: Literary Modernism, Queer Theory, and the Trans Feminine Allegory* (Chicago: Northwestern University Press, 2017).
17. For more comprehensive discussions on the history or the use of the concept, see, for instance, Manuel DeLanda, *A New Philosophy of Society: Assemblage Theory and Social Complexity* (London: Continuum, 2006); and Ian Buchanan, "Assemblage Theory, or, The Future of an Illusion," *Deleuze Studies* 11, no. 3 (2017): 457–74.
18. Gayle Rubin, "The Traffic in Women: Notes on the 'Political Economy' of Sex," in *The Second Wave: A Reader in Feminist Theory, New York*, ed. Linda Nicholson (New York: Routledge, 1997), 59.
19. Jasbir Puar, *Terrorist Assemblages: Homonationalism in Queer Times* (Durham, NC: Duke University Press, 2007), 195.
20. "Power has no essence, it is simply operational." Gilles Deleuze, *Foucault*, trans. Sean Hand (Minneapolis: University of Minnesota Press, 1988), 27.
21. On the relevance of the Deleuzo-Guattarian concept of assemblage for trans studies, see Abraham B. Weil, "Transmolecular Revolution," in *Deleuze, Guattari, and the Schizoanalysis of Trans Studies*, ed. Ciara Cremin (London: Bloomsbury, 2022), 129–50. See also Ciara Cremin on the relevance of Deleuzian schizoanalysis for trans studies: Ciara Cremin, introduction to *Deleuze, Guattari, and the Schizoanalysis of Trans Studies*, ed. Ciara Cremin (London: Bloomsbury, 2022), 1–8.
22. Gilles Deleuze and Félix Guattari, *Kafka: Towards a Minor Literature*, trans. Dana Polan (Minneapolis: University of Minnesota Press, 1986), 81.
23. Proust, *Sodom and Gomorrah*, 5.
24. Susan Stryker, "(De)Subjugated Knowledges: An Introduction to Transgender Studies," in *The Transgender Studies Reader*, ed. Susan Stryker and Stephen Whittle (New York: Routledge, 2006), 3.

25. Susan Stryker and Stephen Whittle, *The Transgender Studies Reader* (New York: Routledge, 2006), 53. Our contemporary use of the term can be traced to the work of John Money and his first experiments of "gender reassignment," tainted by a conservative and racist understanding of social roles.
26. Daniel Welzer Lang, "Introduction: Genre: Travaux en cours . . .," in *Aux frontières du genre*, ed. Arnaud Alessandrin (Paris: L'Harmattan, 2012), 13–14. For a comparison of French and American uses of the terms "gender" and "sexual difference" and the difficulties of their translation, see Chris Coffman, *Queer Traversals: Psychoanalytic Queer and Trans Theories* (London: Bloomsbury, 2022).
27. Simone de Beauvoir, *The Second Sex*, trans. Constance Borde and Sheila Malovany-Chevallier (New York: Vintage, 2011). On Beauvoir's use of the word "sex" and its legacy on French materialist feminism in relation to queer theory and trans studies, see Mat Fournier, "Trans Auntologies: *The Second Sex* and the Ethics of Transmasculinity," *Simone de Beauvoir Studies* 32, no 2 (2022): 265–85.
28. On the incompatibilities between a trans approach and Lacanian psychoanalysis, see Paul Preciado, *Can the Monster Speak? Report to an Academy of Psychoanalysts*, trans. Frank Wynne (Cambridge, MA: MIT Press, 2021). In *Queer Traversals*, Chris Coffman convincingly argues for a trans-positive use of Lacanian psychoanalysis, yet this path remains mostly ignored. On the prevalence of Lacanian psychoanalysis and its impact on French conversations around gender, see Camille Robcis, *The Law of Kinship: Anthropology, Psychoanalysis, and the Family in France* (Ithaca, NY: Cornell University Press, 2013); and Bruno Perreau, *Queer Theory: The French Response* (Stanford, CA: Stanford University Press, 2016).
29. See, for instance, George L. Mosse, *The Image of Man: The Creation of Modern Masculinity* (New York: Oxford University Press, 1996); on the French context specifically, see Judith Surkis, *Sexing the Citizen, Morality and Masculinity in France, 1870–1920* (Ithaca, NY: Cornell University Press, 2006); Mary Louise Roberts, *Civilization Without Sexes: Reconstructing Gender in Postwar France, 1917–1927* (Chicago: University of Chicago Press, 1994); Sandrine Sanos, *The Aesthetics of Hate: Far-Right Intellectuals, Antisemitism, and Gender in 1930s France* (Stanford, CA: Stanford University Press, 2013); and Dean, *The Frail Social Body*.

INTRODUCTION ~ 223

30. Murat, *La loi du genre*, 12–13. All translations of Murat are mine.
31. Murat, *La loi du genre*; emphasis mine.
32. Murat, *La loi du genre*, 24.
33. Kathryn Bond Stockton, *Gender(s)* (Cambridge, MA: MIT Press, 2021), 97.
34. Stockton, *Gender(s)*, 11.
35. Marquis Bey, *Cistem Failure: Essays on Blackness and Cisgender* (Durham, NC: Duke University Press, 2022).
36. See, for instance, Karl Heinrich Ulrichs, *The Riddle of "Man-Manly" Love: The Pioneering Work on Male Homosexuality*, trans. Michael A. Lombardi-Nash (Amherst: Prometheus, 1994). For recent discussions of sexology and early discussions of gender variance, see Heaney, *The New Woman*, 23–38; and Kahan, *The Book of Minor Perverts*.
37. Kahan, *The Book of Minor Perverts*, 46.
38. Hil Malatino, for instance, gives a compelling description of dysphoria in order to theorize trans affects, asserting both their durability and their legitimacy. Hil Malatino, *Side Affects: On Being Trans and Feeling Bad* (Minneapolis: University of Minnesota Press, 2022).
39. See, for instance, Eribon, *Insult and the Making of the Gay Self*; and Robin Brontsema, "A Queer Revolution: Reconceptualizing the Debate Over Linguistic Reclamation," *Colorado Research in Linguistics* 17 (June 2004).
40. APA, "What Is Gender Dysphoria?," August 2022, https://www.psychiatry.org/patients-families/gender-dysphoria/what-is-gender-dysphoria.
41. APA, "DSM-5-Gender-Dysphoria," https://www.psychiatry.org/File%20Library/Psychiatrists/Practice/DSM/APA_DSM-5-Gender-Dysphoria.pdf.
42. Norman M. Fisk, "Gender Dysphoria Syndrome: The Conceptualization That Liberalizes Indications for Total Gender Reorientation and Implies a Broadly Based Multi-Dimensional Rehabilitative Regimen," *Western Journal of Medicine* 120 (May 1974): 388–89.
43. Fisk, "Gender Dysphoria Syndrome," 388.
44. Malatino, *Side Affects*, 2–4.
45. The most distressful aspects of dysphoria have been stunningly described by Andrea Long Chu in her *New York Times* opinion piece

"My New Vagina Won't Make Me Happy," *New York Times*, November 24, 2018.
46. Cremin, *Deleuze*, 5. On the Deleuzo-Guattarian definition of affect, see Brian Massumi, *Parables for the Virtual: Movement, Affect, Sensation* (Durham, NC: Duke University Press, 2021), xxxiii–xli.
47. My use of the term is inspired by Sara Ahmed. See, for instance, Sara Ahmed, *Living a Feminist Life* (Durham, NC: Duke University Press, 2017), 65–88.
48. See Massumi, *Parables for the Virtual*, 48.
49. Michael Snediker, *Contingent Figure: Chronic Pain and Queer Embodiment* (Minneapolis: University of Minnesota Press, 2021), xiv.
50. Snediker, *Contingent Figure*, 62; emphasis mine.
51. Rachel Mesch, *Before Trans: Three Stories from Nineteenth-Century France* (Stanford, University of California Press, 2020), 8. On the difficulty and the necessity of historical discussions of trans lives and concepts, see also Leah DeVun and Zeb Tortorici, "Trans, Time, and History," *Transgender Studies Quarterly* 5, no. 4 (November 2018): 518–39.
52. Susan Stryker, Paisley Currah, and Lisa Moore, "Introduction: Trans, Trans-, or Transgender?," *Women's Studies Quarterly* 36, nos. 3–4 (2008): 12. Cameron Awkward-Rich warns against two opposite yet equally fraught approaches of trans studies: "transsexual theory" and "queer trans theory." The former limits itself to focusing on trans lives; the latter idealizes transness as a site of political contestation. Conceptualizing dysphoria opens a way beyond these dead-ends: dysphoria isn't a site of contestation but a modality of subjection. Cameron Awkward-Rich, *The Terrible We: Thinking with Trans Maladjustment* (Durham, NC: Duke University Press, 2022).
53. Jen Mannion, for instance, has shown how the modern category of trans can become a powerful tool in revealing the entanglement of gender and sexuality and the futility of attempting to analyze them separately when looking at the past. Jen Mannion, *Female Husbands: A Trans History* (Cambridge: Cambridge University Press, 2020).
54. Cael Keegan, for instance, argues that "in response to queer studies' investment in deconstructing the gender binary . . . trans* studies must turn inside out, articulating a constative *but* that asserts *but* gender is

real like this." Keegan underscores how queer theory's involvement against heteronormativity prevents the field from giving an authentic account of gender embodiment. Cáel M. Keegan, "Getting Disciplined: What's Trans* About Queer Studies Now?," *Journal of Homosexuality* 67 no. 3 (2020): 384–97.
55. Heaney, *The New Woman*, 255.
56. Karen Barad, *Meeting the Universe Halfway: Quantum Physics and the Entanglement of Matter and Meaning* (Durham, NC: Duke University Press, 2007), 46.
57. Alexandre Baril and Sarah Cavar underscore how critical disabilities studies can help apprehend trans lives and forms of embodiment. Sarah Cavar and Alexandre Baril, "Disability," in *Trans Bodies, Trans Selves: A Resource by and for Transgender Communities*, ed. Laura Erickson-Schroth (New York: Oxford University Press, 2022), 68–93.
58. Weil, "Transmolecular Revolution," 133; emphasis mine.
59. See, for instance, Judith Jack Halberstam, *In a Queer Time and Place: Transgender Bodies, Subcultural Lives* (New York: New York University Press, 2005); Elizabeth Freeman, *Time Binds: Queer Temporalities, Queer Histories* (Durham, NC: Duke University Press, 2010). I discuss queer and trans temporality in chapter 5.
60. In this regard, my approach is genealogical rather than historical: while I want to read modernist works both as assemblages and as part assemblages of their times (historical, contingent), what I'm interested in is, in Foucault's terms, the "history of the present."
61. Amin has shown how Genet used his popular origins and "honed" his performance as an outlaw to seduce this intellectual bourgeois elite. Amin, *Disturbing Attachments*, 2.
62. For a discussion of these entanglements, see, for instance, Bey, *Cistem Failures*; Marquis Bey, *Black Trans Feminism* (Durham, NC: Duke University Press, 2022).
63. I am indebted to Howard Chiang's concept of transtopia, which enables us to identify "different scales of gender transgression that are not always recognizable through the Western notion of transgender." While the body of work and of ideologies discussed here are precisely at the root of what might be referred to as "Western," using them to pinpoint different scales and forms of gender transgression allows us

to trace diversified and overlapping trajectories while avoiding teleological assumptions of linear progress. Howard Chiang, *Transtopia in the Sinophone Pacific* (New York: Columbia University Press, 2021), 4.

64. On Lili Elbe, see *Lili Elbe, Man Into Woman: The First Sex Change*, ed. Niels Hoyer, trans. James Stenning (London: Blue Boat, 2004); on Violette Norris, see Marie-Josèphe Bonnet, *Violette Norris, histoire d'une scandaleuse* (Paris: Perrin, 2011).
65. Michael Lucey, *Never Say I: Sexuality and the First Person in Colette, Gide, and Proust*, (Durham, NC: Duke University Press, 2006), 4.
66. See Lucey, *Never Say I*, 29–56.
67. Christian Gury, *L'extravagant Maurice Rostand* (Paris: Kimé, 1994), 43–50.
68. Michel Carassou, *René Crevel* (Paris: Fayard, 1989), 135–37.
69. Maurice Rostand, *La femme qui était en lui* (Paris: Ernest Flammarion, 1933).
70. André Gide, *Corydon*, trans. Richard Howard (New York: Farrar, Straus and Giroux, 1983–2015); André Gide, *Madeleine*, trans. Justin O'Brien (Chicago: Elephant Paperbacks, 1952–1989); André Gide, *The Immoralist*, trans. Richard Howard (New York: Knopf, 1970); André Gide, *Strait Is the Gate*, trans. Dorothy Bussy (New York: Knopf, 1949).
71. Bersani, *Homos*, 113–29; Jonathan Dollimore, *Sexual Dissidence: Augustine to Wilde, Freud to Foucault* (Oxford: Clarendon, 1991), 3–18; Michael Lucey, *Gide's Bent: Sexuality, Politics, Writing* (New York: Oxford University Press, 1995), 71.
72. Sedgwick, *Epistemology of the Closet*; Gilles Deleuze, *Proust and Signs: The Complete Text*, trans. Richard Howard (Minneapolis: University of Minnesota Press, 2000); Simon Porzak, "Inverts and Invertebrates: Darwin, Proust, and Nature's Queer Heterosexuality," *Diacritics* 41, no. 4 (2013): 6–34.
73. Sedgwick, *Epistemology of the Closet*, 220.
74. Deleuze, *Proust and Signs*, 170.
75. For a historical perspective on abjection in the context of the French interwar years, see Sanos, *The Aesthetics of Hate*, 75–117.
76. See, for instance, Halberstam, *In a Queer Time and Place*; Lee Edelman, *No Future, Queer Theory and the Death Drive* (Durham, NC: Duke University Press, 2004); and Freeman, *Time Binds*.

77. Raymond Radiguet, *The Devil in the Flesh*, trans. A. M. Sheridan Smith (London: Calder and Boyars, 1968); Colette, *The Vagabond*, trans. Enid McLeod (Westport, CT: Greenwood, 1974).
78. Jean Genet, *Our Lady of the Flowers*, trans. Bernard Frechtman (New York: Grove, 1991); René Crevel, *Mon corps et moi* (Toulouse: Editions Ombres, 2008).

I. A CASE STUDY: SCHIZOPHRENIC SPLITS IN *LA FEMME QUI ÉTAIT EN LUI*

1. Maurice Rostand, *La femme qui était en lui* (Paris: Ernest Flammarion, 1933). All translations of Rostand are mine.
2. Rostand, *La femme qui était en lui*, vii.
3. Léon Laleau, *Maurice Rostand intime* (Paris: Les Editions du Monde moderne, 1926), 101. Laleau compares Rostand to Musset and Shelly and calls him "the last of our romantics." See also Christian Gury, *L'extravagant Maurice Rostand. Un ami de Proust et de Cocteau* (Paris: Kimé, 1994), 76. Gury calls Rostand's work "anachronistic," which he explains by the fact that Rostand "was never able to free himself from his heredity." All translations of Gury and Laleau are mine.
4. Michael Lucey, *Never Say I: Sexuality and the First Person in Colette, Gide, and Proust*, (Durham, NC: Duke University Press, 2006).
5. Gury, *L'extravagant Maurice Rostand*, 18–19.
6. Gilles Barbedette and Michel Carassou, "Entretien avec André Du Dognon," in *Paris Gay 1925*, ed. Gilles Barbedette and Michel Carassou (Paris: Non Lieu, 2008), 61. My translation.
7. Maurice Rostand, *L'homme que j'ai tué* (Paris: Ernest Flammarion, 1925). Theater adaptation: Maurice Rostand, *L'homme que j'ai tué, pièce en trois actes et un prologue de Maurice Rostand d'après son roman* (Paris: Lang, Blanchong, 1930). *Broken Lullaby*, dir. Ernst Lubitsch (1932); *Frantz*, dir. François Ozon (2016).
8. Emma Heaney, *The New Woman: Literary Modernism, Queer Theory, and the Trans Feminine Allegory* (Chicago: Northwestern University Press, 2017).
9. Jean Rostand, *Les problèmes de l'hérédité et du sexe* (Paris: Rieder, 1933), 60, 63.

10. For a trans perspective on endocrinal research in the first decades of the twentieth century, see Kadji Amin, "Glands, Eugenics, and Rejuvenation in *Man Into Woman*: A Biopolitical Genealogy of Transsexuality," *Transgender Studies Quarterly* 5, no. 4 (2018): 589–605.
11. Radclyffe Hall, *The Well of Loneliness* (London: Jonathan Cape, 1928). Translated into French a year before the publication of Rostand's novel, Hall's novel was likely to be known by Rostand, who was frequenting the same Parisian circles as she was.
12. Radclyffe Hall, *Le puits de solitude*, trans. Léo Lack (Paris: Librairie Gallimard, 1932).
13. Heather Love, *Feeling Backward: Loss and the Politics of Queer History* (Cambridge, MA: Harvard University Press, 2009).
14. Guy de Maupassant, *The Horla*, trans. Charlotte Mandel (New York: Melville House, 2005).
15. Heaney, *The New Woman*, 3.
16. Yv E. Nay and Eliza Steinbock, "Critical Trans Studies in and Beyond Europe: Histories, Methods, and Institutions," *Transgender Studies Quarterly* 8, no. 2 (2021): 150.
17. On the relationship between the first diagnoses of schizophrenia and Stevenson's story, see Kieran McNally, *A Critical History of Schizophrenia* (London: Palgrave Macmillan, 2016), 21–22. For a trans perspective on dissociative identity disorder and its relationship to transness, see Cameron Awkward-Rich, *The Terrible We: Thinking with Trans Maladjustment* (Durham, NC: Duke University Press, 2022), 89–116.
18. Benjamin Kahan, *The Book of Minor Perverts: Sexology, Etiology, and the Emergences of Sexuality* (Chicago: University of Chicago Press, 2019), 26–44.
19. Laura Doan and Jay Prosser, "Introduction: Critical Perspectives Past and Present," in *Palatable Poison: Critical Perspectives on "The Well of Loneliness,"* ed. Laura Doan and Jay Prosser (New York: Columbia University Press, 2001), 22.
20. See, for instance, George L. Mosse, *The Image of Man: The Creation of Modern Masculinity* (New York: Oxford University Press, 1996). On the French context, see Mary Louise Roberts, *Civilization Without Sexes: Reconstructing Gender in Postwar France, 1917–1927* (Chicago: University of Chicago Press, 1994); and Judith Surkis, *Sexing the*

Citizen: Morality and Masculinity in France, 1870–1920 (Ithaca, NY: Cornell University Press, 2006).

21. Carolyn Dean, *The Frail Social Body: Pornography, Homosexuality, and Other Fantasies in Interwar France* (Berkeley: University of California Press, 2000), 7.
22. Roberts, *Civilization Without Sexes*, 102–9. Françoise Vergès has described how French natalist policies were only aimed at white women and benefited solely white families. Françoise Vergès, *The Womb of Women: Race, Capital, Feminism*, trans. Kaiama Glover (Durham, NC: Duke University Press, 2020).
23. Nay and Steinbock, "Critical Trans Studies in and Beyond Europe," 150.
24. Karl Heinrich Ulrichs, *The Riddle of "Man-Manly" Love: The Pioneering Work on Male Homosexuality*, trans. Michael A. Lombardi-Nash (Amherst, MA: Prometheus, 1994).
25. Robert Beachy, *Gay Berlin: Birthplace of a Modern Identity* (New York: Knopf, 2014), 6.
26. Heaney, *The New Woman*, 4.
27. Ulrichs, *The Riddle of "Man-Manly" Love*, 36.
28. Ulrichs thus initiated a long tradition of understanding transfemininity as "a woman's soul enclosed in a man's body." Heaney, *The New Woman*, 3.
29. Ulrichs, *The Riddle of "Man-Manly" Love*, 55, 56.
30. On *Männerbund*, see Beachy, *Gay Berlin*, 140–59.
31. André Gide, *Corydon*, trans. Richard Howard (New York: Farrar, Straus and Giroux, 1983–2015), xx.
32. This well-known argument in favor of sexual selection has been contradicted by contemporary biology. In bird species such as peacocks, it is actually the female, not the male, which evolved to lose its bright colors. Joan Roughgarden: *The Genial Gene: Deconstructing Darwinian Selfishness* (Oakland: University of California Press, 2009), 18–21.
33. Gide, *Corydon*, 69.
34. Heaney, *The New Woman*, 24–29.
35. Heaney, *The New Woman*, 6–7.
36. Rostand, *La femme qui était en lui*, 229, 234.
37. Elena Mancini, *Magnus Hirschfeld and the Quest for Sexual Freedom* (London: Palgrave Macmillan, 2010), 51.

38. On Deleuze's conception of the archipelago, see Masato Goda, "Archipelagic System and Deleuze's Philosophy," *Deleuze and Guattari Studies* 12, no. 2 (April 2018): 283–301.
39. Kadji Amin, "Taxonomically Queer? Sexology and New Queer, Trans, and Asexual Identities," *Gay and Lesbian Studies Quarterly* 29, no. 1 (2023): 91–107.
40. Rostand, *La femme qui était en lui*, 13, 12.
41. See, for instance, Rostand, *La femme qui était en lui*, 61.
42. Rostand, *La femme qui était en lui*, 30, 43, 62.
43. Rostand then specifies that the two Weiningers are not related. Rostand, *La femme qui était en lui*, 107.
44. Otto Weininger, *Sex and Character, Authorized Translation from the Sixth German Edition* (New York: G. P. Putnam's Sons, 1906), 89, 92.
45. Fittingly, the opera's plot is based on a tragic love triangle ending with the death of the two lovers.
46. Rostand, *La femme qui était en lui*, 92, 90, 94, 97.
47. Rostand, *La femme qui était en lui*, 72, 126, 73.
48. Rostand, *La femme qui était en lui*, 40, 41.
49. Rachel Mesch has explored the relationship between the decadent trope of monstrous femininity and gender variance through her study of the French decadent writer Rachilde. Rachel Mesch, *Before Trans: Three Gender Stories from Nineteenth-Century France* (Stanford, CA: Stanford University Press, 2021), 123–206. George Mosse has discussed the relationship between the decadent figures of femmes fatales, epitomized by Gustave Moreau's and Huysmans's Salomé, and the crisis of masculine identity at the turn of the century. Mosse, *The Image of Man*, 103.
50. Rostand, *La femme qui était en lui*, 103.
51. Rostand, *La femme qui était en lui*, 54.
52. Brian Glavey, *The Wallflower Avant-Garde: Modernism, Sexuality, and Queer Ekphrasis* (New York: Oxford University Press, 2016), 3.
53. On the European civil war, see Enzo Traverso, *Fire and Blood: The European Civil War, 1914–1945*, trans. David Fernbach (London: Verso, 2017).
54. Mary Louise Roberts has shown how French post–World War I images of femininity oscillate between figures of passivity and sacrifice, on the

one hand, and figures of transgression and danger, on the other. See Roberts, *Civilization Without Sexes*. For a broad discussion of the creation of modern masculinity and the crisis associated with it, see Mosse, *The Image of Man*. For an extensive discussion of the turn-of-the-century masculinity crisis in the French context, see Surkis, *Sexing the Citizen*.

55. Dean, *The Frail Social Body*, 14.
56. Roberts, *Civilization Without Sexes*, 31.
57. Traverso, *Fire and Blood*, 28.
58. Mosse, *The Image of Man*, 115, 110.
59. Traverso, *Fire and Blood*, 210.
60. Maurice Rostand, *Confession d'un demi-siècle* (Paris: La Jeune Parque, 1948), 196.
61. "War met me while I was in boarding school." Rostand, *La femme qui était en lui*, 67.
62. Sandrine Sanos, *The Aesthetics of Hate: Far-Right Intellectuals, Antisemitism, and Gender in 1930s France* (Stanford, CA: Stanford University Press, 2013).
63. Rostand, *La femme qui était en lui*, 35–36.
64. Rostand, *La femme qui était en lui*, 68.
65. Similarly, the novel's insistence on tender fatherly loves reverses the trope of maternal attachment and its resulting in boys' effeminacy, a blame that had been cast repeatedly on Rostand's relationship with his own mother. Gury, *L'extravagant Maurice Rostand*, 15–17.
66. Gury, *L'extravagant Maurice Rostand*, 27–30.
67. Rostand, *Confession*, 196. Maurice Rostand also states that his father was eventually killed by his patriotism, as he likely contracted the influenza that killed him when he attended the celebrations for the 1918 victory.
68. Rostand, *Confession*, 281.
69. Gury, *L'extravagant Maurice Rostand*, 74.
70. Rostand, *La femme qui était en lui*, 233.
71. Rostand, *La femme qui était en lui*, 68, 101, 67. Earth, *la terre*, is feminine in French.
72. Maurice Rostand, *Le pilori* (Paris: Flammarion, 1921).
73. Rostand, *Le pilori*, 95.

74. François Porché, *L'amour qui n'ose pas dire son nom* (Paris: Grasset, 1927).
75. Rostand, *La femme qui était en lui*, 13.
76. Haas Heye was indeed married to the daughter of Prince Philipp of Eulenburg, who was tried in 1907 after accusations of homosexuality, among a group of Kaiser Wilhelm II's cabinet members. The Eulenburg affair had significant repercussions throughout Europe.
77. Rostand, *La femme qui était en lui*, 103. Haas Heye was conscripted in 1916 but released a few months later. He did spend the rest of the war in Basel, where he organized fashion shows.
78. Dean has shown how homosexuality was described as a threat to the social body. Dean, *The Frail Social Body*, 14, 130. But same-sex love wasn't the only form of resistance opposed to the French state's enforcement of heterosexual familialism. Anarchists, feminists, and pacifists concurred in advocating for antifamilialist sexual practices. The anarchist E. Armand, for instance, promoted in his novels a "loving comradeship" and advocated in favor of Malthusianism and contraception, because fewer births meant less cannon fodder for the nation's armies. In the same way, the surrealist avant-garde saw free love as a revolutionary force able to disrupt the bourgeois order. E. Armand, *La révolution sexuelle et la camaraderie amoureuse* (Paris: Zones, 2009); and Xavière Gauthier, *Surréalisme et sexualité* (Paris: Gallimard, 1971).
79. Rostand, *La femme qui était en lui*, 104, 66. Silvestre de Solm is the narrator's first love.
80. Rostand, *La femme qui était en lui*, 39, 16, 188, 234.
81. Elsa Dorlin, *La matrice de la race. Généalogie sexuelle et coloniale de la nation française* (Paris: La Découverte, 2009), 14. My translation.
82. Rostand, *Confession*, 266–68.
83. Pascale Barthélémy, "1931: L'empire aux portes de Paris," in *Histoire mondiale de la France*, ed. Patrick Boucheron (Paris: Seuil, 2017), 818–23. My translation.
84. Ann Laura Stoler, *Carnal Knowledge and Imperial Power: Race and the Intimate in Colonial Rule* (Berkeley: University of California Press, 2002), 42, 62–65.
85. Siobhan B. Sommerville, *Queering the Color Line: Race and the Invention of Homosexuality in American Culture* (Durham, NC: Duke University Press, 2000), 15.

86. Kyla Schuller, *The Biopolitics of Feeling: Race, Sex, and Science in the Nineteenth Century* (Durham, NC: Duke University Press, 2018), 16. Theories of gender deviance either endorsed the racial divide or ignored it. See Heike Bauer, *The Hirschfeld Archives: Violence, Death, and Modern Queer Culture* (Philadelphia: Temple University Press, 2017).
87. Rostand, *La femme qui était en lui*, 105, 234, 124, 230.
88. Rostand, *La femme qui était en lui*, 155.
89. Xine Yao, *Disaffected: The Culture of Unfeeling in Nineteenth-Century America* (Durham, NC: Duke University Press, 2021), 5.
90. Rostand, *La femme qui était en lui*, 106.
91. Weininger, *Sex and Character*, 338. Weininger's theories were adopted by Nazi thinkers including Hans Blüher, the founder of the youth movement Wandervogel, who popularized the expression of "male bonding" (*Männerbund*). On the relationship between virile homoeroticism and fascism, see Andrew Hewitt, *Political Inversions: Homosexuality, Fascism, and the Modernist Imaginary* (Stanford, CA: Stanford University Press, 1996). On the French context, see Sanos, *The Aesthetics of Hate*.
92. Rostand, *La femme qui était en lui*, 232.
93. Rostand, *La femme qui était en lui*, 103.
94. Foucault points out how the emergence of the psychiatrist as "medical character" accompanied the creation of modern psychiatry. Michel Foucault, *History of Madness*, trans. Jean Khalfa and Jonathan Murphy (New York: Routledge, 2013), 503–10. See also Camille Robcis, *Disalienation: Politics, Philosophy, and Radical Psychiatry in Postwar France* (Chicago: University of Chicago, 2021), 122–23.
95. Rostand, *La femme qui était en lui*, 106.
96. Linda De Roche, "A Wizard Cultivator: Zelda Fitzgerald's *Save Me the Waltz* as Asylum Autobiography," *Tulsa Studies in Women's Literature* 11, no. 2 (1992): 247–64. De Roche describes how Switzerland became a therapeutic destination where those in bourgeois circles sought help for their mental health troubles.
97. McNally, *A Critical History of Schizophrenia*, 23–25.
98. Rostand, *La femme qui était en lui*, 110, 119–20, 12.
99. Rostand, *La femme qui était en lui*, 115, 119.

100. To this day, transgender individuals are more likely to be diagnosed with schizophrenia. Sebastian M. Barr, Dominic Roberts, and Katharine N. Thakkar, "Psychosis in Transgender and Gender Nonconforming Individuals: A Review of the Literature and a Call for More Research," *Psychiatry Research* 306 (December 2021).
101. Kahan, *The Book of Minor Perverts*, 15.
102. Glavey, *The Wallflower Avant-Garde*, 3.
103. Ciara Cremin, "Introduction," in *Deleuze, Guattari, and the Schizoanalysis of Trans Studies*, ed. Ciara Cremin (London: Bloomsbury, 2022) 3.
104. Gilles Deleuze and Félix Guattari, *Anti-Oedipus: Capitalism and Schizophrenia*, trans. Robert Hurley, Mark Seem, and Helen R. Lane (Minneapolis: University of Minnesota Press, 1983), 9–16.
105. Rostand, *La femme qui était en lui*, 42 (Sylvestre's "dark eyes"); 109 (the doctor's eyes); 63 (Robert's eyes).
106. Rostand, *La femme qui était en lui*, 64, 169–170.
107. Rostand, *La femme qui était en lui*, 64.
108. Hil Malatino, *Side Affects: On Being Trans and Feeling Bad* (Minneapolis: University of Minnesota Press, 2022), 3.

2. GIDE'S FAILED MARRIAGES

1. André Gide, *Corydon*, trans. Richard Howard (New York: Farrar, Straus and Giroux, 1983–2015), xix.
2. Married in 1895 to his cousin Madeleine Rondeaux, Gide reportedly never consummated his marriage, which lasted until Madeleine's death in 1938.
3. André Gide, *Fruits of the Earth*, trans. Dorothy Bussy (London: Secker and Warburg, 1949–1952).
4. André Gide, *Madeleine*, trans. Justin O'Brien (Chicago: Elephant Paperbacks, 1952–1989).
5. Michael Lucey, *Gide's Bent: Sexuality, Politics, Writing* (New York: Oxford University Press, 1995), 71.
6. Jonathan Dollimore, *Sexual Dissidence: Augustine to Wilde, Freud to Foucault* (Oxford: Clarendon, 1991), 40.
7. See, for instance, Emma Heaney, *The New Woman: Literary Modernism, Queer Theory, and the Trans Feminine Allegory* (Chicago: Northwestern

University Press, 2017), 38–39. Heaney argues that queer theory is rooted in a misogyny, and particularly a trans misogyny, inherited from early-twentieth-century gay male theorists of homosexuality, including Gide.

8. Lucey, *Gide's Bent*, 22.
9. Leo Bersani, *Homos* (Cambridge, MA: Harvard University Press, 1995), 118.
10. André Gide, *The Immoralist*, trans. Richard Howard (New York: Knopf, 1970).
11. Dollimore, *Sexual Dissidence*, 44.
12. Bersani, *Homos*, 123.
13. Bersani, *Homos*, 128.
14. Mat Fournier, "Lines of Flight," *Transgender Studies Quarterly* 1, no. 1 (2014): 121–22.
15. Gilles Deleuze, *Two Regimes of Madness: Texts and Interviews, 1975–1995*, trans. Ames Hodges and Mike Taormina (New York: Semiotext(e), 2007), 124–25.
16. André Gide, *If It Die*, trans. Dorothy Bussy (Middlesex: Penguin, 1977–1982), 256–57.
17. Gide, *If It Die*, 236.
18. Davida Pine, *The Marriage Paradox: Modernist Novels and the Cultural Imperative to Marry* (Gainesville: University Press of Florida, 2005), 3.
19. Judith Surkis, *Sexing the Citizen, Morality and Masculinity in France, 1870–1920* (Ithaca, NY: Cornell University Press, 2006), 3.
20. Surkis, *Sexing the Citizen*, 18.
21. Carolyn Dean, *The Frail Social Body: Pornography, Homosexuality, and Other Fantasies in Interwar France* (Berkeley: University of California Press, 2000), 5.
22. André Gide, *Strait Is the Gate*, trans. Dorothy Bussy (New York: Knopf, 1949).
23. Lucey, *Gide's Bent*, 69, 70.
24. André Gide, *Travels in the Congo*, trans. Dorothy Bussy (New York: Knopf, 1930).
25. Kadji Amin, *Disturbing Attachments: Genet, Modern Pederasty, and Queer Theory* (Durham, NC: Duke University Press, 2017), 4.
26. Bersani, *Homos*, 113.

27. Gide, *Corydon*, xv, xx.
28. Gide identifies three distinct types of male homosexuals: the "pederast," "who ... falls in love with young boys"; the "sodomite," "whose desire is addressed to other men"; and the "invert," who "assumes the role of a woman and desires to be possessed." The last, Gide states, "alone deserved the reproach of moral or intellectual deformation ... that are commonly addressed to all homosexuals." Gide further notes that he himself is a pederast, while "the sodomites are more numerous." André Gide, *Journals*, vol. 1: *1889–1949*, trans. Justin O'Brien (New York: Knopf, 1956).
29. Elena Mancini, *Magnus Hirschfeld and the Quest for Sexual Freedom* (New York: Palgrave Macmillan, 2010), 51.
30. Lucey convincingly refutes the hypothesis that *Corydon* might be apprehended as ironic. Lucey, *Gide's Bent*, 69.
31. In *Corydon* Gide uses the term "uranism" indiscriminately from homosexuality, pederasty, and Greek love. See Richard Howard's preface in Gide, *Corydon*, xiv. For a history of the term "uranism" and Gide's use of it, see Elisabeth Ladenson, *Proust's Lesbianism* (Ithaca, NY: Cornell University Press, 1999), 39.
32. On the accuracy and the sources of Gide's representation of ancient Greece in *Corydon*, see Patrick Pollard, *André Gide: The Homosexual Moralist* (New Haven, CT: Yale University Press, 1991), 141–75. On the influence of German scholarship and particularly Winckelmann's view of pederasty, see Pollard, *André Gide*, 283–84.
33. Gide, *Corydon*, 42, 44.
34. Gide, *Corydon*, 117, 94–95; emphasis in the original.
35. Gide, *Corydon*, 116, 118. On pederasty and pedagogy in Gide, see Ian Fleishman, "Pederasty and/as Narrative Form," *French Forum* 45, no 2 (2020): 155–69.
36. Gide, *Corydon*, 82, 42.
37. James Baldwin, *Collected Essays* (New York: Library of America, 1998), 231.
38. *Madeleine* was published in French under the title *Et nunc manet in te*, from a poem attributed to Virgil. Gide, *Madeleine*, 3.
39. Gide, *Madeleine*, 12, 38, 16.
40. Gide, *Madeleine*, 16.

41. He himself, after all, could perform well enough to have a daughter with another woman. Catherine Gide (1923–2013) was the biological daughter of André Gide and Elisabeth Van Rysselberghe. Gide acknowledged paternity after Madeleine's death.
42. Gide, *Madeleine*, 20, 16.
43. Gide, *Madeleine*, 16–17.
44. Lucey, *Gide's Bent*, 56.
45. Gide, *Madeleine*, 39.
46. Gide, *Madeleine*, 34, 37.
47. Gide, *Madeleine*, 41, 42, 19.
48. Baldwin, *Collected Essays*, 233–34.
49. Gide, *If It Die*, 305.
50. Gide, *Travels in the Congo*.
51. Lucey, *Gide's Bent*, 145, 179.
52. Julien Green, *Journal intégral 1919–1940* (Paris: Robert Laffont, 2019).
53. Green, *Journal intégral*, 1069. My translation. Green reports the conversation on January 6, 1937, but doesn't mention when it actually took place. "Gide me parlait des exigences sexuelles d'Allégret pendant leur voyage en Afrique. Il fallait à Marc des jeunes filles, de vraies jeunes filles et non des putains, dans chaque village. Et cela se passait dans la tente commune, aux pieds de Gide, Marc baisant sur le sol, pour plus de commodité. 'Et, me disait Gide, vous n'imaginez pas les difficultés qu'offre l'amour dit normal. C'est exactement chercher à ouvrir une boîte de sardines dont on a perdu la clé. Alors que pour nous, la chose est si simple !'"
54. On the French context, see, for instance, Christelle Taraud, *La prostitution coloniale. Algérie, Tunisie, Maroc (1830–1962)* (Paris: Payot, 2003).
55. Alan Sheridan, *André Gide: A Life in the Present* (Cambridge, MA: Harvard University Press, 1999), 406.
56. Marc Allégret, *Carnets du Congo. Voyage avec Gide* (Paris: Presse du CNRS, 1987), 108. The 1987 preface to the *Carnets*, written by Daniel Durosay, complacently muses on "these very young girls . . . teenagers . . . barely developed" and pictures Allégret as a Don Juan. Allégret, *Carnets*, 39.

57. GrandPalaisRmn, "About Us," n.d., https://www.photo.rmn.fr/CS.aspx?VP3=SearchResult&VBID=2CMFCI6Z5HLVMZ&SMLS=1&RW=2310&RH=1257.
58. The same argument, describing heterosexual sex as unnatural, was already made in *Corydon*. Men wouldn't be able to find "the specific gesture" if they weren't instructed by women. Gide, *Corydon*, 90.
59. Sheridan, *André Gide*, 186.
60. Gide, *The Immoralist*, 3.
61. As Bersani notes, Michel finds himself surrounded by gay men who all are serving the state, including Ménalque. Michel's is the only case for whom sexual preference seems to involve "renunciation of citizenship." Bersani, *Homos*, 118.
62. Baldwin, *Collected Essays*, 232, 235.
63. Bersani, *Homos*, 113, 116–17.
64. Bersani, *Homos*, 116, 118.
65. Gide, *The Immoralist*, 40–41.
66. Bersani, *Homos*, 119. Author's emphasis.
67. Gide, *If It Die*, 286–87.
68. Bersani, *Homos*, 122–23.
69. Lawrence Schehr, *French Gay Modernism* (Chicago: University of Chicago Press, 2004), 90.
70. Schehr, *French Gay Modernism*, 91.
71. Bersani, *Homos*, 125.
72. Baldwin, *Collected Essays*, 234.
73. Heaney, *The New Woman*, 38–39.
74. Farid Laroussi, *Postcolonial Counterpoints: Orientalism, France, and the Maghreb* (Toronto: University of Toronto Press, 2016), 104.
75. Laroussi, *Postcolonial Counterpoints*, 105.
76. Gide, *If It Die*, 240, 238–39.
77. Laroussi, *Postcolonial Counterpoints*, 89.
78. Dollimore, *Sexual Dissidence*, 17.
79. Laroussi, *Postcolonial Counterpoints*, 92, 99.
80. Sara Ahmed, *Queer Phenomenology: Orientations, Objects, Others* (Durham, NC: Duke University Press, 2006), 7.
81. Gide, *Fruits of the Earth*, 26.
82. Gide, *The Immoralist*, 11.

83. Gide, *If It Die*, 239.
84. Gide, *The Immoralist*, 45.
85. Laroussi, *Postcolonial Counterpoints*, 104.
86. Gide, *Madeleine*, 32.
87. According to his friend Roger Martin Du Gard, Gide was a hypochondriac, constantly discussing the dangers threatening his health and afflicted by an obsessive fear of drafts. Roger Martin du Gard, *Notes sur André Gide, 1913–1951* (Paris: Gallimard, 1951).
88. Gide, *If It Die*, 288.
89. Bersani, *Homos*, 119.
90. Gide, *If It Die*, 345.
91. Lucey's *Gide's Bent*, for instance, doesn't refer to it.
92. Sheridan, *André Gide*, 232.
93. Gide, *The Immoralist*, 169.
94. Gide, *Madeleine*, 5.
95. Gide, *If It Die*, 200–12.
96. Gide, *Strait Is the Gate*, 32, 39, 231, 186.
97. Emily S. Apter, *André Gide and the Codes of Homotextuality*, Stanford French and Italian Studies 48 (Stanford, CA: Stanford University Press, 1987), 105.
98. Lucile's adultery is based on the story of Madeleine's mother, mentioned in *Madeleine* as the "tragic event" and moment when Madeleine "began to play her salutary role in [Gide's] life." Gide, *Madeleine*, 10–11. But the consequences on their personalities are opposite: according to her husband, "that painful secret . . . marked [Madeleine] . . . for life. All her life long she remained like a child who has had a fright." Gide, *Madeleine*, 14. While Madeleine becomes fearful, Alissa subsumes the fear into a sublime rejection of sex.
99. Gide, *Strait Is the Gate*, 15.
100. See, for instance, figures 18, 19, and 20 in Robin Mitchell, *Vénus Noire: Black Women and Colonial Fantasies in Nineteenth-Century France* (Athens: University of Georgia Press, 2020), 113–15.
101. Mitchell, *Vénus Noire*, 137.
102. Mitchell, *Vénus Noire*, 107.
103. Gide, *Strait Is the Gate*, 17.
104. Gide, *Strait Is the Gate*, 26.

105. Gide, *Strait Is the Gate*, 19.
106. Margaret Gray sees in Juliette, Alissa's sister, a true embodiment of femininity. Alissa, who is also in love with Jérôme but sacrifices herself by entering a loveless marriage and becoming, in turn, a mother, thus exposes Jérôme and Alissa's relationship as masquerade. Gray's analysis emphasizes the assimilation of spirituality and masculinity. Margaret Gray, *Stolen Limelight: Gender, Display, and Displacement in Modern Fiction in French* (Chicago: University of Chicago Press, 2022).
107. Gide, *Strait Is the Gate*, 119, 67, 66, 72–73, 21.
108. Gide, *If It Die*, 236.
109. Bersani, *Homos*, 118.
110. Bersani, *Homos*, 123.
111. Gide, *Strait Is the Gate*, 225.
112. Gide, *Fruits of the Earth*, 20.
113. Gide, *Strait Is the Gate*, 119.

3. CROSS-POLLINATION: A TRANS READING OF MARCEL PROUST

1. Marcel Proust, *In Search of Lost Time*, vol. 4: *Sodom and Gomorrah*, trans. C. K. Scott Moncrieff, Terence Kilmartin, and D. J. Enright (New York: Random House, 1992–2003).
2. Gilles Deleuze, *Proust and Signs: The Complete Text*, trans. Richard Howard (Minneapolis: University of Minnesota Press, 2000); Eve Kosofsky Sedgwick, *Epistemology of the Closet* (Berkeley: University of California Press, 1990). Sedgwick often returned to Proust, whom she discusses in several of the essays posthumously gathered in *The Weather in Proust* (Durham, NC: Duke University Press, 2011). This chapter, however, only refers to "The Spectacle of the Closet," the chapter on Proust in the *Epistemology of the Closet*.
3. Anne Sauvagnargues, *Deleuze and Art*, trans. Samantha Bankston (London: Bloomsbury Academic, 2013), 109.
4. Sedgwick, *Epistemology of the Closet*, 3. Whether in *Proust and Signs* or in *Logic of Sense*, Deleuze never uses the term "epistemology," which bears a different meaning in French than in English and refers to critical examination of sciences rather than to a theory of knowledge.

Furthermore, while Sedgwick's use of the term in her *Epistemology of the Closet* is based on a Foucauldian approach, it doesn't coincide with Foucault's notion of "episteme" as conceptualized in *The Order of Things*: "the middle region" where body, words, and things connect and become intertwined in our perception. Michel Foucault, *The Order of Things: An Archeology of the Human Sciences*, trans. Alan Sheridan (New York: Random House, 1994), xxiii. In this regard, Foucault's *episteme* is more comparable to the Deleuzian notion of assemblage.

5. Gilles Deleuze and Félix Guattari, *What Is Philosophy*, trans. Hugh Tomlinson and Graham Burchell (New York: Columbia University Press, 1994), 63.
6. Emma Heaney, *The New Woman: Literary Modernism, Queer Theory, and the Trans Feminine Allegory* (Chicago: Northwestern University Press, 2017).
7. Elisabeth Ladenson, *Proust's Lesbianism* (Ithaca, NY: Cornell University Press, 1999); Michael Lucey, *Never Say I: Sexuality and the First Person in Colette, Gide, and Proust* (Durham, NC: Duke University Press, 2006); and Simon Porzak, "Inverts and Invertebrates: Darwin, Proust, and Nature's Queer Heterosexuality," *Diacritics* 41, no. 4 (2013): 6–34.
8. Leo Bersani, *Homos* (Cambridge, MA: Harvard University Press, 1995); Didier Eribon, *Insult and the Making of the Gay Self*, trans. Michael Lucey (Durham, NC: Duke University Press, 2004).
9. Porzak, "Inverts and Invertebrates," 11.
10. Eliza Steinbock, *Shimmering Images: Trans Cinema, Embodiment, and the Aesthetics of Change* (Durham, NC: Duke University Press, 2019).
11. André Gide, *Journals*, vol. 2: *1914–1927*, trans. Justin O'Brien (New York: Knopf, 1948), 276–77.
12. Bersani, *Homos*, 139; Eribon, *Insult*, 88.
13. Lucey, *Never Say I*, 221.
14. Proust, *Sodom and Gomorrah*, 19.
15. Bersani, *Homos*, 138. Proust confirms this view. See Laure Murat, *La loi du genre. Une histoire culturelle du 'troisième sexe'* (Paris: Fayard, 2006), 316.
16. Eribon, *Insult*, 82, 84–86.
17. Heaney, *The New Woman*, 4.

18. Heaney, *The New Woman*, 205.
19. Deleuze and Guattari, *What Is Philosophy*, 63.
20. Jack Halberstam, *Female Masculinity* (Durham, NC: Duke University Press, 1998).
21. "Having . . . been invested, by a persecution similar to that of Israel, with the physical and moral characteristics of a race." Proust, *Sodom and Gomorrah*, 22. The persecution creates the race, not the other way around.
22. Proust, *Sodom and Gomorrah*, 20.
23. The parallels between antisemitism and the situation of gay men run through the entire narrative. *Sodom and Gomorrah*'s opening, for instance, explicitly mentions the Dreyfus affair. Bracing himself for courage while trying to get closer to Charlus and Jupien, the young narrator reminds himself that he "just fought several duels unafraid on account of the Dreyfus case." Proust, *Sodom and Gomorrah*, 11. In the following chapter, the adult narrator, who is attending a party and realizes that a number of guests belong to the cursed race, is told in secret that the Prince de Guermantes has disclosed a sympathy for Dreyfus. Lucey underscores how this economy of secret and disclosure is central to Proust's ability to describe homosexuality in the first person. Lucey, *Never Say I*, 215–17.
24. Proust, *Sodom and Gomorrah*, 1, 12–13, 16–49. Châtellerault's presence at the party and his arrival at the same time as the narrator are later additions to the manuscript. Lucey demonstrates how gay characters and their connection to the narrator are carefully woven into the narrative. The composition reveals how the part played by Charlus became more significant, as well as how Proust created narrative threads connecting him to a series of characters, including the narrator. Lucey, *Never Say I*, 220–22, 228–29.
25. Murat, *La loi du genre*, 320.
26. In addition to Charlus and Jupien, we can mention Saint-Loup, Morel, Legrandin, Albertine, Andrée, the Duc de Chatellerault, the Prince de Guermantes . . . along with Odette, Gilberte, and la Verdurin, who are said to have had affairs with women.
27. André Gide, *Journal 1889–1939* (Paris: Gallimard, 1948), 694. The English translation uses the word "homosexuality," whereas Gide uses

both the term *homosexuel* (as an adjective) and the word *uranisme* in the same paragraph.
28. Murat, *La loi du genre*, 316, 318.
29. Gilles Deleuze and Félix Guattari, *A Thousand Plateaus*, trans. Brian Massumi (Minneapolis: University of Minnesota Press, 1987).
30. Proust, *Sodom and Gomorrah*, 4–5.
31. Proust, *Sodom and Gomorrah*, 4–5.
32. Proust, *Sodom and Gomorrah*, 5.
33. Alfred de Vigny, *Destinées* (Paris: Michel Lévy Frères, 1864), 81–91.
34. "La Femme aura Gomorrhe et l'Homme aura Sodome / Et, se jetant de loin un regard irrité, / Les deux sexes mourront chacun de son côté." Quoted in Proust, *Sodom and Gomorrah*, 21.
35. Ladenson, *Proust's Lesbianism*, 12. With the exception of Mme Vaugoubert. Ladenson also notes that Albertine herself begins to appear "mannish" to the narrator once he ceases to be interested in her.
36. Ladenson also exposes genealogical motives for the fact that *Sodom and Gomorrah* focuses primarily on Sodom. The two succeeding volumes, *The Captive* and *The Fugitive*, "were originally conceived as parts three and four of *Sodom and Gomorrah*. . . . The fact that what Proust intended to include under the rubric *Sodom and Gomorrah* kept growing in scope, along with the role of Albertine, suggest both the capital importance of what the title designates and also the degree to which the double-barreled name was meant to correspond to a double-barreled inquiry: Sodom, represented chiefly in the form of Charlus's adventures, and Gomorrah, represented by Albertine and her cohorts." Ladenson, *Proust's Lesbianism*, 32.
37. Ladenson, *Proust's Lesbianism*, 32.
38. Ladenson, *Proust's Lesbianism*, 10.
39. Gide, *Journal*, 694.
40. Sedgwick, *Epistemology of the Closet*, 234.
41. Proust, *Sodom and Gomorrah*, 5.
42. Ladenson, *Proust's Lesbianism*, 47, 43.
43. Quoted in Ladenson, *Proust's Lesbianism*, 48.
44. Murat, *La loi du genre*, 326.
45. Proust, *Sodom and Gomorrah*, 44.
46. Emphasis in original.

47. Sedgwick, *Epistemology of the Closet*, 219.
48. Porzak, "Inverts and Invertebrates," 12, 15, 13.
49. Proust, *Sodom and Gomorrah*, 38.
50. Sam See follows a different avenue, emphasizing Darwin's claims that "biological forms undergo . . . a perpetual process of change." Darwin, therefore, describes a "nature without end" whose variations are incompatible with the heteronormative account of sexual selection. This emphasis on change, along with the queer aesthetics of feeling See derives from it, is reflected in Proust's use of botanical metaphors throughout his entire work. Sam See, "Charles Darwin, Queer Theorist," in *Queer Natures, Queer Mythologies*, ed. Christopher Looby and Michael North (New York: Fordham University Press, 2020), 20.
51. Proust, *Sodom and Gomorrah*, 36.
52. Proust, *Sodom and Gomorrah*, 37.
53. "Reverie," 1890: "Since here on earth each soul / Gives someone / Its music, its ardour, / Or its perfume." Trans. Richard Stokes, in Graham Johnson and Richard Stokes, eds., *A French Song Companion* (Oxford: Oxford University Press, 2000). The poem, originally untitled, was part of Victor Hugo's 1837 volume *Les voix intérieures*.
54. Eve Kosofsky Sedgwick, *Epistémologie du placard*, trans. Maxime Cervulle (Paris: Editions Amsterdam, 2008). Deleuze committed suicide in 1995.
55. Deleuze, *Proust and Signs*, 4.
56. Sedgwick, *Epistemology of the Closet*, 220.
57. Porzak, "Inverts and Invertebrates," 7.
58. Deleuze, *Proust and Signs*, 15.
59. Anne Sauvagnargues points out how Deleuze's use of the terms "semantics" and "semiotics" reflects "a philosophy of signs that is irreducible to the linguistic sphere and the rules of language and linguistics." Anne Sauvagnargues, *Deleuze and Art*, trans. Samantha Bankston (London: Bloomsbury, 2013), 4–5.
60. Sauvagnargues, *Deleuze and Art*, 4–5.
61. Deleuze, *Proust and Signs*, 4.
62. Lucey, *Never Say I*, 247–48.
63. Deleuze, *Proust and Signs*, 172.
64. Sedgwick, *Epistemology of the Closet*, 223.

65. Deleuze, *Proust and Signs*, 45.
66. Proust, *Sodom and Gomorrah*, 13.
67. Steinbock, *Shimmering Images*, 12.
68. Sauvagnargues, *Deleuze and Art*, 78.
69. Deleuze, *Proust and Signs*, 128. I quote Sauvagnargues and Bankston's modified translation.
70. Deleuze, *Proust and Signs*, 135.
71. Deleuze, *Proust and Signs*, 136–37. My emphasis.
72. For a trans exploration of the Deleuzo-Guattarian concept of transversality, see Abraham B. Weil, "Psychoanalysis and Trans*versality," in *Transgender Studies Quarterly* 4, nos. 3–4 (2017): 639–46.
73. Mat Fournier, "Lines of Flight," in *Transgender Studies Quarterly* 1, nos. 1–2 (2014): 121–22.
74. Steinbock, *Shimmering Images*, ix.
75. Murat, *La loi du genre*, 332.
76. Deleuze, *Proust and Signs*, 4.

4. ON QUEER CROOKS, ABJECTION, AND MOVING SIDEWAYS: MAURICE SACHS'S DYSPHORIC SMUGGLING

1. Jean Cocteau, *Journal d'un inconnu* (1953), quoted in *Cahiers de L'Herne: Maurice Sachs*, ed. Henri Raczymow (Paris: Editions de L'Herne, 2016), 42. All translations of *Cahiers de L'Herne* are mine.
2. For a detailed bibliography of Sachs's work, see Henri Raczymow, *Maurice Sachs, ou Les travaux forcés de la frivolité* (Paris: Gallimard, 1988), 485–86. All translations of Raczymow are mine.
3. For a historical perspective on abjection in the context of the French interwar years, see Sandrine Sanos, *The Aesthetics of Hate: Far-Right Intellectuals, Antisemitism, and Gender in 1930s France* (Stanford, CA: Stanford University Press, 2013), 75–117.
4. See, for, instance Enzo Traverso, *Fire and Blood: The European Civil War, 1914–1945*, trans. David Fernbach (New York: Verso, 2017), 210.
5. Alan Sheridan, *André Gide: A Life in the Present* (Cambridge, MA: Harvard University Press, 1999), 186.

6. Maurice Sachs, *Witches' Sabbath*, trans. Richard Howard (Sacramento, CA: Spurl, 2020), 162.
7. April 1934. Quoted in Raczymow, *Maurice Sachs*, 223. Author's emphasis.
8. David M. Halperin and Valerie Traub, *Gay Shame* (Chicago: University of Chicago Press, 2009), 4.
9. For discussions of abjection, see Didier Eribon, *Hérésies. Essais sur la théorie de la sexualité* (Paris: Fayard, 2003); and David M. Halperin, *What Do Gay Men Want? An Essay on Sex, Risk, and Subjectivity* (Ann Harbor: University of Michigan Press, 2007). All translations of Eribon are mine.
10. Raczymow has shown how Sachs's enrollment by the Gestapo was motivated by opportunism, not inner antisemitism. Raczymow, *Maurice Sachs*, 424–32.
11. Raczymow, *Maurice Sachs*, 427.
12. Violette Leduc, *In the Prison of her Skin*, trans. Derek Coltman (London: Hart-Davis, 1970); Violette Leduc, *La Batarde*, trans. Derek Coltman (London: Dalkey Archive, 2003); André du Dognon and Philippe Monceau, *Le dernier sabbat de Maurice Sachs* (Paris: Le Sagittaire, 1979) (all translations of Du Dognon and Manceau are mine); Patrick Modiano, *The Occupation Trilogy: La Place de l'Etoile, The Night Watch, Ring Roads*, trans. Caroline Hillier, Patricia Wolf, and Frank Wynne (New York: Bloomsbury, 2015).
13. Raczymow, *Maurice Sachs*, 25.
14. Raczymow, *Cahiers de L'Herne*, 9–10.
15. Jennifer Spitzer shows how W. H. Auden's use of the term "crook" as synonymous with homosexuality reveals "an unstable use of queer characterization," a strategy that shares similarities with Sachs's accounts of his own crookedness. Jennifer Spitzer, *Secret Sharers: The Intimate Rivalries of Modernism and Psychoanalysis* (New York: Fordham University Press, 2023), 89.
16. Gilles Deleuze, *Proust and Signs*, trans. Richard Howard (Minneapolis: University of Minnesota Press, 2000), 170–82.
17. Kadji Amin, *Disturbing Attachments: Genet, Modern Pederasty, and Queer Theory* (Durham, NC: Duke University Press, 2017), 1–10.
18. Tahar ben Jelloun, *Jean Genet, menteur sublime* (Paris: Folio Gallimard, 2013). The opposition between Sachs and Genet I'm building

on here is a simplification, and they might have more in common than their reputations would let us believe. Amin has pointed out, for instance, how Genet worked on his own image. Amin, *Disturbing Attachments*, 2.
19. Raczymow, *Maurice Sachs*, 29.
20. Carlo Jansiti, "Une amitié étincelante et noire," in *Cahiers de L'Herne: Maurice Sachs*, ed. Henri Raczymow (Paris: Editions de L'Herne, 2016), 115.
21. Jansiti, "Une amitié étincelante et noire," 117.
22. David T. Jacobson, "Jews for Genius: The Unholy Disorders of Maurice Sachs," *Yale French Studies* 85 (1994): 195.
23. See, for instance, Jeffery P. Dennis, *The Myth of the Queer Criminal* (New York: Routledge, 2018).
24. Gilles Deleuze and Félix Guattari, *Kafka: Toward a Minor Literature*, trans. Dana Polan (Minneapolis: University of Minnesota Press, 1986), 81–82.
25. Thomas, Clerc, *Maurice Sachs le désoeuvré* (Paris: Allia, 2005), 73. All translations of Clerc are mine.
26. Maurice Sachs, *Le sabbat. Souvenirs d'une jeunesse orageuse* (Paris: Corrêa, 1946); Maurice Sachs, *La chasse à courre* (Paris: Gallimard, 1949); English translation: Maurice Sachs, *The Hunt*, trans. Richard Howard (New York : Stein and Day, 1965); Maurice Sachs, *Abracadabra* (Paris: Gallimard, 1952); Maurice Sachs, *Histoire de John Cooper d'Albany* (Paris: Gallimard, 1955); Maurice Sachs, *La décade de l'illusion* (Paris: Gallimard, 1950); Maurice Sachs, *The Decade of Illusion* (New York: Knopf, 1933).
27. Clerc, *Maurice Sachs le désoeuvré*, 20.
28. Sachs, *Witches' Sabbath*, 58–60.
29. Sachs, *Witches' Sabbath*, 59. My translation. Howard translates "la bassesse bourgeoise" as "middle-class baseness," which is anachronistic and inaccurate. Sachs's family belongs to the Parisian bourgeoisie, which would be closer to a contemporary upper class.
30. Sachs, *Witches' Sabbath*, 60.
31. Raczymow, *Maurice Sachs*, 80–81.
32. Clerc, *Maurice Sachs le désoeuvré*, 13.
33. See Cocteau's account of the event in *Cahiers de L'Herne: Maurice Sachs*, ed. Henri Raczymow (Paris: Editions de L'Herne, 2016), 42.

34. Raczymow, *Maurice Sachs*, 193, 213.
35. Raczymow, *Cahiers de L'Herne*, 5–8.
36. Sachs, *The Hunt*, 10.
37. Raczymow, *Cahiers de L'Herne*, 14.
38. Deleuze and Guattari, *Kafka*, 146–45.
39. Dennis, *The Myth of the Queer Criminal*, 159.
40. Jacobson, "Jews for Genius," 183, 188.
41. Raczymow, *Maurice Sachs*, 135. Interestingly, Sachs attributes the same versatility to his friend the poet Max Jacob, whom he describes as "both Cinderella and her sisters, the ogre, the wolf, and all seven dwarfs." *Witches' Sabbath*, 131.
42. Jacobson, "Jews for Genius," 187.
43. Jacobson, "Jews for Genius," 195.
44. Maurice Sachs, *Mémoire moral* (Paris: Editions de L'Herne, 2016), 17.
45. Sachs, *Mémoire moral*, 17.
46. In French, the word "sabbat" refers to witchcraft rituals, while "shabbat" designates the Jewish holiday. Monceau's and Du Dogon's title uses the spelling "sabbat" in reference to Sachs's *Witches' Sabbath*. But it is also at the same time an antisemitic comment on Sachs's choice of title and an allusion to the unnatural and orgiastic nature of (their version of) Sachs's death.
47. Du Dognon and Monceau, *Le dernier sabbat*, 18. Shortly after his collaboration with Du Dognon, Monceau enrolled in the French military task force sent to oppose the independence of Vietnam, where he went missing. Du Dognon and Monceau, *Le dernier sabbat*, 10.
48. See Raczymow, *Maurice Sachs*, 424–50.
49. Du Dognon and Monceau, *Le dernier sabbat*, 205.
50. Eve Kosofsky Sedgwick, *Tendencies* (Durham, NC: Duke University Press, 1994), xii.
51. Modiano, *The Occupation Trilogy*, 13, 23, 14, 21.
52. Marcel Jouhandeau, "Comment je suis devenu antisemite," in *Cahiers de L'Herne: Maurice Sachs*, ed. Henri Raczymow (Paris: Editions de L'Herne, 2016), 83–84.
53. Sanos, *The Aesthetics of Hate*, 13, 75–76, 11; author's emphasis.
54. Marcel Jouhandeau, *De l'abjection* (Paris: Gallimard, 2006).
55. Eribon, *Hérésies*, 176–78.

56. Eribon, *Hérésies*, 178.
57. Jouhandeau, *De l'abjection*, 71.
58. Eribon, *Hérésies*, 191.
59. On the association of homosexuality and fascism and its aftermath, see Andrew Hewitt, *Political Inversions: Homosexuality, Fascism, and the Modernist Imaginary* (Stanford, CA: Stanford University Press, 1996).
60. Halperin, *What Do Gay Men Want?*, 75, 64.
61. Sachs, *Witches' Sabbath*, 20, 12.
62. Sachs, *Witches' Sabbath*, 19. My translation: Howard uses "error" to translate the French "faute," which erases its moral connotation.
63. Sachs, *Witches' Sabbath*, 18.
64. Raczymow traces Sachs's dramatization of his first memories to the influence of psychoanalysis and his therapy with Allendy. Raczymow, *Maurice Sachs*, 177–83.
65. Sachs, *Witches' Sabbath*, 22, 20.
66. Sachs, *Mémoire moral*, 20, 21, 28, 26. The famous Bibliothèque rose (pink library) is series of children books (publishing titles to this day). But the color pink has its own importance for Sachs, as I will discuss later on.
67. Sachs, *Witches' Sabbath*, 19.
68. Sachs, *Witches' Sabbath*, 116.
69. Marquis Bey, *Them Goon Rules: Fugitive Essays on Radical Black Feminism* (Tucson: University of Arizona Press, 2019), 68.
70. Bey, *Them Goon Rules*, 68.
71. Raczymow, *Maurice Sachs*, 114.
72. Sachs, *Witches' Sabbath*, 130.
73. Jacobson, "Jews for Genius," 186.
74. Lucienne Cantaloube-Ferrieu, "Variations sur une association: *Les pénitents en maillots roses*," *Centre de recherches Max Jacob* 9 (1987): 13.
75. Sachs, *Witches' Sabbath*, 128.
76. Clerc, *Maurice Sachs le désoeuvré*, 104.
77. Sachs, *The Hunt*, 115, 140; author's emphasis.
78. Sachs, *The Hunt*, 138.
79. Leduc had, for instance, given her wedding band to an impoverished Sachs, after refusing his suggestion that she sell her furniture (a

process he would be happy to facilitate) in order to "go on an adventure" with him. Raczymow, *Maurice Sachs*, 390. *The Hunt* briefly mentioned this episode: "T. L. . . . still in love with me . . . made me a present of a small jewel." Sachs, *The Hunt*, 128.
80. Sachs, *Witches' Sabbath*, 147.
81. Sachs, *Witches' Sabbath*, 148.
82. Raczymow, *Maurice Sachs*, 194–201, 393–405.
83. Sachs, *Witches' Sabbath*, 123.
84. J. Jack Halberstam, *In a Queer Time and Place: Transgender Bodies, Subcultural Lives* (New York: New York University Press, 2005), 2–10.
85. Sachs, *The Hunt*, 25. My translation.
86. Maurice Sachs, *Alias* (Paris: Gallimard, 2006), 91. All translations of *Alias* are mine.
87. Sachs, *The Hunt*, 52. The openly gay Maréchal Liautey, who instituted and governed the French colonial empire in North Africa, is more of a literary reference than it seems, since he is likely one of the inspirations for Proust's Charlus.
88. Sachs, *Alias*, 81; author's emphasis.
89. Baptiste Morizot, *Les diplomates, cohabiter avec les loups sur une autre carte du vivant* (Marseille: Wildproject, 2016), 30. Translation mine.
90. Jean Genet, *The Thief's Journal*, trans. Bernard Frechtman (New York: Grove, 1964).
91. See, for instance, Raczymow, *Maurice Sachs*, 74. Raczymow analyzes Sachs's "evil call" through his relationship with his mother, claiming that "Sachs *marries* evil in order to 'marry' his mother." Author's emphasis.
92. Sachs, *The Hunt*, 47–49. The French text uses the word "piperie," referring to loaded dice ("dés pipés"). Here again Sachs relies on a gambling metaphor, emphasizing complex processes and individual skills and knowhow.
93. See, for instance, Sachs, *The Hunt*, 110–11.
94. Sachs, *The Hunt*, 116.
95. Raczymow, *Maurice Sachs*, 381.
96. Jansiti, "Une amitié étincelante et noire," 117.
97. Sachs, *The Hunt*, 128–31.
98. Jansiti, "Une amitié étincelante et noire," 116.

4. ON CROOKS, ABJECTION, AND MOVING SIDEWAYS   251

99. Deleuze and Guattari, *Kafka*, 6.
100. Raczymow, *Maurice Sachs*, 433.
101. Sachs, *Witches' Sabbath*, 10, 236, 164, 111.
102. Sachs, *The Hunt*, 128–29.
103. Raczymow, *Maurice Sachs*, 177–81.
104. Sachs, *Witches' Sabbath*, 22, 192.
105. Sachs, *The Hunt*, 131.
106. Sachs, *Witches' Sabbath*, 10. My translation. Howard translated the French word "conscience" by "awareness," which ignores the text's moral undertone.
107. Sachs, *Witches' Sabbath*, 272–73, 275, 276.
108. Sachs, *The Hunt*, 79.
109. See, for instance, Raczymow, *Maurice Sachs*, 444.
110. Jansiti, "Une amitié étincelante et noire," 115.
111. Adeline Brunschwig, "La plaie et le couteau," in *Cahiers de L'Herne: Maurice Sachs*, ed. Henri Raczymow (Paris: Editions de L'Herne, 2016), 14–15.
112. Samuel Berlin and Sage Brice, "The Ontopolitics of Gender as Transindividual Relation," in *Deleuze, Guattari, and the Schizoanalysis of Trans Studies*, ed. Ciara Cremin (London: Bloomsbury 2022), 15–16.
113. Sachs, *The Hunt*, 78. My translation.
114. Sachs, *The Hunt*, 78.
115. Brunschwig, "La plaie et le couteau," 15.
116. Sachs, *Witches' Sabbath*, 151.
117. Sachs, *The Hunt*, 115.
118. Jacobson, "Jews for Genius," 197.
119. Du Dognon and Monceau, *Le dernier sabbat*, 40.
120. Sachs, *Mémoire moral*, 15.
121. Eribon, *Hérésies*, 181.
122. Sachs, *Alias*, 81, 85, 87; Sachs, *Witches' Sabbath*, 186–88.
123. Similarly, Leduc recalls how "when [Sachs] put a bill in [her] hand . . . it was a message more than a bill." Violette Leduc, quoted in *Cahiers de L'Herne: Maurice Sachs*, ed. Henri Raczymow (Paris: Editions de L'Herne, 2016), 125–26.
124. Gilles Deleuze and Félix Guattari, *A Thousand Plateaus: Capitalism and Schizophrenia*, trans. Brian Massumi (Minneapolis: University of Minnesota Press, 1987), 126.

125. Dennis, *The Myth of the Queer Criminal*, 85.
126. Maurice Sachs, *Au temps du Bœuf sur le toit* (Paris: Grasset, 1987), 31–32.
127. Raczymow, *Maurice Sachs*, 12; Clerc, *Maurice Sachs le désoeuvré*, 66–67.
128. *The Hunt* was published posthumously in 1949, and his title was chosen by its editor Yvon Belaval in reference to Sachs's eponymous theater play.
129. Andrea Long Chu writes that dysphoria "feels like hunger without appetite." Andrea Long Chu, "My New Vagina Won't Make Me Happy," *New York Times*, November 24, 2018.
130. Violette Leduc, quoted in *Cahiers de L'Herne*, 124.

5. INTERMITTENT MIRACLES: QUEER TIME AND TEMPORAL DYSPHORIA

1. Colette, *The Vagabond*, trans. Stanley Applebaum (Mineola, NY: Dover, 2010); Raymond Radiguet, *The Devil in the Flesh*, trans. A. M. Sheridan Smith (London: Calder and Boyars, 1968); Jean Genet, *Our Lady of the Flowers*, trans. Bernard Frechtman (New York: Grove, 1991); René Crevel, *Mon corps et moi* (Toulouse: Editions Ombres, 2008). An English translation of the book is available, but I choose to refer here to the French text because I find this translation to be often inaccurate. René Crevel, *My Body and I*, trans. Robert Bonnono (New York: Archipelago, 2005).
2. Elizabeth Freeman, *Time Binds: Queer Temporalities, Queer Histories* (Durham, NC: Duke University Press, 2010); Judith Jack Halberstam, *In a Queer Time and Place: Transgender Bodies, Subcultural Lives* (New York: New York University Press, 2005); Lee Edelman, *No Future: Queer Theory and the Death Drive* (Durham, NC: Duke University Press, 2004).
3. Crevel, *Mon corps et moi*, 84.
4. Freeman, *Time Binds*, x, 3.
5. Edelman, *No Future*, 2. I do not mean to imply that Edelman's and Freeman's description of temporality are one and the same but to stretch out common traits pertaining to my argument.
6. I borrow this expression from Kathryn Bond Stockton, *The Queer Child, or Growing Sideways in the Twentieth Century* (Durham, NC: Duke University Press, 2009).

7. Heather Love, *Feeling Backwards: Loss and the Politics of Queer History* (Cambridge, MA: Harvard University Press, 2009), 24.
8. Leah Devun and Zeb Tortorici, "Trans, Time, and History," *Transgender Studies Quarterly* 5, no. 4 (2018): 522.
9. Love, *Feeling Backward*, 31.
10. Devun and Tortorici, "Trans, Time, and History," 521.
11. Crevel, *Mon corps et moi*, 9. All translations of Crevel are mine.
12. Halberstam, *In a Queer Time and Place*, 2, 4, 11.
13. Devun and Tortorici, "Trans, Time, and History," 533–34.
14. Colette, *The Vagabond*, 108, 67–69.
15. The English translation, "Big Ninny," doesn't convey the animal metaphor typical of Colette's sensibility.
16. Colette, *The Vagabond*, 15. The French text is more explicit: "L'ardent désir qu'il a de moi le gêne comme une arme encombrante." Colette, *La vagabonde* (Paris: Albin Michel, 1990), 76.
17. Colette, *The Vagabond*, 104.
18. Colette, *The Vagabond*, 127, 126.
19. Michael Lucey, *Someone: The Pragmatics of Misfit Sexualities, from Colette to Hervé Guibert* (Chicago: University of Chicago Press, 2019), 7–48.
20. Judith Thurman, *Secrets of the Flesh: A Life of Colette* (New York: Knopf, 2000), 190.
21. Kadji Amin, "Ghosting Transgender Historicity in Colette's *The Pure and the Impure*," *L'Esprit Créateur* 53, no. 1 (2013): 115.
22. Colette, *The Vagabond*, 188.
23. Amin, "Ghosting Transgender Historicity," 116.
24. Lucey, *Someone*, 19.
25. Colette, *The Vagabond*, 167.
26. Colette, *The Vagabond*, 162.
27. Stockton, *The Queer Child*, 4.
28. Radiguet, *The Devil in the Flesh*, 5.
29. Radiguet, *The Devil in the Flesh*, 5.
30. Stockton, *The Queer Child*, 4, 12.
31. On virginity and marriage in the early twentieth century, see Aïcha Limbada, *La nuit de noces. Une histoire de l'intimité conjugale* (Paris: La Découverte, 2023).
32. Radiguet, *The Devil in the Flesh*, 5, 9.

33. Radiguet, *The Devil in the Flesh*, 48.
34. Radiguet, *The Devil in the Flesh*, 65.
35. Radiguet, *The Devil in the Flesh*, 126, 127.
36. Jean-Paul Sartre, introduction to Genet, *Our Lady of the Flowers*, 1.
37. Sartre, introduction to Genet, *Our Lady of the Flowers*, 1. According to Genet's biographer Edmund White, the lost manuscript was in fact another book, titled *Specter of the Heart* (*Le spectre du coeur*). In Genet's account of the destruction, the manuscript was simply taken from his cell, and he was punished with three days in solitary confinement for his misuse of the material entrusted to him. Edmund White, *Genet: A Biography* (New York: Vintage, 1993), 210.
38. White, *Genet*, 196.
39. Genet, *Our Lady of the Flowers*, 56.
40. In the English translation, Mignon has become "Darling." I will use his original name here, since Mignon, literally "cute," retains an aesthetic dimension and because of the second meaning of the word, a mignon, which is the same in French and in English. In naming a pimp "Mignon," Genet is emphasizing the ambiguity of the character.
41. Genet, *Our Lady of the Flowers*, 70.
42. Genet, *Our Lady of the Flowers*, 307.
43. Agnès Fontvieille-Cordani, "Surexposition de la métaphore . . . au risque de sa dissolution. Jean Genet, *Journal du voleur*," in *Stylistiques?*, ed. Judith Wulf and Laurence Bougault (Rennes: Presses Universitaires de Rennes, 2010), 295–96.
44. I am referring here to the French definition of the hyperbaton (*hyperbate*), which is used by Fontvieille.
45. Genet, *Our Lady of the Flowers*, 153.
46. Agnès Fontvieille, "Jean Genet: la phrase qui tombe à pic," in *L'hyperbate aux frontiers de la phrase*, ed. Anne-Marie Paillet et Claire Stolz (Paris: Presses de l'Université Paris-Sorbonne, 2011), 300.
47. Genet, *Our Lady of the Flowers*, 71, 224.
48. Genet, *Our Lady of the Flowers*, 77, 84.
49. Fontvieille, "Jean Genet," 19.
50. White, *Genet*, 211.
51. Genet, *Our Lady of the Flowers*, 76, 134.
52. Halberstam, *In a Queer Time and Place*, 6.
53. Crevel, *Mon corps et moi*, 9.

54. Crevel, *Mon corps et moi*, 75.
55. Michel Carassou, *René Crevel* (Paris: Fayard, 1989), 41–45.
56. Crevel, *Mon corps et moi*, 94, 40.
57. Genet, *Our Lady of the Flowers*, 215, 51, 55.
58. Sartre, introduction to Genet, *Our Lady of the Flowers*, 2.
59. Genet, *Our Lady of the Flowers*, 56.
60. Crevel, *Mon corps et moi*, 69.
61. Crevel, *Mon corps et moi*, 115.
62. Carassou, *René Crevel*, 265–66.
63. Crevel, *Mon corps et moi*, 77.
64. Crevel, *Mon corps et moi*, 84.

BIBLIOGRAPHY

Ahmed, Sara. *Queer Phenomenology: Orientations, Objects, Others*. Durham, NC: Duke University Press, 2006.
Awkward-Rich, Cameron. *The Terrible We: Thinking with Trans Maladjustment*. Durham, NC: Duke University Press, 2022.
Amin, Kadji. *Disturbing Attachments: Genet, Modern Pederasty, and Queer History*. Durham, NC: Duke University Press, 2017.
——. "Ghosting Transgender Historicity in Colette's *The Pure and the Impure*." *L'Esprit Créateur* 53, no. 1 (2013): 114–30.
——. "Glands, Eugenics, and Rejuvenation in *Man Into Woman*: A Biopolitical Genealogy of Transsexuality." *Transgender Studies Quarterly* 5, no. 4 (2018): 589–605.
——. "Taxonomically Queer? Sexology and New Queer, Trans, and Asexual Identities." *Gay and Lesbian Studies Quarterly* 29, no. 1 (2023): 91–107.
Apter, Emily S. *André Gide and the Codes of Homotextuality*. Stanford French and Italian Studies 48. Stanford, CA: Stanford University Press, 1987.
Barad, Karen. *Meeting the Universe Halfway: Quantum Physics and the Entanglement of Matter and Meaning*. Durham, NC: Duke University Press, 2007.
Barr, Sebastian M., Dominic Roberts, and Katharine N. Thakkar. "Psychosis in Transgender and Gender Non-conforming Individuals: A Review of the Literature and a Call for More Research." *Psychiatry Research* 306 (December 2021).
Beachy, Robert. *Gay Berlin: Birthplace of a Modern Identity*. New York: Knopf, 2014.

Beauvoir, Simone de. *The Second Sex*. Trans. Constance Borde and Sheila Malovany-Chevallier. New York: Vintage, 2011.

Berlin, Samuel, and Sage Brice. "The Ontopolitics of Gender as Transindividual Relation." In *Deleuze, Guattari, and the Schizoanalysis of Trans Studies*, ed. Ciara Cremin. London: Bloomsbury, 2022.

Bersani, Leo. *Homos*. Cambridge, MA: Harvard University Press, 1996.

Bey, Marquis. *Black Trans Feminism*. Durham, NC: Duke University Press, 2022.

——. *Cistem Failure: Essays on Blackness and Cisgender*. Durham, NC: Duke University Press, 2022.

——. *Them Goon Rules: Fugitive Essays on Radical Black Feminism*. Tucson: University of Arizona Press, 2019.

Buchanan, Ian. "Assemblage Theory, or, The Future of an Illusion." *Deleuze Studies* 11, no. 3 (2017): 457–74.

Clerc, Thomas. *Maurice Sachs le désoeuvré*. Paris: Allia, 2005.

Coffman, Chris. *Queer Traversals: Psychoanalytic Queer and Trans Theories*. London: Bloomsbury, 2022.

Colette. *The Vagabond*. Trans. Enid McLeod. Westport, CT: Greenwood, 1974.

Cremin, Ciara. Introduction to *Deleuze, Guattari, and the Schizoanalysis of Trans Studies*, ed. Ciara Cremin, 1–8. London: Bloomsbury, 2022.

Crevel, René. *Mon corps et moi*. Toulouse: Editions Ombres, 2008.

Dean, Carolyn. *The Frail Social Body: Pornography, Homosexuality, and Other Fantasies in Interwar France*. Berkeley: University of California Press, 2000.

DeLanda, Manuel. *A New Philosophy of Society: Assemblage Theory and Social Complexity*. London: Continuum, 2006.

Deleuze, Gilles. *Foucault*. Trans. Sean Hand. Minneapolis: University of Minnesota Press, 1988.

——. *Proust and Signs: The Complete Text*. Trans. Richard Howard. Minneapolis: University of Minnesota Press, 2000.

——. *Two Regimes of Madness: Texts and Interviews 1975–1995*. Trans. Ames Hodges and Mike Taormina. New York: Semiotext(e), 2007.

Deleuze, Gilles, and Félix Guattari. *Anti-Oedipus: Capitalism and Schizophrenia*. Trans. Brian Massumi. Minneapolis: University of Minnesota Press, 1983.

———. *Kafka: Towards a Minor Literature*. Trans. Dana Polan. Minneapolis: University of Minnesota Press, 1986.

———. *A Thousand Plateaus: Capitalism and Schizophrenia*. Trans. Brian Massumi. Minneapolis: University of Minnesota Press, 1987.

———. *What Is Philosophy*. Trans. Hugh Tomlinson and Graham Burchell. New York: Columbia University Press, 1994.

Dennis, Jeffery P. *The Myth of the Queer Criminal*. New York: Routledge, 2018.

DeVun, Leah, and Zeb Tortorici. "Trans, Time, and History." *Transgender Studies Quarterly* 5, no. 4 (November 2018): 518–39.

Doan, Laura. *Disturbing Practices: History, Sexuality, and Women's Experience of Modern War*. Chicago: University of Chicago Press, 2013.

Doan, Laura, and Jay Prosser. "Introduction: Critical Perspectives Past and Present." In *Palatable Poison: Critical Perspectives on "The Well of Loneliness,"* ed. Laura Doan and Jay Prosser. New York: Columbia University Press, 2001.

Dollimore, Jonathan. *Sexual Dissidence: Augustine to Wilde, Freud to Foucault*. Oxford: Clarendon, 1991.

Dorlin, Elsa. *La matrice de la race. Généalogie sexuelle et coloniale de la nation française*. Paris: La Découverte 2009.

Du Dognon, André, and Philippe Monceau. *Le dernier sabbat de Maurice Sachs*. Paris: Le Sagittaire, 1979.

Edelman, Lee. *No Future: Queer Theory and the Death Drive*. Durham, NC: Duke University Press, 2004.

Eribon, Didier. *Hérésies. Essais sur la théorie de la sexualité*. Paris: Fayard, 2003.

———. *Insult and the Making of the Gay Self*. Trans. Michael Lucey. Durham, NC: Duke University Press 2004.

Fisk, Norman M. "Gender Dysphoria Syndrome: The Conceptualization That Liberalizes Indications for Total Gender Reorientation and Implies a Broadly Based Multi-Dimensional Rehabilitative Regimen." *Western Journal of Medicine* 120 (May 1974): 386–391.

Fleishman, Ian. "Pederasty and/as Narrative Form." *French Forum* 45, no. 2 (2020): 155–69.

Foucault, Michel. *History of Madness*. Trans. Jean Khalfa and Jonathan Murphy. New York: Routledge, 2013.

———. *The Order of Things: An Archeology of the Human Sciences*. Trans. Alan Sheridan. New York: Random House, 1994.

Fournier, Mat. "Trans Auntologies: *The Second Sex* and the Ethics of Transmasculinity." *Simone de Beauvoir Studies* 32, no. 2 (2022): 265–85.
Freeman, Elizabeth. *Time Binds: Queer Temporalities, Queer Histories.* Durham, NC: Duke University Press, 2010.
Genet, Jean. *The Thief's Journal.* Trans. Bernard Frechtman. New York: Grove, 1964.
———. *Our Lady of the Flowers.* Trans. Bernard Frechtman. New York: Grove, 1991.
Gide, André. *Corydon.* Trans. Richard Howard. New York: Farrar, Straus and Giroux, 1983–2015.
———. *Fruits of the Earth.* Trans. Dorothy Bussy. London: Secker and Warburg, 1949–1952.
———. *If It Die.* Trans. Dorothy Bussy. Middlesex: Penguin, 1977–1982.
———. *The Immoralist.* Trans. Richard Howard. New York: Knopf, 1970.
———. *Journals 1889–1949.* Vol. 1. Trans. Justin O'Brien. New York: Knopf, 1956.
———. *Madeleine.* Trans. Justin O'Brien. Chicago: Elephant Paperbacks, 1952–1989.
———. *Strait Is the Gate.* Trans. Dorothy Bussy. New York: Knopf, 1949.
Glavey, Brian. *The Wallflower Avant-Garde: Modernism, Sexuality, and Queer Ekphrasis.* New York: Oxford University Press, 2016.
Gray, Margaret. *Stolen Limelight: Gender, Display, and Displacement in Modern Fiction in French.* Chicago: University of Chicago Press, 2022.
Green, Julien. *Journal intégral, 1919–1940.* Paris: Robert Laffont, 2019.
Gury, Christian. *Lyautey-Charlus.* Paris: Kimé, 1998.
Halberstam, Judith Jack. *In a Queer Time and Place: Transgender Bodies, Subcultural Lives.* New York: New York University Press, 2005.
Halperin, David M. *What Do Gay Men Want? An Essay on Sex, Risk, and Subjectivity.* Ann Harbor: University of Michigan Press, 2007.
Heaney, Emma. *The New Woman: Literary Modernism, Queer Theory, and the Trans Feminine Allegory.* Chicago: Northwestern University Press, 2017.
Hewitt, Andrew. *Political Inversions: Homosexuality, Fascism, and the Modernist Imaginary.* Stanford, CA: Stanford University Press, 1996.
Jacobson, David T. "Jews for Genius: The Unholy Disorders of Maurice Sachs." *Yale French Studies* 85 (1994).
Johnson, Graham, and Richard Stokes, eds. *A French Song Companion.* Oxford: Oxford University Press, 2000.

Jouhandeau, Marcel. "Comment je suis devenu antisemite." In *Cahiers de L'Herne: Maurice Sachs*, ed. Henri Raczymow. Paris: Editions de L'Herne, 2016.

———. *De l'abjection*. Paris: Gallimard, 2006.

Kahan, Benjamin. *The Book of Minor Perverts: Sexology, Etiology, and the Emergences of Sexuality*. Chicago: University of Chicago Press, 2019.

Ladenson, Elisabeth. *Proust's Lesbianism*. Ithaca, NY: Cornell University Press, 1999.

Lang, Daniel Welzer. "Introduction: Genre: Travaux en cours . . ." In *Aux frontières du genre*, ed. Arnaud Alessandrin. Paris: L'Harmattan, 2012.

Laroussi, Farid. *Postcolonial Counterpoints: Orientalism, France, and the Maghreb*. Toronto: University of Toronto Press, 2016.

Love, Heather. *Feeling Backward: Loss and the Politics of Queer History*. Cambridge, MA: Harvard University Press, 2009.

Lucey, Michael. *Gide's Bent: Sexuality, Politics, Writing*. New York: Oxford University Press, 1995.

———. *Never Say I: Sexuality and the First Person in Colette, Gide, and Proust*. Durham, NC: Duke University Press, 2006.

———. *Someone: The Pragmatics of Misfit Sexualities, from Colette to Hervé Guibert*. Chicago: University of Chicago Press, 2019.

Malatino, Hil. *Side Affects: On Being Trans and Feeling Bad*. Minneapolis: University of Minnesota Press, 2022.

Mancini, Elena. *Magnus Hirschfeld and the Quest for Sexual Freedom*. London: Palgrave Macmillan, 2010.

Mesch, Rachel. *Before Trans: Three Stories from Nineteenth-Century France*. Stanford, CA: University of California Press, 2020.

Mitchell, Robin. *Vénus Noire: Black Women and Colonial Fantasies in Nineteenth-Century France*. Athens: University of Georgia Press, 2020.

Mosse, George L. *The Image of Man: The Creation of Modern Masculinity*. New York: Oxford University Press, 1996.

Murat, Laure. *La loi du genre, Une histoire culturelle du 'troisième sexe.'* Paris: Fayard, 2006.

Nay, Yv E., and Eliza Steinbock. "Critical Trans Studies in and Beyond Europe: Histories, Methods, and Institutions." *Transgender Studies Quarterly* 8, no. 2 (2021).

Perreau, Bruno. *Queer Theory: The French Response*. Stanford, CA: Stanford University Press, 2016.

Pine, Davida. *The Marriage Paradox: Modernist Novels and the Cultural Imperative to Marry*. Gainesville: University Press of Florida, 2005.
Porzak, Simon. "Inverts and Invertebrates: Darwin, Proust, and Nature's Queer Heterosexuality." *Diacritics* 41, no. 4 (2013).
Preciado, Paul. *Can the Monster Speak? Report to an Academy of Psychoanalysts*. Trans. Frank Wynne. Cambridge, MA: MIT Press, 2021.
Proust, Marcel. *In Search of Lost Time*. Vol. 4: *Sodom and Gomorrah*. Trans. C. K. Scott Moncrieff and Terence Kilmartin. Rev. D. J. Enright. New York: Random House, 2003.
Puar, Jasbir. *Terrorist Assemblages: Homonationalism in Queer Times*. Durham, NC: Duke University Press, 2007.
Raczymow, Henri. *Maurice Sachs ou Les travaux forcés de la frivolité*. Paris: Gallimard, 1988.
Radiguet, Raymond. *The Devil in the Flesh*. Trans. A. M. Sheridan Smith. London: Calder and Boyars, 1968.
Robcis, Camille. *The Law of Kinship: Anthropology, Psychoanalysis, and the Family in France*. Ithaca, NY: Cornell University Press, 2013.
Roberts, Mary Louise. *Civilization Without Sexes: Reconstructing Gender in Postwar France, 1917–1927*. Chicago: University of Chicago Press, 1994.
Rostand, Jean. *Les problèmes de l'hérédité et du sexe*. Paris: Rieder, 1933.
Rostand, Maurice. *Confession d'un demi-siècle*. Paris: La Jeune Parque, 1948.
———. *La femme qui était en lui*. Paris: Ernest Flammarion, 1933.
———. *L'homme que j'ai tué*. Paris: Ernest Flammarion, 1925.
———. *L'homme que j'ai tué, pièce en trois actes et un prologue de Maurice Rostand d'après son roman*. Paris: Lang, Blanchong, 1930.
Rubin, Gayle. "The Traffic in Women: Notes on the 'Political Economy' of Sex." In *The Second Wave: A Reader in Feminist Theory*, ed. Linda Nicholson. New York: Routledge, 1997.
Sachs, Maurice. *The Decade of Illusion*. New York: Knopf, 1933.
———. *The Hunt*. Trans. Richard Howard. New York: Stein and Day, 1965.
———. *Witches' Sabbath*. Trans. Richard Howard. Sacramento, CA: Spurl, 2020.
Sanos, Sandrine. *The Aesthetics of Hate: Far-Right Intellectuals, Antisemitism, and Gender in 1930s France*. Stanford, CA: Stanford University Press, 2013.
Schehr, Lawrence. *French Gay Modernism*. Chicago: University of Chicago Press, 2004.

Schuller, Kyla. *The Biopolitics of Feeling: Race, Sex, and Science in the Nineteenth Century.* Durham, NC: Duke University Press, 2018.
Sedgwick, Eve Kosofsky. *Between Men: English Literature and Male Homosocial Desire.* New York: Columbia University Press, 1985.
———. *Epistemology of the Closet.* Oakland: University of California Press, 1990.
———. *The Weather in Proust.* Durham, NC: Duke University Press, 2011.
Sheridan, Alan. *André Gide: A Life in the Present.* Cambridge, MA: Harvard University Press, 1999.
Snediker, Michael. *Contingent Figure: Chronic Pain and Queer Embodiment.* Minneapolis: University of Minnesota Press, 2021.
Sommerville, Siobhan B. *Queering the Color Line: Race and the Invention of Homosexuality in American Culture.* Durham, NC: Duke University Press, 2000.
Spitzer, Jennifer. *Secret Sharers: The Intimate Rivalries of Modernism and Psychoanalysis.* New York: Fordham University Press, 2023.
Steinbock, Eliza. *Shimmering Images: Trans Cinema, Embodiment, and the Aesthetics of Change.* Durham, NC: Duke University Press, 2019.
Stockton, Kathryn Bond. *Gender(s).* Cambridge, MA: MIT Press, 2021.
———. *The Queer Child: Or, Growing Sideways in the Twentieth Century.* Durham, NC: Duke University Press, 2009.
Stoler, Ann Laura. *Carnal Knowledge and Imperial Power: Race and the Intimate in Colonial Rule.* Berkeley: University of California Press, 2002.
———. *Race and the Education of Desire: Foucault's "History of Sexuality" and the Colonial Order of Things.* Durham, NC: Duke University Press, 1995.
Stryker, Susan. "(De)Subjugated Knowledges: An Introduction to Transgender Studies." In *The Transgender Studies Reader*, ed. Susan Stryker and Stephen Whittle. New York: Routledge, 2006.
Stryker, Susan, Paisley Currah, and Lisa Moore. "Introduction: Trans, Trans-, or Transgender?" *Women's Studies Quarterly* 36, nos. 3–4 (2008).
Stryker, Susan, and Stephen Whittle, eds. *The Transgender Studies Reader.* New York: Routledge, 2006.
Surkis, Judith. *Sexing the Citizen: Morality and Masculinity in France, 1870–1920.* Ithaca, NY: Cornell University Press, 2006.
Traverso, Enzo. *Fire and Blood: The European Civil War, 1914–1945.* Trans. David Fernbach. London: Verso, 2017.

Ulrichs, Karl Heinrich. *The Riddle of "Man-Manly" Love: The Pioneering Work on Male Homosexuality*. Trans. Michael A. Lombardi-Nash. Amherst, MA: Prometheus, 1994.

Vergès, Françoise. *The Wombs of Women: Race, Capital, Feminism*. Trans. Kaiama L. Glover. Durham, NC: Duke University Press, 2020.

Yao, Xine. *Disaffected: The Culture of Unfeeling in Nineteenth-Century America*. Durham, NC: Duke University Press, 2021.

Weil, Abraham B. "Transmolecular Revolution." In *Deleuze, Guattari, and the Schizoanalysis of Trans Studies*, ed. Ciara Cremin, 129–50. London: Bloomsbury, 2022.

Weininger, Otto. *Sex and Character, Authorized Translation from the Sixth German Edition*. New York: G. P. Putnam's Sons, 1906.

INDEX

Abel (character in *Strait Is the Gate*), 103
abjection: Eribon on, 177; queer transgression and, 157; Sachs and, 29, 140–142, 147, 156–158, 168
abnormal heterosexuality, in *Strait Is the Gate*, 104
Adelair (character in *Alias*), 167–168, 177, 178
adolescence, as queer time, 196
affect, dysphoria as, 18–19
Ahmed, Sara, 96
Albertine (character in *In Search of Lost Time*), 113, 119, 123, 124
Alias (Sachs), 167, 178, 179
Alias, Blaise (character in *Alias* and *Au temps du Boeuf sur le toit*), 167, 178
Alissa (character in *Strait Is the Gate*), 81, 98–105
Allégret, Marc, 80, 90–92
Allendy, René, 172
American Psychiatric Association (APA), on gender nonconformity, 16

Amin, Kadji: on classification systems, comparison of, 46–47; on Genet, 7–8, 144, 225n61, 247n18; mentioned, 221n16; on queer studies, 80; on *The Vagabond*, 192
ancient Greece, as trope in *Corydon*, 82, 83–84
animals, as companions, 191
Annamite, the, (character in *La femme qui était en lui*), 62–63, 64
antisemitism: antisemitic animal metaphors, 155; antisemitic markers, role of, 63; antisemitic tropes, 119; cursed race and, 117; in *La femme qui était en lui*, 38; French, 155; gay men's situation, parallels with, 242n23; Sachs, antisemitic collective assemblage shaping portrayals of, 153; ugliness as trope of, 176; visibility of, 6; Weininger's, 63–64
APA (American Psychiatric Association), on gender nonconformity, 16

Apter, Emily, 100
archipelagic systems, 46–47
Armand, E., 232n78
assemblage, about, 8–12. *See also* gender assemblage
Au temps du Boeuf sur le toit (Sachs), 178
Auden, W. H., 246n15
authenticity, Sachs and, 171, 172
autobiography, differences from fiction, 24–25
Awkward-Rich, Cameron, 224n52

Baldwin, James, 85, 89–90, 93, 95
Barad, Karen, 21
Baril, Alexandre, 225n57
Baudelaire, Charles, 101, 186
beauty, association with death, 51
Beauvoir, Simone de, 13, 14
Belaval, Yvon, 252n128
Ben Jelloun, Tahar, 144
Berlin, Samuel, 175
Bersani, Leo: critique of Proust's homophobia, Sedgwick and, 130; on Gide, 74, 75, 76; on homosexuals, 80; on *The Immoralist*, 93–94, 238n61; mentioned, 105, 111; on *Sodom and Gomorrah*, 112; on *Strait Is the Gate*, 104
Bey, Marquis, 14, 161–162
Bibliothèque rose, 249n66
"Big Canary" ("Grand-Serin," Max, character in *The Vagabond*), 188–193, 195
bildungsroman, *In Search of Lost Time* as, 131

Blaise Alias (character in *Alias*), 167
Bleuler, Eugen, 65–66
Blüher, Hans, 233n91
bodies and embodiment: bodies as spaces, 212; Brown bodies, in *La femme qui était en lui*, 60; cassocks and, 162; Charlus's embodiment, 133; disposable female bodies, 92, 102; female bodies, desire and, 84; female bodies, men and, 73; female embodiments, 20, 97; in *La femme qui était en lui*, 41, 69; forms of embodiment, relationship to gender assemblage, 109; in Gide's writings, 102; in *The Immoralist*, 94; impossible embodiments, 68–70; male bodies, as nation's body, 53–54; Mignon's body, in *Our Lady of the Flowers*, 205–206; nature and bodies, 194, 195; in Proust, 110; queer and dysphoric time and, 186; of Rondeaux (Madeleine), 88–89; Sachs and bodies, 174–175; severed heads, in *My Body and I*, 210; shimmering bodies, 133–138; in *Strait Is the Gate*, 101–102, 103, 105, 105; temporal dysphoria and, 184–185; time and, 211–214. *See also* dysphoria
borderlands, 64, 65
Bosch, Frau, as nickname for Charlus in *In Search of Lost Time*, 137
botanical metaphors, 28

Breton, André, 215
Brice, Sage, 175
bridges, Creve's versus Genet's, 216
Brunschwig, Adeline, 174–175, 176
Burghölzi (Zürich University psychiatric research hospital), 66

Cahiers de L'Herne (journal), on Sachs, 143, 151
Cantaloube-Ferrieu, Lucienne, 163
Carnets (Allégret), 91
cats, cheese and, 197
Cavar, Sarah, 225n57
chameleon, Sachs as, 153, 155, 178
Chanel, Coco, 169
Charlus (character in *In Search of Lost Time*): colonialism and, 7; as conceptual figure, 132–133, 136; Deleuze and Sedgwick on, 132; as embodiment of change, 136–137; feminization of, 116, 120–121, 124; Jupien, encounter with, 113–114, 117–118, 126, 127, 128, 129, 134; on male homosexuality, 118; nickname for, 137; reversals in, 119; Sachs, comparison with, 29, 143; sex of, 3, 4–5; smile of, 11, 125
Chiang, Howard, 225n63
Child (character in *The Vagabond*), 191
Christianity, modern, attitudes toward women, 83
chronic pain, 19
chrononormativity: characteristics of, 183; as concept, 182–183; disruptions of, 199, 200, 201; escapes from, 192, 193; Freeman on, 182, 183; gender binary and, 208; of marriage, 195; outside of, 214–217; queer time versus, 189; queerness and dysphoria versus, 184, 217; space and, 209, 210; violence of, 216; war and, 196
Chu, Andrea Long, 223–224n45, 252n129
cistem failure, gender as, 14
citizenship, 38, 53–54
civilization: dysphoria and, 31–35; sex difference and, 61–62
class, Sachs and, 145–146
Clerc, Thomas, 149, 163
closet, the, 24–25, 109, 132
Cocteau, Jean: influences on, 33; on *Our Lady of the Flowers*, 202; on Sachs, 139, 140, 153; Sachs and, 149, 169
Coffman, Chris, 222n28
Colette: challenges faced by, 23; futureless behaviors, association with, 184; mentioned, 182; temporal boundaries in, 208; *The Vagabond*, 29–30, 182, 186–195
collective assemblage of enunciation, 146–147, 151–152, 171, 174
colonialism: coloniality of being, 36; colonization, warfare of, 38; construction of modern gender and, 6; Gide and, 90–92; Paris Colonial Exposition, 61, 64; racial divide of, 7
conceptual abysses, 129–133

conceptual personae, 109, 111
Confession d'un demi-siècle (Rostand), 54
confessions, 170–173
confinement, effects of, 188
conscious pariahs, 152
contamination, as a trope, 119
contradictions, in shimmering signs of inversion, 134
Corydon (character in *Corydon*), 82
Corydon (Gide): delayed publication of, 71; the erotic of misogyny in, 81–85; on femininity as nature, 89; on homosexuality, 71–72, 75, 104; introduction to, 79; on masculinity, 78; on third-sex theory, 43; on women, 92
counterfeiters, 144
Cremin, Ciara, 68
Crevel, René: futureless behaviors, association with, 184; Gide and, 26; mentioned, 182; *My Body and I*, 30, 182, 187–188, 209–217; on queer time, 182; on solitude, 186; suicide, 215
criminality, relation to queerness, 146
crook, Auden's use of term, 246n15
cross-dressing, in *Witches' Sabbath*, 163
Culafroy, Louis (character in *Our Lady of the Flowers*), 202–203, 205, 207
cursed race, homosexuality as, 111, 116–120

Darwin, Charles, and Darwinism, 28, 126, 244n50. *See also* evolutionary biology
de Chatellerault, Duc (character in *Sodom and Gomorrah*), 118
De l'abjection (On abjection, Johandeau), 157
De Roche, Linda, 233n96
dead ends, in *Sodom and Gomorrah*, 114
Dean, Carolyn, 7, 37, 53, 232n78
death: beauty, association with, 51; marriage as, 98–105
Decade of Illusion, The (Sachs), 177
deidentification, in *Strait Is the Gate*, 104–105
Deleuze, Gilles: on archipelagic systems, 46; on assemblage, 9; on Charlus, 132–133; on collective assemblages, 146–147; on contagion, 119; on desire, 76; on gender, 10, 138; gender and sexuality, response to discussions of, 135; on literature, 151; mentioned, 28; on nonconceptual figures, 115; Proust, analysis of, 108; on Proust, comparison with Sedgwick, 129–131; on reading Proust, 4–5; on Sachs, 178; on schizophrenia, 68–69; Sedgwick, comparison with, 108–109; on signs, 137; on smuggling, 170–171; suicide, 244n54; terminology uses, 240n4, 244n59; on transversality, 134; on writing, 1

delight, 163
delle Donne, Marie, 162
Dennis, Jeffery, 152, 178
desire: in *Corydon*, 84–85; in Crevel versus Genet, 212; femininity and, 124; in Gide, 76; Gide's mother and, 87; homosexual desire, 135, 165; love and, 87; in Proust, 4, 114; sex, love, and spirituality and, 75–77; in *Strait Is the Gate*, 102; of women, 89
Devil in the Flesh, The (Radiguet): introduction to, 187; mentioned, 29–30, 182; queer temporality and chrononormativity in, 195–201; temporal boundaries in, 208
Devun, Leah, 8, 185, 186
Diagnostic and Statistical Mental Disorders (DSM-5), 15–16
Dinshaw, Carolyn, 8, 185
disorientation, in *The Immoralist*, 96
Disturbing Attachments (Amin), 7–8
Divine (character in *Our Lady of the Flowers*), 202–203, 205–208, 211, 214
Doan, Laura, 6
Dollimore, Jonathan, 73, 74, 75, 94, 96
Dorlin, Elsa, 60
Dreyfus affair, 117, 242n23
DSM-5 (*Diagnostic and Statistical Mental Disorders*), 15–16
Du Dognon, André, 154, 176, 248n46
Durosay, Daniel, 237n56
Duval, Jeanne, 101

dysphoria: about, 14–19; as affect, 36; author's experiences of, 2; characteristics of, 125, 185–186; of Charlus, 116; civilization and, 31–35; conceptualization of, 224n52; descriptions of, 175; dysphoric pacifism, 39, 52–57; dysphoric smuggling (*See* Sachs, Maurice); dysphoric temporality, in *Our Lady of the Flowers*, 203; dysphoric time, comparison with queer time, 184–185; effects of, 17–19; in *La femme qui était en lui*, 68–69; gender, relationship to, 17; gender assemblage and, 133; gender dysphoria, 15–16, 67; homosexuality, relationship to, 57–58; impact of, 137; insatiable hunger of, 179; inverts as embodiments of, 109; musical, 68–70; nature of, 21, 35–41, 109, 110; in Proust, 116, 122; queerness versus, 3; in Sachs, 29; Sachs's, 140, 160, 176; Sachs's dysphoric guilt, 158; solitude of, 214; sources of, 11. *See also* bodies; Sachs, Maurice
dysphoric assemblage. *See* gender assemblage

Earth, personification in *La femme qui était en lui*, 57
Edelman, Lee, 182, 183
embodiment. *See* bodies and embodiment
embryology, Ulrichs's reliance on, 42

Emmanuel (character in *La femme qui était en lui*), 35, 45, 58, 59–60, 64
Emmanuel (character in *Le Pilori*), 57
empires, as borderlands, 64
enunciation, collective assemblage of, 146–147, 151–152, 171, 174
episteme, as term, 241n4
epistemology of the closet, 130, 131
Epistemology of the Closet (Sedgwick), 108, 129–132
erasure and visibility, in Sachs's writings, 172
Eribon, Didier, 111, 112, 114, 157, 177
Ernestine (character in *Our Lady of the Flowers*), 207
erotic of misogyny, 81–85, 90
Ettinghausen, Maurice. *See* Sachs, Maurice
European civil war, 53
European imperialism, 38
evolutionary biology (Darwinism): Gide and, 43, 44; influence of, 107; as trope in *Corydon*, 82–83; Ulrichs and, 42, 44
evolutionary theory, gendered birth of modern citizenship and, 38
existentialist freedom, 202
exorcisms, 66

failed marriages. *See* Gide, André
families, white nuclear, 183
fantasy, in *La femme qui était en lui*, 35
far-right movements, sources of, 54
fascism, 156
fathers, 48, 58

feeling, biopolitics of, 63
Feeling Backward (Love), 8
femininity: *Corydon* on, 82; desire and, 124; in France in interwar years, 52; gender/sexuality seesaw and, 45; influence of wars on, 37–38; masculinity, differences from, 120–125; monstrous femininity of decadent femmes fatales, 51; oppressiveness of, 74–75; in Proust's men-women, 116; tragic enigma of, 49–52; Ulrichs and Gide on, 44; violence of, 57. *See also* transfemininity; women
Fernande (character in *La femme qui était en lui*), 47, 49–50
fertilization, 126, 128, 129, 134–135
fiction, differences from autobiography, 24–25
Fisk, Norman F., 16–17
Fitzgerald, Zelda, 65
flexibility, survival using, 155
folds, image of, 168
Fontvieille, Agnès, 204
Forel, August, 66
Forel, Oscar, 65
form, of content and expression, 170–171
Fossette (bulldog in *The Vagabond*), 191
Foucault, Michel, 20, 74, 135, 233n94, 241n4
Fournier, Mat: dysphoria of, 18; experiences as trans man, 1–2; Proust, response to, 4–5; theoretical approach of, 225n60

INDEX ɞ 271

fragility, Gide's use of term, 97–98
France: colonial empire, as
  enforcing white masculinity, 27;
  colonial empire, in gender
  assemblage of *La femme qui était
  en lui*, 61; colonial empire,
  nature of, 27–28, 90; familialist
  politics, 53; French imperialism,
  discriminative systems in, 23;
  heterosexual familialism,
  enforcement of, 232n78; during
  interwar years, 37; masculinity
  in, at end of WWI, 53;
  Morocco, colonization of, 7;
  natalist policies, targets of,
  229n22
freedom, existentialist, 202
Freeman, Elizabeth, 182, 183
Fregoli, Leopoldo, 163
French Equatorial Africa, Gide in,
  90–92
French literature: during interwar
  years, 25–30; misogynist and
  heterocentrist tradition in,
  122–123; modernist canon, class
  of authors of, 146; modernist
  canon, influence of, 8;
  modernist writers, on gender
  assemblage, 5–6
French literature, undoing gender
  in: *La femme qui était en lui*
  (Rostand), 31–70; Gide, André,
  71–105; introduction to, 1–30;
  Proust, Marcel, trans reading
  of, 107–138; queer time and
  temporal dysphoria, 181–217;
  Sachs, Maurice, 139–180

Fruits of the Earth (Gide), 72, 84
fugue, femininity as, 120–125
futurity, productive and
  reproductive, 183–184

Gallimard publishing house, 150
gaslighting, in *Madeleine*, 85–86
gay men: Proust on, 4; as
  transfeminine women, 115. *See
  also* homosexuals and
  homosexuality; inverts and
  inversion
gay sex, in Sachs's memoirs, 165
gay shame, 141–144
gender(s): abjection as gendered,
  157; about, 12–14; author's use of
  term, 12–14; dysphoria,
  relationship to, 17;
  entanglements of, 9; in *La
  femme qui était en lui*, 47–48;
  gender deviance, 20, 35–36,
  64–68; gender dissolution, in *La
  femme qui était en lui*, 64; gender
  euphoria, 70; gender fluidity, in
  Our Lady of the Flowers, 205;
  gender nonconformity, APA
  on, 16; gender politics, Bey's
  question on, 161–162; gender
  reassignment technologies
  during interwar years, 23–24;
  gender transgression, nature of
  understanding of, 225–226n63;
  gendered service, 183; gendering
  of white colonizers, 61; Gide's
  mapping of, 74; Hirschfeld's
  understanding of, 46–47;
  intersectional aspects of, 9;

gender(s): *(continued)*
  modern, as racialized construct, 6; as operational, 10; queerness of, 14; sexuality and, in Proust, 107–108; subjectivity of, 21; timing of, 204–208; violence of, 56; writing of, during interwar years, 25–30. *See also* men; trans; women
gender assemblages: contradictions of, 60; in *Corydon*, 85, 93; discussion of, 211–214; dysphoria of, 25, 68, 216; in *La femme qui était en lui*, 53, 61; forms of embodiment, relationship to, 109; French modernist writers on, 5–6; Gide's, 72–73, 76, 78–81; of interwar years, Sachs and, 147; mapping of, 136; marriage as, 77; masculinity and, 125; misogyny of, 75; in Proust, Charlus and, 133; purposes of, 21–22; question of navigation of, 24; schizophrenic divides in, 35–36; in *Strait Is the Gate*, 102, 103, 105; tensions in, 32; time and, 181–182
gender binary: as coded system, 130; *Corydon* on, 82; in France at end of WWI, 53; materialization of question of, 36; modern, violence of, 6; oppressive nature of, 20; in *Our Lady of the Flowers*, 208; as process of subjectification, 74; in Proust, 107–108, 130; Sachs and, 144, 145; in *Strait Is the Gate*, 105

gender dysphoria: diagnosed as psychosis, 67; DSM-5 definition of, 15–16
Gender Dysphoria Program (Stanford University), 16
Genet, Jean: futureless behaviors, association with, 184; gay shame and, 141; mentioned, 182; Sachs and, 26, 144–145, 168; sexual abjection and, 158; spaces of, 211, 212; *The Thief's Journal*, 168. See also *Our Lady of the Flowers*
genre, French use of term, 12–13
Gérard, Rosemonde, 32
Gestapo, Sachs as informant for, 150, 171
Gide, André, 71–105; chronology of discussion of works of, 78–79; complexity of reception of, 75; Crevel and, 26; dysphoric assemblage of, 78–81, 86; father's death, 99; homosexuality as nature and a practice of, 75–77; as hypochondriac, 239n87; *If It Die*, 76, 90, 96–98, 104; introduction to, 71–75; love, sex, desire, and spirituality and, 75–77; *Madeleine* as marriage of heaven and hell, 85–90; marriage of, 28, 85; marriage paradox and, 77–78; Orient, metamorphoses in, 95–98; overview of, 27–28; paradox of, 73; physical descriptions in writings of, 101; portrayals of, 27; Proust and, 26, 136; Sachs, comparison with, 140; sexual

preference of, 7; *Strait Is the Gate*, 77, 81, 98–105; terminology, use of, 242–243n27; travels in French Equatorial Africa, 90–92. See also *Corydon*; *Immoralist, The*

Gide, André, views of: Arab boys, fetishization of, 95; attitude toward his mother, 87; on families, 71; on homosexuality and marriage, 71; on male homosexuals, types of, 236n28; on marriage, 189; misogyny of, 93, 164; Orientalism of, 80; on *Sodom and Gomorrah*, 112

Gide, Catherine, 237n41

glass closets, 24–25

Glavey, Brian, 52, 68

Gomorrah (in *Sodom and Gomorrah*), 122, 243n36

Gonzalès, Alvaro (character in *La femme qui était en lui*), 62, 64

"Grand-Serin" ("Big Canary," Max, character in *The Vagabond*), 188–193, 195

Graves, Robert, 183

Gray, Margaret, 240n106

Green, Julien, 91, 237n53

growing up, process of, 196–197

Guattari, Félix: on assemblage, 9; on collective assemblages, 146–147; on contagion, 119; on literature, 151; on nonconceptual figures, 115; on reading Proust, 4–5; on Sachs, 178; on schizophrenia, 68–69; on smuggling, 170–171; on transversality, 134; on writing, 1

Gury, Christian, 227n3

Haas-Eye, Otto, 58–59

Hahn, Reynaldo, 128

Halberstam, Jack: mentioned, 116, 179; on queer places, 208–209; on queer time, 182, 186; on sex scenes, chronology of, 166

Hall, Radclyffe, 34

Halperin, David, 157, 158

Heaney, Emma: on *Corydon*, 95; on femininity, 45; on Foucault, 135; on homosexuality, Ulrichs's and Gide's models of, 44; on modernist literature, 109; on queer theory, 20, 22, 235n7; transmisogyny, analysis of, 110; on Ulrichs, 41, 115; on women, 33

heaven and hell, Gide and, 79

heteronormativity: as coded system, 130; heteronormative familialism, in *Strait Is the Gate*, 100, 102; heteronormative temporality, 186, 187

heterosexuality: abnormal, in *Strait Is the Gate*, 104; *Corydon* on, 83; heterosexual marriage, dysfunctionality of, 27; heterosexual reproduction, improbability of, 126; heterosexual sex, 87, 194; *The Immoralist* and, 94; influence of horror of, 102; in Proust, 123; social enforcement of, 164–165

Heye, Haas, 232nn76–77
Hirschfeld, Magnus, 38–39, 42, 46–47, 69, 81
homosexuals (male homosexuals) and homosexuality: *Corydon* on, 83; as cursed race, 111, 116–120; defense of, 57–60; dysphoria, relationship to, 57–58; *La femme qui était en lui* as defense of, 57; homosexual sex, as akin to spirituality, 84; homosexuality as high stakes, 165; homosexuals as the other, 54; *Madeleine* on, 87; as nature and a practice, 75–77; Proust's conception of, 28, 107–108; Sachs's understanding of, 165; self, relationship to, 76; site of homosexuality in *In Search of Lost Time*, 122–123; white masculine homosexuals, 95. *See also* gay men; inverts and inversion; lesbians and lesbianism; men-women
"How I Became Antisemitic" (Jouhandeau), 156
Howard, Richard, 251n106
Hugo, Victor, 128, 129
hunger, of dysphoria, 179
Hunt, The (Sachs): on clothing, 163; fake transparency in, 169–170; preface of, 151; queer sex in, 167; queer temporality in, 166; schemes depicted in, 179; self-description in, 175
hyperbatons, in *Our Lady of the Flowers*, 204–205, 206

If It Die (Gide), 76, 90, 96–98, 104
illness, association with Orient, 96–97
Immoralist, The (Gide): contact with nature in, 194; introduction to, 80–81; on masculinity, 78; problematic nature of, 92–95; on sexuality, 75; on state-sanctioned conjugality, 77; *Strait Is the Gate*, similarities to, 99
In a Queer Time and Place (Halberstam), 208–209
individuality, loss of, in *Our Lady of the Flowers*, 208
In Search of Lost Time (Proust): Albertine (character in), 113, 119, 123, 124; Deleuze on, 108, 131; Eribon on, 114; female inverts in, lack of, 122; femininity and desire in, 124; the future as focus of, 129, 131; gender divisions in, 121; interruptions to chronological narrative of, 114; inversion in, 111; Legrandin (character in), 119; lesbians in, 109; male homosexuality in, 112; male romance in, 128; Murat on, 118; production of meaning in, 129; site of homosexuality in, 122; teenage narrator of, 3. *See also* Charlus; *Sodom and Gomorrah*
intensity, in *Strait Is the Gate*, 98, 104
intermediaries, Sachs and, 167–170
intermittent miracles, 182, 188. *See also* queer time and temporal dysphoria

International Writers Congress in Defense of Culture, 215
invertebrate crossing, 127
inverts and inversion: contagions, similarity to, 111, 119; as embodiment of dysphoria, 109; as embodiment of gender binary, 111; fertilization and, 136; gender/sexuality seesaw of, 36; Gide on, 236n28; inversion in Proust, 137; inverts as conceptual figures, 132; late-nineteenth-century theories of, 38–39; normal pederasts versus, 82; as practice of embodiment, 110; in Proust, 28, 108, 109–110; Proust's use of term "invert," 118; shimmering signs of inversion, 134; theorization of, 41–45; trope of, 39. *See also* homosexuals and homosexuality; men-women investment, heterosexuality as, 165
"It's a Queer Time" (Graves), 183, 194

Jacob, Max, 139, 163, 248n41
Jacobson, David J., 153
Jacques (character in *The Devil in the Flesh*), 198–200
jellyfish metaphor, 128
Jérôme (narrator of *Strait Is the Gate*), 81, 98–105
Jews and Judaism: Jewish men, Weininger on, 63–64; Jews as the other, 54; Sachs as Jewish, 152. *See also* antisemitism; Sachs, Maurice

J./Julian (character in *The Hunt*), 171–172
Jouhandeau, Marcel, 141, 156, 157–158, 166, 168
Journel (Green), 91
Jouvenel, Bertrand de, 200
Jouvenel, Henry de, 188
joy, 76, 105
Jupien (character in *In Search of Lost Time*): Charlus, encounter with, 113–114, 117–118, 126, 127, 128, 129, 134

Kahan, Benjamin, 6, 15, 36, 46
Keegan, Cáel M., 224–225n54

Lacanian psychoanalysis, 13
La colère de Samson (Samson's anger, Vigny), 121
Ladenson, Elisabeth, 122, 123, 124, 243nn35–36
La femme qui était en lui (Rostand), 31–70; civilization and dysphoria, 31–35; dysphoria in, 35–41; dysphoric pacifism in, 39, 52–57; femininity, tragic enigma of, 39, 49–52; gender/sexuality seesaw, 41–45; homoeroticism, defense of, 39, 57–60; inversion, theorization of, 41–45; musical dysphoria, 40, 68–70; overview of, 26–27; racial divide in, 40, 60–64; schizophrenia, gender deviance as, 40, 64–68; tender masculinity in, 39, 46–48; women in, 47
La loi du genre (Murat), 118

lamps, symbolism of, 100
Lang, Daniel Welzer, 12–13
La Place de l'Etoile (Modiano), 142, 155
Laroussi, Farid, 95, 96, 97
Laurens, Paul, 96
"Law of *Gender*, The" (Murat), 13–14
Le dernier sabbat de Maurice Sachs (*Maurice Sachs's Last Sabbath*, Dognon and Monceau), 142, 154
Leduc, Violette, 139, 142, 164, 165, 170
Legrandin (character in *In Search of Lost Time*), 119
Le horla (Maupassant), 35
Le pilori (Rostand), 57
lesbians and lesbianism: Colette's fascination with, 192; as object of Proustian love, 123–124; in *In Search of Lost Time*, 109, 111–112, 122, 123
Les pénitents en maillots roses (Penitents in pink tights, Jacob), 163
Les problèmes de l'hérédité et du sexe (Rostand), 34
L'homme que j'ai tué (Rostand), 33, 55–56
Liautey, Maréchal, 250n87
ligne de fuite (line of flight), 136
lines of flight: Charlus's smile as, 21; desire as, 76; dysphoric time as, 216; femininity as, 125; in gender assemblage in Gide, 76, 81; in *The Immoralist*, 94; inversion as, 136; from male desire, 82; of manly love, 84; queer time as, 216; in *Strait Is the Gate*, 105; writers' use of, 23
linguistic reclamation, 15
literary canon: engagement with, 22–25; modernist canon, paradox of, 73–74. *See also* French literature
loneliness, 128
love: desire and, 87; Gide on, 76–78; sex, desire, and spirituality and, 75–77
Love, Heather, 8, 35, 185, 186
lovers, in *La femme qui était en lui*, 48
Lubitsch, Ernst, 33
Lucey, Michael: on Colette's unintelligibility, 191, 192–193; on collective identity, emergence of, 24–25; on Gide, 27, 87; on Gide and Bersani, 74; mentioned, 6; on Proust, 132, 242nn23–24; on representation of gay identity, 32
Lucile (character in *Strait Is the Gate*), 101–104
Lyautey, Louis Hubert Gonzalve (Maréchal), 7, 61, 167

Madeleine (character in *Madeleine*), 98, 100. *See also* Rondeaux, Madeleine
Madeleine (Gide), 72, 79, 85–90
Malatino, Hil, 17, 70, 223n38
male homosexuals. *See* homosexuals (male homosexuals) and homosexuality

"Male Prison, The" (Baldwin), 85
Manceau, Philippe, 176
Mannion, Jen, 224n53
Marcel (character in *Sodom and Gomorrah*), 113
Marceline (character in *The Immoralist*), 93, 97, 99–100
Maritain, Jacques, 139, 149
marriage: chrononormativity of, 195; Colette on, 189; as death, 98–105; dysfunctionality of, 27; as gendering anchor, 86; in *The Immoralist*, 93, 94; marriage paradox, 77–78; nature of, 72; temporality and, 181–182. *See also* Gide, André
Marthe (character in *The Devil in the Flesh*), 197–200, 211, 216
Martin Du Gard, Roger, 239n87
masculinity: abjection and, 157; *Corydon* on, 82; femininity, differences from, 120–125; Gide on, 78; influence of wars on, 37–38, 53–54; of narrator's father in *La femme qui était en lui*, 54–55; oppressiveness of, 74–75; prison of, 93; Sachs's relationship to, 140; tender masculinity, 46–48. *See also* men
masks: authenticity as, in Sachs's writings, 172; masculinity as, 120–125
masturbation, 166, 202, 213, 217
materiality, 21, 204
maternal attachment, 231n65
Matthews, Gladys, 150, 165
Maupassant, Guy de, 35

Maurice Sachs's Last Sabbath (*Le dernier sabbat de Maurice Sachs*, Du Dognon and Monceau), 142, 154
Max ("Grand-Serin," "Big Canary," character in *The Vagabond*), 188–193, 195
méduse, 128
Mémoire moral (*Moral memoirs*, Sachs), 159–160, 176
men: fragility of, 98; male desire, 36, 84–85; male gaze, 88–89, 122–123; male romance, 128–129; male superiority, 49. *See also* homosexuals (male homosexuals) and homosexuality; masculinity
men-women: as conceptual figures, 116; fugue state of, 125; in Proust, 4, 112, 114–116. *See also* homosexuals (male homosexuals) and homosexuality; inverts and inversion
Mesch, Rachel, 19, 230n49
Michel (narrator in *The Immoralist*), 80, 92–96, 98, 99, 141, 143
Mignon (character in *Our Lady of the Flowers*), 202, 203, 205–208, 214
miracles, 127. *See also* queer time and temporal dysphoria
misfits, 25
misogyny: erotics of, 27–28, 90; Gide's, 93; racialized, 92
missed encounters, 113–116
Mitchell, Robin, 101

modernist texts, problematic nature of, 23
Modiano, Patrick, 142, 155, 167
Monceau, Philippe, 154, 248nn46–47
Money, John, 222n25
Moral Memoirs (*Mémoire moral*, Sachs), 159–160, 176
Morizot, Baptiste, 168
Morny, Mathilde de, 191–192
Mosse, George, 54, 230n49
moving sideways. See Sachs, Maurice
MtF sex-reassignment surgery, 67
Murat, Laure, 13–14, 118–119, 124
music: Glavey on, 52; as marker of elitism, 55; musical dysphoria, 68–70; musical talent as feminine, 51
My Body and I (Crevel): introduction to, 187–188; mentioned, 30, 182; space in, 216; temporal dysphoria and, 209–217

narratives: nonlinear, 187; of possession, 35–36
narrator (of *La femme qui était en lui*): confession of, 56; death of, 45; Emmanuel and, 50; gender, understanding of, 47; inner Woman of, 49, 50, 51, 62, 69; inner Woman of, separation from, 35, 56, 65, 67–68; love, romantic longing for, 52; men, relationships with, 58, 59, 62; musical talent, 51; racialized helpers, 60, 64; schizophrenic divides faced by, 69; self-description, 34; servants and, 40; splits surrounding, 36; tender masculinity and, 48, 54; unmentioned diagnosis of, 66
narrator (of *L'homme que j'ai tué*), 37
Nathaniel (character in *Fruits of the Earth*), 105
nature, question of nature of, 21
Nay, Yv E., 36
Néré, Renée (narrator of *The Vagabond*), 188–195, 208, 209, 211
Never Say I (Lucey), 24
New Woman, The (Heaney), 20
nonlinear narratives, 187
normal pederasts, inverts versus, 82

object choice, question of stabilization of, 37
old war, 56–57
oppositions, in *Witches' Sabbath*, 163
orchid-bumblebee metaphor, 28, 110, 130
order, in *The Devil in the Flesh*, 200
Orient: illness, association with, 96–97; metamorphoses in, 95–98; Oriental inscrutability, trope of, 63
other, the: abjection and, 142, 158; homosexuals as, 54; Jews as, 54; racialized otherness, white masculinity and, 95; Woman as, 52. See also abjection
Our Lady of the Flowers (character in *Our Lady of the Flowers*), 202, 207–208, 214

Our Lady of the Flowers (Genet): bodies in, 211, 212; introduction to, 187–188; mentioned, 30, 182; opening of, 212–213; primary themes of, 213; temporal dysphoria and, 201–208, 210–211
Ozon, François, 33

pacifism, 39, 52–57; as guise for dysphoria, 37–38
pain, chronic, 19
Paris Colonial Exposition (1931), 61, 64
pederasty, 43, 82, 236n28
people of color: Rostand's alienation of, 33; Sachs's claim of being mixed race, 153. *See also* race and racism
Philipp of Eulenburg (prince), 232n76
Pines, Davida, 77, 98
pink color, 162–163
piperie as term, 250n92
place-making practices, 208–209
plurality, in *Our Lady of the Flowers*, 207
Porzak, Simon, 28, 112, 126, 128, 130
poststructuralism, comparison with queer theory, 108
Prangins Clinique, 65
present, the: literary influences on history of, 7–8; as queer time, 195
progress, problematic nature of, 22
Proust, Marcel: challenges faced by, 23; on Charlus, sex of, 1; Darwinian references, 133; on gender, 138; Gide and, 26, 136; on homosexuality, 113, 123; on race, 155; Rostand and, 26; Sedgwick versus Deleuze on, 129–131; shifting of focus from sexuality to gender, 123; Ulrichs and, 42
Proust, Marcel, trans reading of, 107–138; conceptual abysses, 112, 129–133; homosexuality as cursed race, 111, 116–120; introduction to, 107–112; masculinity and femininity, differences in, 111–112, 120–125; overview of, 28; shimmering bodies, 112, 133–138; *Sodom and Gomorrah*, missed encounters in, 111, 112–116; *Sodom and Gomorrah*, queer fertilization in, 112, 125–129
Proust and Signs (Deleuze), 108, 129–131, 134, 137
psychiatry, influence on gender assemblage splits, 36
psychic denudation, 105
Puar, Jasbir, 9–10
Pure and the Impure, The (Colette), 192, 193

queer, author's experiences as, 2–3
queer communities, linguistic reclamation by, 15
queer criminal, Sachs as, 168, 170
queer crooks. *See* Sachs, Maurice
queer fertilization, in *Sodom and Gomorrah*, 125–129

queer historiography, Love on, 8, 185, 186
queer places, temporality of, 208–209
queer sex, as source of freedoms, 167
queer signs, in narratives, 130–131
queer theory, 7–8, 20, 108, 235n7
Queer Time and Place (Halberstam), 208–209
queer time and temporal dysphoria (queer temporality), 181–217; chrononormativity, outside of, 214–217; in *The Devil in the Flesh*, 195–201; dysphoric assemblages, 211–214; genders, timing of, 204–208; introduction to, 181–188; in *My Body and I*, 209–217; in *Our Lady of the Flowers*, 201–208, 210–217; overview of, 29–30; in *Queer Time and Place*, 208–209; sex scenes and, in Sachs, 166–167, 179; temporal dysphoria, 208–211; in *The Vagabond*, 188–195
queer traitors, 178
queer trans theory, limitations of, 224n52
queer transgression, 157
queerness, 3, 143, 146

race and racism: modern gender as racialized construct, 6; Proust on race, 155; races, creation of, 117; racial divide in *La femme qui était en lui*, 40, 60–64; racial divide of colonialism, 7; racialized misogyny, 92; racialized otherness, white masculinity and, 94; Sachs's racial invisibility, 162; structural racism in modernist texts, 23. *See also* people of color; white people

Raczymow, Henri, 142, 144–145, 170, 246n10, 249n64, 250n91
Radiguet, Raymond, 26, 182, 184, 208
Rastignac, Eugène de (character in *La comédie humaine*), 177
religion, relationship to spirituality, 76–77
repressive hypothesis, of Urnings, 42
reproduction, fertilization versus, 126
Réunion des Musées Nationaux, 91
reversal, 118–119. *See also* inverts and inversion
Rheinau mental asylum, 65
Roberts, Mary Louise, 230–231n54
Rondeaux, Madeleine, 71, 85, 86, 88–89, 234n2
Rostand, Edmond, 32, 55
Rostand, Jean, 34, 66
Rostand, Maurice: on father's death, 231n67; Gury on, 227n3; life of, 32–33; on male homosexuality, 59; mentioned, 196; pacifism, 55; paradoxical literary profile of, 32–33; Proust and, 26; on woman, 31. *See also La femme qui était en lui*
Rubin, Gayle, 9

sabbat, shabbat versus, 248n46
Sachs, Andrée, 149–150
Sachs, Maurice, 139–180; *Alias*, 167, 178, 179; cassock, wearing of, 161–163; Catholicism, conversion to, 149–150; challenges faced by, 23; class, understanding of, 145; confessional writings of, 170–173; criminal activities, reasons for, 145–146; death of, 154, 180; family status, 247n29; Genet and, 26; Gide, relationship with, 141; on his own sexuality, 159; intermediaries and, 167–170; introduction to, 139–141; on Jacob, 248n41; Jouhandeau and, 156; obscurity in memoirs of, 169; overview of, 28–29; psychoanalysis, experience of, 172; Radiguet and, 26; refugees, smuggling of, 170, 171–172; reputation of, 142, 148–150; self-creation of, 147; at seminary, 161–163; serial confessions of, 170–173; writing by and being written, 174–176; writings of, 148, 178–180. See also *Hunt, The*; *Witches' Sabbath*
Sachs, Maurice, characteristics of: abjection, 29, 140–142, 147, 156–158, 177; animality, 156–157; bodily distress, 175; body positivity, 166; as chameleon, 152–155, 175; as collective assemblage of enunciation, 146–148, 151–152, 171; contempt for productive futurity, 184; crookedness of, 144–146; dysphoria of, 158–161, 176; femininity of, 159, 160; gambling of, 164–167; gender incongruity of, 159–161; guilt of, 158–160; laterality of, 177–178; misogyny of, 164; as self-generative legend, 148–150; as self-made collective assemblage, 151–152; shamelessness of, 141–144; as ugly seducer, 153
sagas, in *Our Lady of the Flowers*, 203, 204–205, 207
Sanos, Sandrine, 54, 156–157
Sartre, Jean-Paul, 202, 213
Sauvagnargues, Anne, 131, 244n59
Schehr, Lawrence, 94
schizoanalysis, 68–69
schizophrenia, 64–68. See also *La femme qui était en lui*
science, influence on gender assemblage splits, 36
scientia sexualis (sexology), 61, 65, 67–68
Second Sex, The (Beauvoir), 13, 14
Sedgwick, Eve Kosofsky: on Charlus, 132–133; Deleuze, comparison with, 108–109; on femininity and desire in *In Search of Lost Time*, 124; on gender, 138; mentioned, 28, 48; on Proust, 129–132, 240n2; on queerness, 155; on *Sodom and Gomorrah*, 126
See, Sam, 244n50
sensuality, queer time of, 193

sentences, types of, in *Our Lady of the Flowers*, 204
serial confessions, 173
servants, 48
service, in chrononormativity, 183
sex: gay, in Sachs's memoirs, 165; heterosexual, 87, 194, 199; homosexual, as akin to spirituality, 84; love, desire, and spirituality and, 75–77; masturbation, 166, 202, 213, 217; meanings to men and to women, 190–191; with men, in *The Immoralist*, 94; sex/gender system, 9, 10–11. *See also* heterosexuality; homosexuals (male homosexuals) and homosexuality; sexuality; trans
Sex and Character (Weininger), 49, 63–64
sex changes, legal, during interwar years, 23–24
sexe, French use of term, 13
sexism, in modernist texts, 23
sexology. *See scientia sexualis*
sexuality: female, contagiousness of, 124; gender and, in Proust, 107–108, 123; in Gide's gender assemblage, 76; in *My Body and I*, 212; Sachs's idea of good and, 141; sexual difference, 13, 43–44, 120–125, 126; sexual dimorphism, 83; sexual dissidence, 74; sexual inclinations, Hirschfeld's types of, 46–47; sexual selection, 43, 229n32. *See also* femininity; heterosexuality; homosexuals (male homosexuals) and homosexuality; masculinity; trans
shabbat, sabbat versus, 248n46
Shackelton, Anna, 87, 99
shimmering bodies, 133–138
Shimmering Images (Steinbock), 133
signs: Proustian, 134; Sedgwick versus Deleuze on, 129–130
Silvestre (character in *La femme qui était en lui*), 51, 52, 59
sins, of the flesh or love, 57–60
smugglers and smuggling, 140, 143, 168, 170–171
Snediker, Michael, 19
social processes, race as, 117
Sodom (in *Sodom and Gomorrah*), 122, 243n36
Sodom and Gomorrah (Proust): botanical metaphors in, 126; epigraph to, 121; missed encounters in, 112–116; opening scene of, 107; queer fertilization in, 125–129; seminal moment of, 120–121
sodomy, Gide on, 236n28
solitude, 52, 214
sorcerers, 65
Sorel, Julien (character in *The Red and the Black*), 177
Soutine, Chaïm, 139
space: in *My Body and I*, 209–211, 216; in *Our Lady of the Flowers* and *My Body and I*, 201–202, 203, 210; queer temporality and, 208–209; of rooms, 213; in *Strait Is the Gate*, 105; temporality of, 30

speed, in Sachs's writings, 178–180
spirituality: as akin to homosexual sex, 84; in Gide's gender assemblage, 76; love, sex, and desire and, 75–77; religion, relationship to, 76–77
Spitzer, Jennifer, 246n15
split personality, 66
Stanford University, Gender Dysphoria Program, 16
Steinbock, Eliza, 36, 112, 133, 136
Stockton, Kathryn Bond, 14, 196, 198
Stoler, Ann Laura, 61
Strait Is the Gate (Gide), 77, 81, 98–105
Stryker, Susan, 11
subjectification, 72, 74
subjectivity, 21
Sue, Eugène, 152
Surrealist Group, 215
Suze (Sachs's nurse), 159, 160
Switzerland, as therapeutic destination, 65, 233n96

temporality. *See* time and temporality
tender masculinity, 29, 31, 37, 46–48, 54, 62
Terrorist Assemblages (Puar), 9
Thief's Journal, The (Genet), 168
Third Republic, conjugality in, 77
third sex, 13–14, 41–42
time and temporality: dysphoric time (temporal dysphoria), 182, 184–185, 208–211, 215–216; of lesbianism, 192; in *Madeleine*, 89; normative temporal linearity, 181; the present, 7–8, 195; productive and reproductive futurity, 183–184; progress versus, 22; temporality, in *Our Lady of the Flowers*, 206–208; temporality of queer places, 208–209; time in *My Body and I*, 210; unbinding time, 197. *See also* chrononormativity; queer time and temporal dysphoria
Tortorici, Zeb, 8, 185, 186
trans: as analytical method, 109; Deleuze's fetishization of, 135; groups designated by, 20; as a strategy, 19–22; trans analysis, objects of, 110; trans ontologies, Steinbock on, 133; trans studies, 11, 23, 108; trans*historicities, 185, 186; transmisogyny, 20, 110; transness in Proust's works, 116; transsexual theory, limitations of, 224n52; transsexuality, basis for, 135; transtopia, 225n63; transversality, 134–136
transfemininity: in *La femme qui était en lui*, 49; transfeminine allegory, 33, 45; transfeminism, 20; Ulrichs on, 229n28
transitioning, limitations of, 70
Travel in the Congo (Gide), 79–80, 90–92
turbans, 9–10

Ulrichs, Karl Heinrich, 38–39, 41, 115, 229n28

United States, notion of gender in, 12
Uranism and Uranists, 82, 118, 236n31
Urnings, 41–42

Vagabond, The (Colette), 29–30, 182, 186–187, 188–195
Van Rysselberghe, Elisabeth, 237n41
variation in nature, 127
Vénus noire, trope of, 101
Vergès, Françoise, 228n11
Vigny, Alfred de, 121–122
violence: of chrononormativity, 216; of colonialism, 90–92; of femininity, 57; of modern gender binary, 6; of war and gender, 56
visibility and erasure, in Sachs's writings, 172
Vouillemont Hotel, 149, 162

Wandervogel (youth movement), 233n91
wars: effects on chrononormativity, 196; influence on femininity, 37–38; influence on masculinity, 37–38, 53–54; old war, 56–57; violence of, 56; World War I, as Great War, 53
Weil, Abraham, 21
Weininger, Otto, 49, 63–64
Weininger, Saül (character in *La femme qui était en lui*), 63, 64, 65, 66–67
Well of Loneliness, The (Hall), 34, 35, 36–37, 228n11

White, Edmund, 206, 254n37
white people: service by, 183; white cismasculinity, 24; white male supremacy, violence of, 91; white masculine homosexuals, 95; white masculinity, racialized otherness and, 94
White Rose (anti-Nazi resistance group), 146
Witches' Sabbatsh (Sachs): body positivity in, 166; on enforced heterosexuality, 164–165; on familial connections to literary scene, 177; loops in, 173; mentioned, 171; pink/black opposition in, 162–163; on Sachs's bodily changes, 175–176; Sachs's cossack in, 162; Sachs's guilt in, 158–159, 160; Sachs's movements in, 179; Sachs's sexualized early memories in, 172
Within a Budding Grove (Proust), 123
Woman (character in *La femme qui était en lui*), 45; characteristics of, 49–50; as dysphoric, 69–70; first appearance of, 51, 59; gender violence and, 56; mentioned, 47; narrator's love of, 59–60; as Other, 52; schizophrenia and, 66; Vietnamese servant of, 60, 62–63
women: animality of, 85; *Corydon* on, 86, 89; disposable female bodies, 92; embodiment of, 97; female bodies, desire and, 84;

female characters in Proust, 124; female inverts in Proust, lack of, 122; feminine selves, nature of, 97; in *La femme qui était en lui*, 47, 49–50; fragility of, 97–98; Gide's attitude toward, 72; in Gide's marriages, 73; guilt of, 72; modern Christianity's attitudes toward, 83; Rostand's reification of, 33; Sachs's views on, 164; solitude of, 52; Weininger on, 49. *See also* femininity

World War I, as Great War, 53

writing: nature of, 186; space for queer time in, 193

Yao, Xine, 63

Zemmour, Eric, 220n8

Zürich University hospital Burghölzi, 66

GPSR Authorized Representative: Easy Access System Europe, Mustamäe tee 50, 10621 Tallinn, Estonia, gpsr.requests@easproject.com